2-

HANDCRAFT
~ILLUSTRATED~
~1994~

Published by
Boston Common Press
17 Station Street
Brookline Village, Massachusetts 02146

ISBN: 0-9640179-2-X
ISSN: 1072-0529

BC = back cover

BC = back cover

BC = back cover

NUMBER ONE ◆ CHARTER ISSUE

$4.00 U.S./$4.95 CANADA

HANDCRAFT
~ ILLUSTRATED

How to Antique Urns

An Inexpensive Plaster Urn Is Quickly Antiqued with a Verdigris Finish

Heirloom Wreaths

Four Basic Techniques Yield Eight Holiday Wreaths

The Secrets of Gilding

New Techniques Make Gilding Fast and Easy

Curly Maple Dresser

Watercolor Paints Transform a Store-Bought Pine Dresser into a Masterpiece

10-MINUTE FLOWER ARRANGEMENTS

•

NO-SEW POTPOURRI SACHETS

•

VICTORIAN DRIED FLOWER BOUQUET

•

QUICK VELVET CHRISTMAS ORNAMENTS

•

SPECIAL INSERT:
ANTIQUE ROSE DECOUPAGE

0 74470 83731 2

TABLE
OF CONTENTS

**THE SECRETS OF
QUICK GILDING**
page 26

SCENTED HANGER
page 8

**HOW TO WRAP
A WINE BOTTLE**
page 22

NO-SEW LACE SACHETS
page 11

**PAINTED CURLY
MAPLE DRESSER**
page 12

QUICK PROJECTS
page 33

HANDCRAFT
~ ILLUSTRATED ~

Editor
CAROL ENDLER STERBENZ

Senior Editor
MICHIO RYAN

Managing Editor
MAURA LYONS

Directions Editor
ELEANOR LEVIE

Copy Editor
DAVID TRAVERS

· · · · · · · · · · ·

Art Director
MEG BIRNBAUM

Contributing Photographers
TOM MCCAVERA
RICHARD FELBER

· · · · · · ·

Publisher and Founder
CHRISTOPHER KIMBALL

Editorial Consultant
RAYMOND WAITES

· · · · · · · · · · ·

Circulation Director
ADRIENNE KIMBALL

Circulation Manager
MARY TAINTOR

Circulation Assistant
JENNIFER KEENE

Production Director
JAMES MCCORMACK

Treasurer
JANET CARLSON

Office Manager
JENNY THORNBURY

Handcraft Illustrated (ISSN 1072-0529) is published bimonthly by Natural Health Limited Partners, 17 Station Street, Box 509, Brookline, MA 02147. Copyright 1993 Natural Health Limited Partners. Application to mail at second class postage rates is pending at Boston, MA and additional mailing offices. Editorial office: 17 Station Street, Box 509, Brookline, MA 02147; (617) 232-1000, FAX (617) 232-1572. Editorial contributions should be sent to: Editor, *Handcraft Illustrated*, 17 Station Street, Brookline, MA 02147. We cannot assume responsibility for manuscripts submitted to us. Submissions will be returned only if accompanied by a large self-addressed stamped envelope. Subscription rates: $24.95 for one year; $45 for two years; $65 for three years. (Canada: add $3 per year; all other foreign add $12 per year.) Postmaster: Send all new orders, subscription inquiries, and change of address notices to *Handcraft Illustrated*, P.O. Box 51383, Boulder, CO 80322-1383, or telephone (800) 873-6141. Single copies: $4 in U.S., $4.95 in Canada and foreign. PRINTED IN THE U.S.A.

EDITORIAL

CAROL ENDLER STERBENZ

After a decade of pursuing a path that has led us farther and farther from home, we find ourselves now turning back, drawn by the yearnings of the spirit to reaffirm our connection to home and family. The journey has altered us and the rhythms of our everyday lives, but our sense of home has remained unchanged. We still like to think of home as a place that is at once comfortable, warm, welcoming, and utterly self-sufficient.

To me, home is the fragrance of cotton sheets dried in fresh air, the simple charm of polished floors, the heft of handmade quilts lifted from a cedar chest on the first cold night in fall. I especially love my quilts, with their colors softly faded from many washings and the crepe-like texture formed by the tiny, evenly spaced quilting stitches. I appreciate them as much for their pleasing aesthetic as for the memories they summon of the children they have kept warm and the guests they have comforted.

Of particular cherished value is a quilt I stitched, a kind of illustrated family record made of cuttings from garments long outgrown — my daughters' baby dresses, my son's cotton shirts, a worn apron, each patch filled with sentimental remembrance. The small quilt is framed and hangs on a wall. It really doesn't "match" anything, it simply testifies to the things I hold most dear.

I have always loved crafts and over the years I have tried my hand at almost every craft that has come my way — painting, woodworking, stained glass, to name a few. I used to work on the second floor of our house in a little room with a window, under the eaves — not just any window, but one that allowed me a view of the bay outside. The water's surface changed in color and texture as it mirrored the skies and was ruffled by the winds. And if the size of the room created an occasional battle with claustrophobia, and the low ceiling caused me to scrape my raised hands or bump my forehead from time to time, the designs I conceived there were borne of exhilaration.

This is not to say that there weren't enormous frustrations in those early years as I attempted to learn a new craft skill or searched for new craft designs. Books and magazines often inspired me with their compelling photographs of wonderful craft projects, but, more often than not, written directions were confusing and incomplete; or, if the directions were comprehensible, the project was of the string-around-the-orange-juice-can variety. If I could have imagined a publication back then, one that could have provided me with the great designs I looked for and the straightforward information I needed to accomplish them, I would have envisioned the magazine you hold in your hands, *Handcraft Illustrated.*

Conceived in the same tradition that prizes handcrafts of exceptional beauty and integrity, *Handcraft Illustrated* is intrinsically more. It approaches making things by hand in a completely unique and practical way. In *Handcraft Illustrated,* crafts are reconceptualized and made user-friendly. Behind the scenes, designers and craft professionals examine each craft, reinterpreting archaic methods, scrutinizing techniques and products, and translating and editing each step of the crafting process so that only the most precise, practical, and effective techniques and the best products remain, ones that consistently yield the project featured.

This approach can be seen in the clear, easy-to-follow directions that lead you step by step, and in the concise illustrations that further support and clarify the instructional text. Additional tips and advice from experts tell you what to look out for and help you solve problems if and when they occur. There is no advertising to disrupt the flow of ideas or to try to persuade you to use a particular product. We give you candid, dependable information that will reward you with a completed project of quality, high style, and fine craftsmanship. And all the while you will be learning new skills or mastering old ones.

Consider our gilded fruit project, for example (*see* "The Secrets of Quick Gilding," page 26). You might initially resist making this attractive gilded pear, thinking that gilding is a complicated, esoteric method suitable only to relics of a religious or political nature. But *Handcraft Illustrated* has developed a simple gilding technique and applied it to an appealing decorative object. In an hour, you can gild enough fruit (or other ornamental objects) to fill a bowl to overflowing or to decorate an entire Christmas tree.

There is no better time than the holidays to engage in handcrafts, making something by hand, one at a time, with no two exactly the same. Handcrafts can help us get in touch with what we like, what we value, and what we need to create a dwelling place for the spirit. *Handcraft Illustrated* is here to welcome you home. ◆

DEAR READER,

Since this is our first issue, I decided to feature questions that are representative of those frequently asked of me as I toured the country in the last year. In future issues, I look forward to including your letters and helping you find the answers to all your questions related to handcrafts — what brand of glue gun is the best (we'll test every brand available and tell you what's best); what new approaches have been developed that allow you to try your hand at otherwise intimidating crafts (we'll teach you about soft-firing and how to paint your own decorative ceramics); and, in every issue, a "what-is-it" question (we'll demystify odd tools and objects that are related to past and present craft techniques). Please write. We look forward to hearing from you.

— CS

FOLK ART METAL CUT-OUTS

I have long admired the look of metal cut-outs used in folk art weathervanes. Is there a way to create the look of metal so that I can make some smaller decorations for my kitchen windowsill?

Aleene Jackson of Artis, Inc. suggests faking the look of metal by using burnt brown bags and her Aleene's Tacky Glue. You can imitate the look of metal ornaments quite inexpensively. Simply trace a shape onto a heavy brown grocery bag and cut out through two thicknesses. Glue them together. Brush glue over one side, and immediately burn directly over a candle flame. Rotate the piece so the flame burns all the wet glue on the surface; it will look very black and sooty. Take a facial tissue and lightly wipe away the soot. Then, with a slightly heavier pressure, ruffle the surface to texture it. If you break the skin, simply reburn. Let dry overnight, and rub lightly with a soft cloth. Dip a finger into gold paint; wipe excess on newspa-

ORNAMENTAL DRIED FRUIT

I love the look of dried apples and citrus slices and I see them used in floral arrangements and on wreaths. Is there a simple way to make these myself?

Making your own dried fruit slices is very easy and inexpensive. Use your sharpest knife to slice apples, lemons, limes, oranges, and pink and yellow grapefruit into 1/8" slices. Simply place the citrus fruit on a cutting board, cutting across the fruit so that each slice reveals the star-shaped pattern of each section. Slice the citrus in half again for half-moon shapes. When cutting apples, you can cut top to bottom so that the heart shape with seeds shows, or you can cut across the fruit to reveal the star pattern. Rub lemon on both sides of the apple slices to prevent too much browning, and string them on crochet cotton. Or place them along with other fruit slices on a window screen or on cheese-

cloth spread over a quilting hoop or frame. Turn the slices every few days to reduce curling edges. Whether you use the dried slices singly as ornaments or as part of a floral arrangement, keep them out of direct sunlight and store them in a dry place.

per and lightly highlight the ridges. Let dry, and repeat on reverse side. Afterwards, you can curl, bend, or shape the piece if you like. For a window decoration, glue several animal shapes on a wood strip and lean against the window.

CARING FOR STENCILS

How can I take care of my precut acetate stencils so that they can be used again and again?

After use, lay the stencil in a pan of warm, soapy water to loosen any paint. Lay an old terrycloth towel on a flat surface and place the stencil painted side up. Gently scrub the residual paint with a used soft toothbrush until the stencil is clean. Be careful not to push down on the "bridges" to avoid breaking them. Wipe the entire stencil with a soft cloth and store between sheets of brown paper until ready to use.

EGGSHELL MOSAIC

How do you create eggshell mosaic? I would like to decorate a small hinged box.

First, soak eggshells in household bleach for at least 48 hours; this will break down the mem-

branes lining the shell and make it easier for the shell to adhere to the surface being decorated. Remove the eggshell sections from the bleach solution, rinse in equal parts vinegar and water, then lay sections on paper towels. Using a wide brush, paint a coating of white glue on the surface of the object to be decorated and press sections of eggshell gently in place until it crackles and adjusts to the gentle contours of the object. When the object is covered as desired and the glue is dry, rub tile grout between the crevices until a smooth surface is achieved. (If you wish, you can mix in dry pigments with the grout.) Let the grout dry. Protect the eggshell surface with a coat of varnish or spray-paint it gold, bronze, copper, or any other color you prefer. The end result is a beautiful, decorative finish reminiscent of Delft pottery.

TIPS ON PROLONGING THE LIFE OF CUT FLOWERS

Although cut flowers are expensive to buy at the florist, I usually indulge myself during the holidays. Can you suggest some ways to extend their vase life?

Before arranging your freshly cut flowers, condition them as follows: using a sharp knife, cut ½"

1" off the bottom of the stems on a long slant under running water. Recutting the stems maximizes water intake by removing any blockage caused by bacteria, air, or debris. Underwater cutting is good for tight bud flowers that are prone to wilting, such as roses.

Smash the hard, woody stems of such trees and shrubs as holly and evergreen with a hammer; or, make a vertical cut in the end of the stem and scrape away the bark in order to help it better absorb water. If possible, place the conditioned stems in a deep container with tepid water (temperature range of 100° to 110°) and leave them in a cool, dimly lit place for several hours to plump up the plants' cells.

Once the arrangement is put together, fill the container to the water line and add special cut-flower food that you dissolve in the water to keep your cuttings fresh. Alternately, add a teaspoon of household bleach or a small piece of charcoal into the bottom of the container to prevent rotting and bacterial growth.

To perk up a wilted flower, remove the flower from the arrangement and strip off as much foliage as possible. Re-cut the stem on an angle and lay the flower horizontally in a tub of shallow water so that it is completely submerged and it can absorb water through all of its parts.

REUSING GIFT WRAP

I am reluctant to throw away beautiful gift wrap after I unwrap a gift. Can you suggest some creative ways to reuse it?

You can cut out single motifs from the gift wrap and apply them to small accessories such as blank stationery and gift cards, notebooks, and photo albums. Gift wrap is not as fragile a medium as you might expect, but it is subject to shrinking and stretching — be sure to apply a thin, even coat of glue to larger sheets to prevent buckling and tearing. To extend its durability, spray on acrylic sealer, laminate it with clear self-adhesive plastic

WEAVING A HEART BASKET

Do you have a pattern for a woven heart basket used to hang on a Christmas tree?

Trace the pattern and use to cut two heart pieces, one each from light and dark paper. Using a ruler and an X-Acto knife, slash each piece along solid lines. Fold in half, right-sides out, along dash line. Position folded shapes on work surface as shown in illustration 1. Weave strips as shown in illustrations 2 and 3. When weaving is completed, straighten woven sections by pulling gently in both directions, being careful not to tear the paper. For handle, cut a strip of matching paper, 1¼" x 7½". Fold in half lengthwise; glue ends inside each basket at inner points of heart as in illustration 3. Fill with candy.

Copy the pattern to enlarge to desired size and use as a template to cut out two heart pieces.

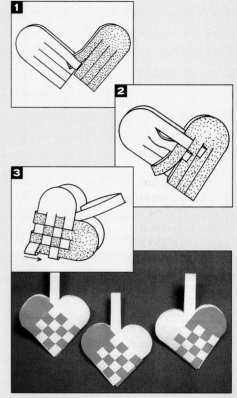

Three woven heart baskets

(Con-Tact), or back it with muslin, using a spray adhesive.

You can make several little shopping bags that can hold baked goods or cosmetics. Simply purchase a small shopping bag to use as your pattern. Carefully open the gift bag along its glued edges and spread it on a sheet of gift wrap. Move the pattern around until you find an unwrinkled section. Using a sharp pencil, trace around the gift bag; cut out gift wrap. Strengthen the gift wrap by laminating with self-adhesive plastic. Make fold lines and glue overlapping sides using rubber cement. Cut and glue lengths of cord to opposite

sides of top edge for handles. Fill with tissue paper and small gifts.

MAKING A FLOOR CLOTH

Can you suggest an easy way to make a small painted floor cloth for use as a kitchen accent?

For a hunter green cloth with a design stenciled in cranberry, buy a 36" x 50" piece of primed artist's canvas, 1 quart flat dark green acrylic paint, a paint roller, one jar acrylic paint in cranberry, a stencil (as desired), a stencil brush, craft glue, and polyurethane varnish.

To prepare the surface of the canvas, smooth away any wrinkles by ironing them. Turn the short edges 2" to the wrong side and hem by gluing down with craft glue; repeat with long edges. Spread newspaper on the floor under canvas and apply two or three coats of green acrylic paint with a roller, running over the edges to seal all threads. Let each coat dry completely before applying the next coat. Stencil pattern to canvas as follows: Lay stencil over designated area. Dip stencil brush into cranberry paint, holding brush vertically; do not overfill brush. With a light tapping motion, paint area of stencil cut-out. Move stencil to next area to be painted and repeat painting process. Let dry. To finish floor cloth, vacuum cloth to remove any dust. Apply three coats of varnish, letting each coat dry and dusting before applying the next coat. ◆

ALL THAT GLITTERS...

Some of my Christmas ornaments have great sentimental value but look dingy and dusty. I don't want to throw them away. Is there any way to perk them up?

You'll be surprised at how a light coat of very fine glitter over part of each decoration gives it a subtle glow that is appealing for the holidays. But any ornament can benefit from a little sparkle, especially clear glass balls. Spray them lightly or mask off a section using artist's white masking tape or stick-on stars to create other subtle patterns. Consider

spraying some glitter on wrapped gifts, windows, and plants, too.

Quick Tips

Pearl Grape Cluster Ornament

These ornaments can be made in a great variety of sizes and styles. Although our version uses costume sweet-water pearls, you can substitute any style or color of bead, from faceted crystals in garnet and amber to baubles encrusted in rhinestones. To make one grape ornament, you will need nine sweet-water pearls: two gold tone (18mm), five white pearl tone (14mm), one copper tone, and one bronze tone (both 10mm); two metallic grape leaves; beading wire and wire cutters.

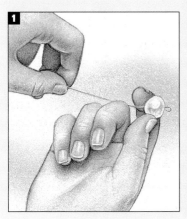

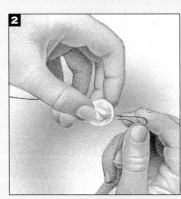

1. Cut nine 5" lengths of beading wire, one for each bead. On each length of wire, make a narrow U-shaped hook on one end and insert the opposite end of the wire into the bead.

2. Slide the bead down the wire feeding the U-shaped hook into the hole until the hook is just inside the bead. Repeat for all beads.

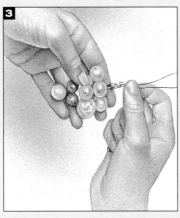

3. On your free hand, arrange the wired beads to resemble a bunch of grapes. Twist the wires together at the top to form a stem.

4. Attach metallic grape leaves by wiring them in place at the top of the grape cluster. Bend wires into a hook and hang as desired.

5. A finished pearl grape cluster.

Making a Garland

A garland may be a long, flexible boa of decorative material — usually fresh evergreen, foliage, and flowers — that is draped over mantels and doorways, or wound around columns and stairway banisters. To determine the length of the garland you want, measure the total length of the object to be draped and add 10" to each end of the garland to allow for a graceful drape. This measurement determines the length of the base wire.

To make a garland, you will need a base wire or cord that is strong enough to support the decorative material. For the evergreen garland pictured, you will need heavy-gauge (14) spool wire for the base; 90 stems total of fresh spruce, fir, and/or balsam evergreens; 15 stems of dusty miller; pinecones; floral tape; medium-gauge (24) spool wire; garden shears; and wire cutters.

1. Cut stems of plant material to identical lengths and use medium-gauge wire to bind individual bouquets (four to six stems each) of the same evergreens.

2. Measure and cut a length (following the directions above) of heavy-gauge wire for the base and wrap with floral tape to prevent bound bouquets from slipping. Form a loop at one end of the base wire. Insert first bouquet into loop and twist to secure.

3. Lay the head of the next bouquet over the stems of the first bouquet, binding in place with medium-gauge wire. Continue across the length of base wire.

4. To decorate, add single pinecones by twisting a 6" length of medium-gauge wire around the bottom collar of scales, allowing one long end to form a false stem. Twist long end around base wire. Add bow as desired.

ILLUSTRATIONS BY HARRY DAVIS

The French Bow

T his bow is made from French wire-edge ribbon, which is available in an exquisite range of colors and widths, and which holds its shape well when manipulated.

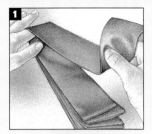

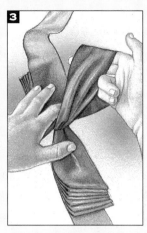

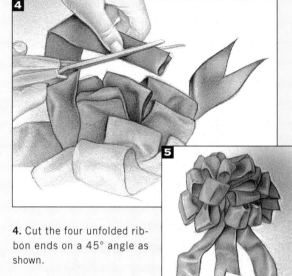

1. From a 7-yard length of ribbon, 2" wide, cut a 12" length and set it aside. This will be used to tie the stack of loops together. Fold the remaining ribbon into accordion pleats that are 9" wide, leaving 5" unfolded at either end.

2. Secure the pleats by tying the reserved 12" length of ribbon around the center of the stack of pleats, leaving two loose ends as streamers.

3. Hold the stack of pleats in place with one hand and open each loop with the other hand, giving each loop a 45° twist. Gently fluff the bow until it is a uniform size.

4. Cut the four unfolded ribbon ends on a 45° angle as shown.

5. The finished bow.

Homemade Beeswax Candles

B eeswax candles are easy to make, can be decorated according to your personal taste, and are less expensive than store-bought. For one candle you will need a sheet of beeswax, a square braid wick, a small amount of any wax to melt, brown paper (greaseproof), and a pair of scissors. Before beginning, lay the sheet of beeswax in a shallow pan of cold tap water. Prime the wick by immersing it in melted wax; remove wick from wax, pull straight, and lay on greaseproof brown paper until hard.

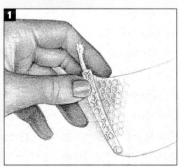

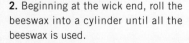

1. Cut a rectangle measuring 10" x 2" from a sheet of beeswax. Cut a 2½" length of primed wick and lay it on the short side of the beeswax. Press gently into place.

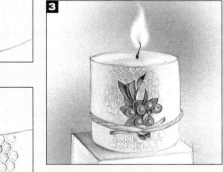

3. Decorate the candle with a raffia and berry decoration made by using a sprig of boxwood and pepperberry, an artificial cluster, fresh leaves, small beads attached with a pin, sequins, or any other suitable material. Remove decoration before lighting a narrow candle to prevent decoration from burning.

2. Beginning at the wick end, roll the beeswax into a cylinder until all the beeswax is used.

Quick and Plump Tassels

T assels are easy to make — this method yields a slightly plumper variety by sandwiching a thick silk cord between two sheaves of thread. You will need a 12" length of twisted silk cord, two skeins of silk thread in a matching color, a darning needle, scissors, and a piece of cardboard.

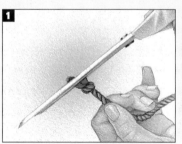

1. Tie a knot at the end of the twisted silk cord, trimming ends even.

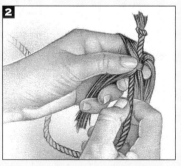

2. Make a sheaf of thread by winding the silk thread about 50 times around a piece of cardboard measuring 2½" wide. Slip a threaded needle under the loops at one end and tie loops securely. Cut the loops at the opposite end. Repeat to make second sheaf. Sandwich the thick cord between the sheaves.

3. Bind sheaves in place with silk thread. Pull the knot down to meet the binding thread.

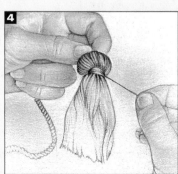

4. Hold the cord so that all threads hang down. Arrange threads evenly around the cord and bind in place with silk thread. Tie off. ◆

How to Create a Verdigris Finish

A plaster urn can be given an antique, verdigris finish in minutes, replicating the look of an ancient piece of bronze.

With a widely available verdigris kit, nonmetal objects can now be "antiqued" with a special paint that contains copper powder.

Applying a Verdigris Finish

1. Using a bristle brush, apply undercoat of copper paint with horizontal strokes to outside surface and inner rim of urn. Let dry. **2.** Apply a second coat of copper paint using strokes perpendicular to those of the first coat. Let dry for only 5 to 10 minutes. **3.** When second coat is still tacky, apply up to six coats of oxidizing solution allowing each layer to dry before applying next coat.

A verdigris finish is most often associated with ancient metal vessels that were buried for centuries. The outside surface of the bronze oxidized, creating an uneven green-gray patina. Literally translated from Old French, verdigris means "green of Greece" and refers to the green color of the corrosion on Greek artifacts. This look became fashionable as early as the Renaissance when the Classical Age was considered the ideal. It became a matter of status and culture to have a garden containing objects with a verdigris finish. Verdigris is still popular for its antique, archaeological look.

Today, any metal or nonmetal object can be made to develop the look of verdigris. Preparation requires just a few minutes and the technique is simple. You can purchase a verdigris kit at most craft stores. The kit contains the two basic components: a base paint containing copper powder, which oxidizes almost immediately (a full-blown verdigris finish will appear overnight), and an oxidizing solution. (There are enough materials in the kit to cover about 10 square feet.) The result is not a faux finish. The copper powder actually oxidizes, although the process takes hours instead of centuries.

Neoclassical urns with richly patinated surfaces can be a graceful complement to contemporary interiors. The urn can be used as a centerpiece or as an indoor planter. You can verdigris virtually anything that can be painted, including fiberglass resin, synthetic stone, concrete, terra-cotta, wood, and even plastic.

CREATING A VERDIGRIS FINISH

Be sure to wear gloves for all steps and to work in a clean, dust-free, and well-ventilated area.

1 urn or other item to verdigris
1 Patina Antiquing Kit by
   Modern Options containing:
   Copper Topper acrylic paint
   Metal Master surface cleaner
   Patina Green oxidizing
    solution
   Primo Primer and Sealer
4 disposable bristle brushes

1 foam brush
Emery cloth
Natural sponge
Latex gloves

Additional items needed:
Stiff wire brush or putty knife
Super-fine steel wool
  (grade 0000)
Tack cloth (cheesecloth
  impregnated with
  linseed oil)
Small disposable cups, such as
  empty yogurt containers

*Additonal items needed when
  working with metal objects:*
1 1" foam or bristle brush
Zinc chromate or epoxy primer
Noxon 7
Denatured alcohol
Very fine steel wool (grade 00)
Razor blade
Nail
Rags

PHOTOGRAPH BY TOM MCCAVERA, ILLUSTRATIONS BY LINDA FENNIMORE

10 Quick Ideas for Verdigris Projects

1. Architectural plaster *brackets*
2. Oval *picture frames* of solid brass
3. Solid brass *sundial* and *garden ornaments*
4. *Electrical switch plates* (must be sealed well with two coats of sealer to withstand daily use)
5. *Tiebacks* and *curtain rods*
6. Large *mirror frames*, especially frames with relief decoration
7. *Wrought iron furniture,* such as plant stands
8. *Old lamps* (Baroque-style lamps with cast details are great.) These look terrific when finished with either an off-white linen lampshade or a less expensive parchment paper lampshade.
9. Solid brass *candlesticks*
10. Solid brass *wind chimes*

---

1. To prepare surfaces for verdigris finish: Surface preparation is an important first step because paint will not adhere properly to an oily or dirty surface. Use wire brush and/or putty knife to remove any loose, old paint on surface to be finished, if necessary. Dull new, shiny surfaces with emery cloth. Remove any remaining dust with tack cloth.

2. If the urn is metallic, follow directions in "Tips on Working with Metal Objects" before continuing.

3. If the urn is nonmetallic, begin with Primo Primer and Sealer included in kit to promote good adhesion of copper paint. Pour a small amount of primer/sealer into a cup and apply an even coat with a foam brush. Fiberglass and plastics will take primer coat well. Very porous surfaces such as raw plaster, terracotta, or unpainted wood need special attention to assure an adequate seal: a second coat may be necessary. Allow to dry about 1 hour.

4. Use bristle brush to paint outside surface and inner rim of prepared urn with undercoat of Copper Topper acrylic paint; use horizontal strokes. Shake bottle well to distribute copper evenly, and stir container frequently while painting to keep copper suspended. Allow to dry for at least 1 hour or until dry to touch.

5. Apply second coat, using strokes perpendicular to those of first coat to reduce any visible brush marks. Dry for only 5 to 10 minutes, until surface is no longer wet but still tacky. Be careful — copper paint dries quickly, and timing is critical. If you wait too long, the oxidizing solution will not react with the copper particles. If this happens, repaint before brushing on layers of oxidizing solution.

6. Brush on coat of Patina Green oxidizing solution using a bristle brush. In just minutes, patches of yellow-green will appear. After 10 to 15 minutes, surface will be fairly dry and green. If an even, green patina has not appeared after it has completely dried (1 hour maximum), second coat of copper paint may have been allowed to dry too long; repaint (repeat steps 5 and 6).

7. The verdigris patina will probably be fairly thin, with raised areas still showing copper through the verdigris. These high areas were the first to dry. Because oxidizing solution collects in the urn's crevices, more green will appear there. When completely dry, add another coat of oxidizing solution to deepen the finish, if desired. (Six coats were used to reach the level of patination seen in the photograph.) Allow to dry thoroughly after each coat. When left to dry overnight, surface will "bloom" fully by next day. To control degree of patination, apply 1 coat of oxidizing solution each day and see how much blooming occurs the next day.

8. Keep in mind that, unlike painting, patination is a chemical reaction not subject to strict control: every patina finish will look different. However, you do have some control. For example, you might prefer not to coat the urn evenly. This will result in highlights featuring an ashy haze over exposed copper (little oxidizing solution was brushed over these areas) combined with darker, greener areas in crevices, which stayed wet longer. If urn is too evenly green, gently buff with steel wool to bring back some copper highlights. For an even more mottled look, dab on additional oxidizing solution with sponge instead of a brush.

9. After desired patination has been achieved, let urn cure 3 days (urn may be used after drying overnight), then apply light coat of primer/sealer with foam brush. Sealer will kill hazy look and brighten copper highlights. Urn can be left unsealed, if preferred — colors are durable — but finish will be susceptible to oil spots and finger marks. For most households, sealer is recommended. Urn is for decorative purposes only; not for use with food. Metal objects can be used outside if sealer coat has dried for at least 1 week. Nonmetal objects such as plaster are best left indoors. Never use an object finished in verdigris as a vase for liquids. For fresh flowers, line vase with plastic or use a plastic insert such as a food storage container. However, a verdigris urn is ideal for dried flower arrangements (see "Victorian Dried Flower Bouquet," page 10). ◆

The Patina Antiquing Kit by Modern Options supplies most of the materials needed to verdigris a nonmetal object. The extras needed are a few household supplies. Only one additonal solution is necessary to verdigris metallic objects.

Tips on Working with Metal Objects

The easiest way to work with metal objects (except aluminum, iron, or steel) is to follow the steps for nonmetal objects. To actually patinate a metallic object, though, you need to determine what the object is made of. Objects can be separated into three categories: aluminum, iron, and steel; solid metals (brass, bronze, and copper); or plated metals (brass, bronze, and copper). Metal surfaces such as aluminum, iron, or steel must be primed in order to produce a nonpermeable barrier between the metal substrata and the patina reagent. Solid brass, bronze, and copper are easily patinated, although they must be stripped of any lacquer to expose the metal surface to allow the reaction to occur with the oxidizing solution. Plated metal objects, however, present a problem with patination because the plating may be thin or worn and the oxidizing solution may react with the metal underneath, causing rust spots and possibly even removing the plating.

1. *Metal surfaces such as aluminum, iron, or steel* must be primed with zinc chromate or epoxy primer using brush. Follow manufacturer's directions and allow to dry overnight. Then follow steps 4 through 9 of main directions.

2. *To determine if a brass, bronze, or copper item is solid or plated,* use a nail to scratch surface in an inconspicuous area (under base, for example). If underlying metal is the same as or a brighter color than surface, the piece is solid (go to step 4 to test for lacquering). However, if a silver color peeks through, it is plated and must be primed.

3. *For plated objects,* use brush to prime with zinc chromate or epoxy primer. Follow manufacturer's directions and allow to dry overnight. Then follow steps 4 through 9 from main directions.

4. *To determine if solid object is lacquered,* run edge of razor blade over surface of metal. If blade raises an ashy burr or flakes, surface is lacquered.

5. *For lacquered objects,* wear latex gloves and remove coating with Noxon 7 or denatured alcohol using very fine steel wool. Remove any Noxon 7 residue with a rag and denatured alcohol.

6. *For unlacquered objects and objects with lacquer removed,* wear gloves to brush on a coat of Metal Master metal cleaner using a clean bristle brush. Rinse with cold water and dry thoroughly. Then follow steps 6 through 9 of main directions.

Scented Hanger

Trimmed with ribbon roses, this lavender-scented coat hanger is a memento of Victorian times.

The Victorian needlewoman had access to a vast range of ribbons in many widths and colors, from the palest greens to the most vibrant pinks. Ribbonwork was a popular afternoon recreation for women, and they often used their abilities to great effect. Today, it would be extremely difficult to recreate the tiny delicate rosettes found on old picture frames and nightwear, but with a little skill and an eye for color, modern versions of these ribbon roses can easily be made and used to decorate lingerie, bed linen, and other soft furnishings.

The technique that follows is simple to learn and requires a minimum of sewing skill. The ribbon roses used for this project were made from ⅝" wide satin ribbon in pastel shades, but they would look equally stunning made in a darker French navy and violet color combination. For a more dramatic effect, silver and gold roses could be used to complement a hunter-green silk hanger.

For fragrance, you can substitute other essential oils, especially rose oil, for the lavender oil if you decorate with dusty pink and jasmine roses offset by a pure white fabric on the hanger. The oil can be sprinkled on tissue paper which is then used to wrap the hanger before the padding is attached.

SCENTED HANGER WITH RIBBON ROSES

1 ounce dried lavender flowers
   Few drops of essential oil of lavender
1 wooden hanger with screw-on hook
½ yard silk or satin fabric in desired colors
½ yard medium-weight quilt batting
1 skein 6-strand embroidery floss to match fabric or ribbon
½ yard each of ⅝" wide single-faced satin ribbon in 5 colors, as desired
   Thread to match fabric and ribbons
   Clear-drying tacky glue
   Sewing needle
   Straight pins
   Scissors
   Ruler
   Iron

1. *For the hanger,* put lavender flowers in small glass or china bowl and sprinkle with essential oil. Stir well and let sit for a few hours until all oil has been absorbed. Unscrew hook from hanger and set aside.

2. Place hanger on wrong side of silk or satin fabric and trace around it.

3. Remove hanger and draw a sewing line around traced area, ¾" from its perimeter. Mark cut line ⅜" beyond sewing line. Cut fabric.

4. Pin cut fabric to remaining fabric, with right sides together. Use cut piece of fabric as template to cut identical piece for back. Measure and mark center of top edge. Starting from center and leaving a small gap, machine-stitch together 2 pieces of cut fabric outward to ends. Press open edges ⅜" to wrong side. Trim seams and clip curves. Turn cover right side out. If necessary, use a needle to push out corners.

5. Cut batting into rectangle 8" wide and 2" longer than hanger. Stir lavender flowers again and sprinkle over batting. Center hanger at bottom edge of batting. Fold batting around and around hanger, pulling tightly and easing over curves. Trim any excess batting. Secure batting by whip-stitching all raw edges along sides and bottom. Use hook to make a hole in batting so that it can later be reinserted when cover is completed.

6. Gently push hanger into cover, compressing batting with your fingers as necessary. Slip-stitch bottom edge closed.

7. Put small amount of glue on outer tip of hook and tightly wrap embroidery floss around hook, pushing strands close together so no metal shows through. When screw is reached, use glue to anchor thread. Let dry. Screw hook back into hanger.

8. *For the ribbon roses,* with matte side of ribbon facing you, fold corner down to form a right triangle.

9. To form center, roll end of ribbon 3 turns to make a tight tube. Pinch base of tube together with thumb and forefinger and stitch tightly with matching thread; leave thread attached.

10. Fold ribbon diagonally outwards, then

Other dried flowers and essential oils, especially rose oil, can be substituted for the evocative lavender flowers and oil used to scent this covered and crafted hanger.

curve it loosely around center to form first petal. Pinch base together and make 1 or 2 stitches to secure petal.

11. Continue rolling and folding, staggering folds for each round, until rose is of desired fullness.

12. Trim ribbon end, turn under, and stitch to base of rose.

13. For each leaf, cut a short length of ribbon. Bring cut edges down as shown to form triangle; make sure satin side faces out. Pin to secure.

14. Knot a length of matching thread and run a row of tiny basting stitches along lower edge through all thicknesses of ribbon. Remove pin and trim ends straight.

15. Pull basting stitches up tightly to gather, and wrap with thread, ending with 2 to 3 small stitches to secure.

16. Stitch several ribbon roses and leaves to hanger at base of hook. ◆

Julia Jones, a designer based in England, is the coauthor of *The English Country Craft Collection* (David & Charles, 1991).

PHOTOGRAPH BY JON DAVIDSON

How to Cover the Hanger

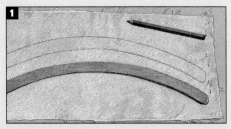

1. Remove hook and place hanger on wrong side of fabric and trace around it.

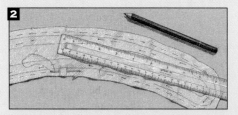

2. Draw a sewing line around traced area ³⁄₄" from its perimeter. Mark cut line (dotted line above) ³⁄₈" beyond sewing line. Cut fabric.

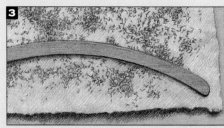

3. Sprinkle lavender flowers over batting and center hanger at bottom edge of batting.

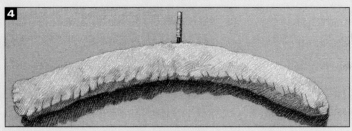

4. Fold batting around and around hanger until all the batting is used. Trim and stitch. Insert hook to make a hole in batting.

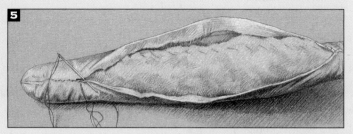

5. Push hanger into cover, compressing batting, and slip-stitch bottom edge closed.

How to Make a Ribbon Rose

Note: Wider ribbon used in illustrations to show detail.

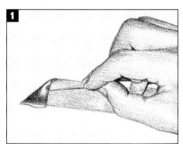

1. With matte side of ribbon facing you, fold corner down to form a right triangle.

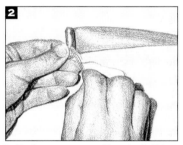

2. To form center, roll end of ribbon three times to make a tube; pinch base and hand stitch tightly.

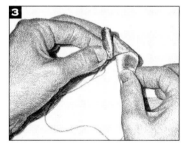

3. Fold ribbon diagonally outwards.

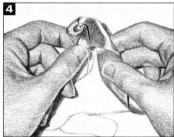

4. Curve ribbon loosely around center to form first petal; pinch base and hand stitch in place.

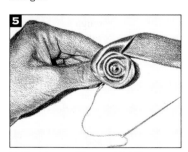

5. Continue rolling and folding, staggering folds until rose reaches desired fullness.

6. Trim ribbon end and stitch to base.

7. For leaf, form triangle with short length of ribbon.

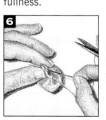

8. Hand stitch across lower edge through all thicknesses of ribbon.

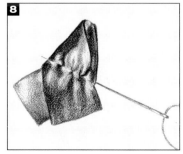

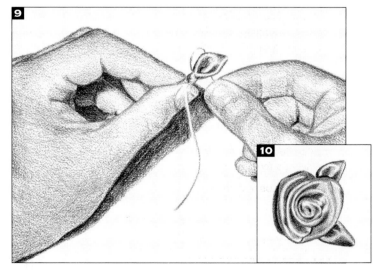

9. Pull stitches tightly together and wrap with thread.

10. Finished rose with leaves stitched to base.

Victorian Dried Flower Bouquet

A grand centerpiece is made with a quick, casual arrangement of dried hydrangea, golden ivy, and bittersweet.

This arrangement of dried flowers combines easily found materials in a range of earth tones — cinnabar, rust, sienna, yellow, and beige — with ripples of satin gold leaves against the dense gray-black background of the urn. The texture of this bouquet runs from silky cascades of gold foliage to crinkly masses of hydrangea, brushy tufts of dried astilbe, and knobby fists of dried pomegranate. The container featured in the photograph is an antique cast-iron urn of the sort that was used in nineteenth-century gardens. Choose an urn that is higher than it is wide so that the vines can cascade over the rim and down the front. Because the urn will not need to hold water, it can be made of plaster or almost any other material. Any muted color and finish will do (for a verdigris finish, *see* "How to Create a Verdigris Finish," page 6), but if you wish to duplicate the finish of this particular urn, purchase lampblack (used to polish wood stoves) and follow the manufacturer's directions. To age the finish, use rottenstone (a decomposed shale powder used to polish furniture). Dust the urn with rottenstone using a brush and then remove the excess with a dry cloth. The gray powder will lodge in the crevices and soften the overall finish.

VICTORIAN DRIED FLOWER BOUQUET

1 large decorative urn or vase, 14" tall, 10" in diameter
8 large heads dried mop-headed hydrangea
3 dried baby artichokes
2 dried pomegranates
2 branches dried bittersweet
1 2' wired vine of silk leaves, such as ivy
1 long twig of beech
2 stems dried astilbe, dryandra, or other natural flowers
3 clusters red berry; artificial (optional)
1 can gold enamel spray paint
4 sheets newspaper to cover floor and for wadding
2 blocks dry floral foam (4½" x 9" x 3")
Sharp 10"-12" scalloped bread knife
Hot-glue gun and glue sticks
Medium-gauge wire
Floral picks

1. Prepare the plant materials. For pomegranate, hot-glue a floral pick to the bottom center of dried pomegranate to form a false stem (this will resemble candied apples).
2. For baby artichoke, twist one end of wire around the bottom collar formed by the first row of scales, leaving 6" or so of straight wire to form a false stem.
3. For 5 hydrangea, cut stems, leaving 6" to 8" of bare stem from cut end to base of mop-headed hydrangea. Crumble other 3 for filler.
4. For leafy vine, hold over newspaper by end of wire and spray-paint gold along front and back surface, then lightly spray some of hydrangea with gold paint. Allow to dry overnight.
5. With tightly wadded newspaper, fill urn to within 4" of top rim. (If foam is not large enough to cover mouth of urn, connect 2 foam blocks by inserting floral picks in between.) Press joined blocks onto rim of urn to form an indentation.
6. With a sharp knife, slice along indentation made by rim.
7. Round and taper foam edges to fit urn just below rim. Wedge into

Four natural materials — pomegranate, baby artichoke, hydrangea, and bittersweet — are arranged in less than 15 minutes.

container with palms of hands to avoid denting foam.

8. To arrange plant materials, insert 5 prepared hydrangea stems close to rim along sides and back of urn. Nestle remaining hydrangea pieces to cover surface of foam.
9. Add stems of bittersweet and crimp (but do not break) the stem where it emerges from foam so bittersweet cascades over rim, just off-center. Repeat this step with beech (but do not crimp).
10. Insert astilbe or other flower overhanging left rim.
11. Insert prepared artichokes and pomegranates, leaving heads above low hydrangea. Insert leafy vine at the back of foam, bending stem to arch gracefully over top to cascade down front of urn and cover crimped bittersweet.
12. Add berry clusters for additional decoration, if desired. ◆

How to Use Floral Foam

1. Place two blocks of joined floral foam on top of vase and press to create an indentation.

2. Slice along indentation with a sharp knife.

3. Insert five hydrangea into foam around sides and back of urn.

4. Nestle remaining hydrangea blossoms over surface of foam to cover and then add remaining plant materials.

 PHOTOGRAPH BY TOM MCCAVERA, DESIGNED BY RAYMOND WAITES, ILLUSTRATIONS BY LINDA FENNIMORE

No-Sew Lace Sachets

*An English rose potpourri captured in lace handkerchiefs
makes luxurious no-sew sachets.*

A piece of muslin secured with a rubber band is used to contain the potpourri, which is then wrapped with a new or antique handkerchief.

Nothing could be simpler yet more elegant than a beautiful lace handkerchief redolent of the lush, sweet scent of a rose or citrus potpourri wrapped inside. In just a few minutes, you can wrap and finish several sachets using either one of the recipes provided here or a commercial potpourri.

I use antique handkerchiefs, beautiful wisps of batiste and lace, although many newly purchased handkerchiefs will do just as well. The potpourri is placed in a small muslin bag, which is twisted closed and held together with a rubber band. This sachet is then wrapped in a handkerchief and tied with a piece of ribbon.

For the potpourri, I am always attracted to roses. Their lush petals create rich ruffles in pale pinks and deep fuchsias, and they always smell as lovely as they look. I use them in flower arrangements all summer and dry them for potpourri. In winter, the rose potpourri and floral waters and the sachets I've made with them tide me over until spring arrives.

My favorite garden, Sissinghurst, in Kent, England, is filled with the shrub roses that Vita Sackville-West planted. She saved many of these species, some of which are hundreds of years old, from extinction. The Bagatelle Gardens in Paris are a sight to behold in May and June, when the roses are blooming on trellises and trained into garlands. These gardens contain the old-fashioned roses that have grown in Europe for centuries and whose fragrances are overwhelming.

This is exactly the kind of scent you'll discover in the Old-English Rose Potpourri recipe printed below, which I discovered in one of my eighteenth-century herb books. I have also included a second recipe for a potpourri with a citrus fragrance. Once you've made the sachet, you can hang it in the clothes closet or tuck it into drawers between your sweaters or bed linens. The captivating scent will linger. Sachets may also be wrapped in cellophane for gift giving.

LACE HANDKERCHIEF SACHET

- 1 square lace handkerchief
- 1 piece of cotton muslin
- 1 length of pretty ribbon, ¼" wide
- 1–2 ounces of potpourri, depending on the size of your handkerchief
  Rubber band

1. Cut the piece of muslin 1" smaller than handkerchief. Edges can be cut with pinking shears to give a more finished look.

2. If homemade potpourri is too oily, add more dried floral material. Place potpourri in center of muslin square and make a ball of it, twisting top and securing with rubber band.

3. Place potpourri sachet in middle of lace handkerchief.

4. Pull corners up and tie around middle with ribbon. Make bow and trim ends as desired.

CHERCHEZ'S OLD-ENGLISH ROSE POTPOURRI

- 7 ounces rose petals (mixed colors for open display, if desired)
- 2 ounces cream globe amaranth
- 2 ounces cut lemongrass
- 1 ounce powdered orrisroot
- 15 drops rose, tea rose, or rose geranium oil

Mix all ingredients thoroughly in a glass bowl or in a glazed pottery bowl. To cure, place mixture in brown paper bag lined with waxed paper for a week or two, shaking every so often.

CITRUS POTPOURRI

- 4 ounces cut orange peel
- 4 ounces marigold flowers
- 3 ounces chamomile flowers
- 1 ounce cut lemongrass
- 1 ounce powdered orrisroot
- 20 drops lemon or lemon verbena oil

For a potpourri with a tangy, citrusy fragrance, combine these ingredients using the directions above. ◆

Barbara Milo Ohrbach is the author of several books, including *The Scented Room* (Clarkson Potter, 1986) and *Simply Flowers, Practical Advice and Beautiful Ideas for Creating Flower-Filled Rooms* (Clarkson Potter, 1993). She lectures throughout the United States on antiques, gardening, and decorating.

Painted Curly Maple Dresser

An inexpensive, unfinished pine dresser is transformed into a show-stopping period piece featuring watercolor imitations of burl and curly maple finishes.

With a few simple materials — a feather, watercolor paint, apple cider vinegar, a few brushes, and some putty — you can transform a plain store-bought piece of pine furniture into a stunning replica of the country-painted American pieces reminiscent of the 1840s. The work can be done in less than a day (not including drying time), using new materials and techniques developed for the home enthusiast. The materials and techniques can also be used on previously finished furniture.

Nineteenth-century craftspeople used a mixture of powdered pigments and beer to make paints. A simpler, easy-to-apply paint is made with artists' tube watercolors combined with apple cider vinegar. This project uses three paint mixtures: burnt sienna, a mixture of burnt sienna and burnt umber, and Prussian blue. There are two basic methods resulting in two different wood grain finishes: burl and curly maple. The burl grain, which is used on the drawer fronts and on the top of the dresser, is created by applying a base layer of burnt sienna paint topped with highlights of Prussian blue and then the burnt sienna/burnt umber mixture. Glazing putty and gloved fingers are used to mottle the surface, creating a layered, burled appearance. The curly maple finish, which is not "curly" at all, but striated in appearance, is used on the sides and front of the dresser framework and for decorative borders on the top and the drawer fronts. It is created by brushing on a coat of the burnt sienna/burnt umber mixture and then brushing it with a turkey feather to create a ribbed look, with alternating thin stripes of darker paint separated by sections of lighter tones. A "molding" accent is then added to the drawer fronts with a narrow rectangle of Prussian blue paint; this detail creates the look of expensive, inlaid wood. A final coat of shellac is used to protect and harden all painted finishes.

Although this is a substantial project which will take the better part of a day, these same techniques can be applied to a small chest, a box, or a tray. You can even create painted

This inexpensive pine dresser cost just $129 and was painted in a faux burl and curly maple finish with less than a single day's work.

wooden picture frames or apply these finishes directly to a door or to moldings.

We suggest that you test the paints and techniques described below on practice boards as you procede to each new step, until the combination of paints is correct and you develop sufficient skills to work quickly. When working on either the practice boards or the actual project, you can remove paint with apple cider vinegar and a cloth and then wipe or dab the area dry with a clean, dry cloth.

PAINTED CURLY MAPLE DRESSER

All wood surfaces, either raw or previously finished, must be prepared for painting (*see* "How to Prepare Wood for Painting," page 14 as well as the painting tips from profess-

ABOUT MASKING TAPES

The sides and front of the dresser famework will be painted in a curly maple finish without any decorative borders. However, the top and drawer fronts will be painted with a center panel of country burl and an outside border of curly maple. The drawer fronts will also feature an "inlay" strip of Prussian blue. The best technique for marking off areas not to be painted is to use masking tape. The best masking tapes to use are white artists' tape because the adhesive is not overly sticky and it removes cleanly and painters' tape that has an adhesive on just a portion of the width.

White artists' tape is used to mask the outer edges of the drawer fronts before painting.

PHOTOGRAPH BY TOM MCCAVERA, ILLUSTRATION BY TONY DELUZ

ionals on page 15, for additional information).

1 ½-ounce tube each of high-quality watercolor paint in burnt sienna and burnt umber
1 ¼-ounce tube of high-quality watercolor paint in Prussian blue
1 bottle apple cider vinegar
1 1" foam brush
3 2" foam brushes
1 3" foam brush
3 ¼" soft-bristled brushes
1 quart of glazing putty, rolled into walnut-size balls
12 sheets plastic wrap, torn into 12" wide strips
1 package of turkey feathers (10 per package) with barbs cut to ¼" along convex edge
1 roll 1" wide white artists' tape
1 roll 2" wide painters' masking tape (adhesive on portion of width only)
   Tack cloths (cheesecloth impregnated with linseed oil)
1 sheet #220 sandpaper
1 pint shellac, 3-pound cut (cut indicates degree of dilution)
   Denatured alcohol (optional, for thinning shellac for a faster drying coat)
1 pint semigloss finish
   Wooden stir sticks for paint
3 smooth-bottomed containers for mixing paint
   Measuring cup
1 set measuring spoons
1 pair vinyl gloves
1 package cotton swabs
   Section of Styrofoam
   Cheesecloth
   Hair dryer (optional)

Making the Paints

Mix paint and vinegar in a smooth-bottomed container, mashing paint against sides and bottom until all lumps are dissolved. The amounts specified will provide a quantity large enough for practicing the technique and rendering the chest. Because brands of paint differ, you may have to add more vinegar if the paint is too opaque, or more pigment if the color is not strong enough and/or if the mixture is too thin.

1. Mix ½-ounce tube of burnt sienna paint with ¼ cup of apple cider vinegar; divide into 2 batches.

2. Mix ½-ounce tube of burnt umber paint with ¼ cup of apple cider vinegar and combine with 1 batch of burnt sienna mixture.

3. Mix ¼-ounce tube of Prussian blue with 2 tablespoons of apple cider vinegar.

Creating the Burl Finish

This technique is used for the dresser top and the drawer fronts. The knobs should be unscrewed and removed from the drawer fronts. Gloves may be worn throughout; always paint in a dust-free, well-ventilated area.

1. Apply 1" tape to dresser top from outside edges in, creating a 1" border all around. Press edges down firmly to prevent paint seepage.

2. Stir burnt sienna paint. Dip a 2" foam brush about halfway into paint.

3. Spread paint over surface with a "scrubbing-in" motion. Paint will probably clump unevenly, revealing circles of base coat; this will actually enhance final look of burl.

4. Stir Prussian blue paint. Dip a ¼" brush halfway into paint and, holding brush vertically, dab tips of bristles randomly into wet areas of burnt sienna paint, about 1¼" to 1½" apart. Avoid a tight repetition of dot patterns.

5. Dip second ¼" brush halfway into burnt sienna paint or use a corner of same foam brush used in step 2. Dab this on top of Prussian blue dots.

6. Form one of prepared balls of glazing putty into a 4" roll, then fold it over so that it has creases in it (creases provide additional texture). Starting at left end of painted surface, roll putty as if it were a rolling pin from bottom to top, repeating this motion on whole surface. Keep recreasing putty. The object is to pull off paint and rearrange what is left. Make a fresh roll of putty when piece you are using no longer removes paint. Work quickly.

7. Dip third ¼" brush halfway into burnt sienna/burnt umber mixture, and apply randomly over surface.

8. Crumple a piece of plastic wrap and roll over surface to break up and redistribute paint.

9. Repeat step 7.

10. Press gloved fingertips lightly into darker areas of paint to create a blurred, less distinct pattern.

Building a Burl Finish

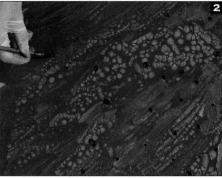

1. Using a 2" foam brush, apply burnt sienna paint with a "scrubbing-in" motion.

2. Dab Prussian blue paint randomly into wet areas of burnt sienna paint.

3. Dip corner of foam brush into burnt sienna paint and dab on top of Prussian blue dots.

4. Roll log of glazing putty as if it were a rolling pin, in order to rearrange paint on surface.

5. Use a ¼" brush to apply dots of burnt sienna/burnt umber mixture.

6. Roll crumpled piece of plastic wrap over surface to break up and redistribute paint.

7. After repeating step 7 and using gloved fingertips to blur the pattern, add dabs of Prussian blue and then use putty to break them up.

Faux-Finish Details

Side of dresser: Columns of curly maple finish appear striated when painted and feathered correctly, with alternating lighter and darker tones.

Top of dresser: The border is made with the curly maple finish; the center section is painted with the burl finish.

Drawers: These are painted in the same manner as the top with the addition of a "molding accent" of Prussian blue that resembles inlaid wood.

11. With brush used in step 4, dab Prussian blue randomly and very lightly on surface.

12. With a gloved finger and/or putty, touch each dab to break it up. Then use a light circular motion to blend it into surface.

13. Examine surface and make corrections. Desired effect is a random mottling of paints and base-coat color, yielding lighter and darker hues. Use a gloved finger to eliminate any harsh edges. You may also add burnt sienna/burnt umber mixture or Prussian blue paint for further contrast. A hair dryer may be used to shorten drying time.

14. Apply shellac when surfaces are thoroughly dry. (For a faster-drying, thinner finish, dilute shellac up to 50% with denatured alcohol.) Because this is a relatively quick process, you may use a 2" foam brush for shellacking even though they are not generally recommended for this task as they tend to disintegrate (regular brushes will leave individual bristles stuck in shellac). *Do not use a hair dryer on shellac.*

15. Remove tape. Let surfaces dry thoroughly.

16. Clean paint seepage on unpainted areas with cotton swab and apple cider vinegar.

17. Repeat steps 1 through 16 for each drawer front.

Creating the Curly Maple Finish

1. *For the borders of the drawer fronts,* start with top left corner of a drawer. Place strip of 1" tape diagonally from corner of drawer to edge of painted burl finish. (Tape will run at 45° angle to edge of drawer — width of tape will block adjacent border.) This will give borders a mitered look. Repeat this for top right corner of drawer. Press tape down firmly.

2. Place a piece of 2" tape lengthwise across drawer, with top edge even with top of burl finish.

3. Repeat steps 1 and 2 for bottom edge of drawer.

4. Dip 1" foam brush partway into burnt sienna/burnt umber mixture and apply to exposed top edge between strips of tape. Do not be concerned if paint brushes over tape.

5. Pick up a turkey feather by the quill, close to where barbs begin (for more detailed work, you can hold feather closer to tip). If you are right-handed, start at left edge of surface you are painting. Use trimmed edge of feather (it should be perpendicular to edge of work surface) and press firmly into paint, pushing to left to form a small ridge of paint. Lift feather off work surface and place just to right of beginning of preceding stroke.

6. Repeat step 5, pushing each successive stroke over end of prior stroke.

7. Touch tip of the 1" foam brush, held vertically, to fill in any broken lines or gaps. Final pattern should be a series of dark thin lines separated by wider bands of lighter paint. Use a delicate touch.

8. Repeat process for bottom of drawer front.

9. Remove all tape. Let dry (or use hair dryer) and then apply shellac. Let dry. *Do not use a hair dryer on shellac.*

10. When dry, tape unpainted sides of drawer front, following steps 1 through 3.

11. Repeat steps 4 through 9 on these taped, unpainted areas.

HOW TO PREPARE WOOD FOR PAINTING

To Prepare Furniture for Painting You Will Need:

1 quart latex primer*
1 quart flat latex interior house paint* (Benjamin Moore 1148 or another "raw sienna" color)
1 sheet #220 sandpaper
1 2" natural bristle brush
1 2" foam brush
  Tack cloth

To Prepare Already Finished Surfaces You Will Also Need:

1 can naphtha
½ pint spackling compound
1 sheet #120 sandpaper
  Putty knife
  Rag

New raw wood surfaces, like the chest used in this project, require a primer to seal the wood. We prefer alkyd to latex because latex paint does not sand well. To begin, wipe the area to be painted with a tack cloth. Use a 2" bristle brush to apply a primer coat, let dry, and sand with #220 sandpaper. Remove dust with a tack cloth. Use a 2" foam brush and apply a flat latex interior house paint (*see* below).

Older surfaces that have been previously finished will usually require additional preparation. With a rag, rub naphtha (a highly flammable substance — follow manufacturer's safety directions) on the surface to remove any wax and let dry. Using a putty knife, fill holes with spackle; when spackle has hardened, sand entire area to be painted with #120 sandpaper to provide an even surface to which the primer coat will adhere. Remove dust with a tack cloth. Apply primer and latex undercoat as instructed above.

* Note: We have recommended a latex paint and primer only because flat alkyd interior paint and primer is not available in some states due to local laws. If you can legally purchase alkyd interior paints and primer, we recommend their use.

PHOTOGRAPHS BY NICK SIMONE

12. Repeat steps 1 through 11 for each drawer.

13. *For the border of the dresser top,* follow steps 1 through 11.

14. *For the sides and front framework of the dresser,* lay dresser on side.

15. Starting on long back edge, use a 3" foam brush to apply burnt sienna/burnt umber paint mixture in 12" to 15" long strips. Longer strips may dry before you have feathered them.

16. Repeat feather manipulations used on drawer fronts. Use both hands, holding feather by tip and by quill.

17. When you are 2" from end of paint strip, apply another 15" strip of paint with foam brush. Repeat steps 15 to 17 until side is completed.

18. Let paint dry (or use hair dryer). Shellac with a 2" foam brush and let dry. *Do not use a hair dryer on shellac.*

19. Repeat steps 15 to18 for other side and front framework of dresser.

Creating the Inlaid Molding on Drawer Fronts

1. Cover curly maple border around drawer front with 2" tape. Leave exposed a hairline where curly maple meets burl.

2. Apply tape parallel to curly maple border all around drawer front to cover burl, but leaving an exposed area of burl that is ¼" wide. This will create a thin rectangle of exposed burl. Press tape down firmly.

3. Fold sandpaper and crease edge. Sand exposed areas, paying particular attention to area right next to tape. Sand until all shine is removed, otherwise additional paint will not adhere to surface. Remove dust by wiping with tack cloth.

4. With ¼" brush, paint Prussian blue mixture on sanded area. Wipe off with cheesecloth or other cloth. (Sanding and first coat will break surface tension and form a "matte tooth.") Apply a second coat of Prussian blue paint.

5. Press a ball of glazing putty into paint and dab it repeatedly until whole band of "molding" is mottled. Let paint dry (or use hair dryer).

6. Shellac with 2" foam brush and let dry. *Do not use a hair dryer on shellac.* Remove tape. Clean up paint seepage between painted areas with a cotton swab and apple cider vinegar.

7. Repeat steps 1 through 6 for each drawer.

Painting the Drawer Knobs
The knobs were removed from the drawer fronts in an earlier step. Push bolts/screws that protrude from back of knobs into a section of Styrofoam to secure. Follow directions for painting the burl finish. Shellac and allow to dry.

Applying the Final Finish
Apply a semigloss finish with a 2" foam brush to all painted surfaces. Dry thoroughly. Replace knobs on drawers when completely dry.

Painting Tips from Professionals
• Take the time to prepare surfaces for painting, especially when painting over an existing finished surface.

• When applying base coats to the dresser, also coat a practice board. Use the board at each stage of the project to practice new techniques.

• To paint items that have bolts or screws attached to them, remove them from the furniture and then push the bolt/screw into a section of Styrofoam to secure.

• When taping, be sure to firmly press the edges of the tape to the surface to prevent paint from seeping underneath the tape.

• For crisp painted edges, always paint over the edge of the tape.

• Purchase the highest quality paints available. These paints contain a higher proportion of pigments to other ingredients, resulting in better coverage.

• Use interior, not exterior, paints.

• Water-based paints will "crawl" or float on a surface that has not been properly prepared (e.g., sanded).

• When shellacking, load your brush fully or it will drag. *Do not use a hair dryer on shellac* (this can be dangerous). Be sure to use fresh shellac. ◆

Ina Brosseau Marx, Allen Marx, and **Robert Marx** are codirectors of The Finishing School in Port Washington, New York. They coauthored *Professional Painted Finishes — A Guide to the Art and Business of Decorative Finishes* (Watson-Guptill, 1991). The Marxes have also produced six videos that include many of the techniques featured in the book.

Painting the Inlaid Molding

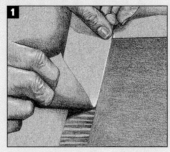

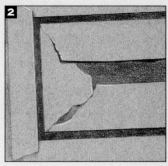

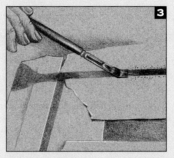

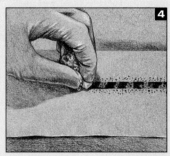

1. Cover curly maple border around drawer fronts with 2" tape. Leave a hairline where the curly maple meets the burl finish.

2. Apply tape parallel to curly maple border, leaving an exposed strip of burl, ¼" wide.

3. Sand exposed area and paint with Prussian blue paint.

4. Use putty to mottle surface of paint.

Painting the Curly Maple Finish

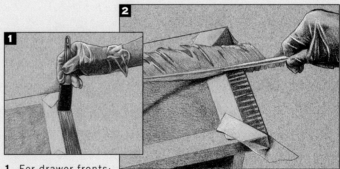

1. For drawer fronts: After masking, paint burnt sienna/burnt umber mixture onto borders with foam brush.

2. Press turkey feather into wet paint, pushing to left to create small ridges of paint. Continue for length of border.

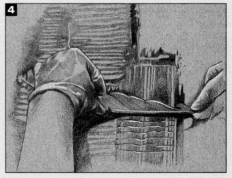

3. For dresser sides: Paint a 12" to 15" long strip of burnt sienna/burnt umber mixture on side of dresser.

4. Use feather to create striated pattern. Continue painting and feathering until side is completed.

Rose Decoupage Lampshade

Use the Pierre-Joseph Redouté roses printed in this issue and an easy cutting method to quickly decorate a lampshade.

D ecoupage, from the French verb *couper* (to cut), is the art of applying cut-out printed images to articles of wood, glass, metal, parchment, plastic, and ceramic. Images can be found almost everywhere; antique and print shops may have collections of chromolithography and Dover Publications publishes three sumptuous volumes of public-domain art (illustrations that are not copyrighted and can be used freely) that are perfect to use on decoupage projects.

When selecting images, it is important to assess the quality of the print and the type of paper used. Paper that is the thickness of two magazine pages is the easiest to work with. Make certain that any printing on the reverse side will not show through when glued. Colors must not bleed; to test, apply a small dab of sealer (*see* below) to a dot-size portion of the print; if the dab acquires a halo, do not use the print.

One of the most inventive solutions to using any image — valuable prints or fine art that you do not want to cut, or images printed on thin paper that might allow the reverse side to show through — is to make a color laser copy of it. Color copiers can also reduce or enlarge the image, and the colors can be manipulated to achieve any color you prefer. Keep in mind that copy colors fade in strong light, and that copy paper is often rather thin and may wrinkle.

We have provided two pages of variously sized images of a full-color reproduction of a painting by Pierre-Joseph Redouté (1759–1840), a botanical painter famous for his renderings of roses. Applied to a black lampshade trimmed in gold, it combines the formal elegance and casual charm of eighteenth-century French decoupage.

Do not be intimidated by the de-

A print with a black background, affixed to a black shade, renders cut edges invisible.

tail on the rose image; we have intentionally used a black background in order to provide for a wide range of cutting ability and accuracy; the cut black margins will disappear when applied to the black lampshade. Remember, it will take some practice to develop confidence and skill in cutting; consider using the smallest rose images for practice and apply them to a smaller object such as a box. Virtually any flat surface or one with a smooth contour is appropriate for decoupage.

ROSE DECOUPAGE LAMPSHADE

Rose print (*see* special insert, following pages)

HOW TO CUT INTRICATE DECOUPAGE

P rints with intricate contours may hold great appeal for decoupage, but are often difficult to cut out. The technique illustrated here, which uses both household and manicure scissors, will make the job easier.

Cut out the decoupage image with household scissors, leaving a 1" border around the image. Hold the manicure scissors in your right hand, with the curved blade pointing to the right and the palm of your right hand facing up slightly. Feed the paper *into* the blades with your left hand, turning the paper as you cut and wiggling it slightly; this motion creates a minutely beveled, feathered edge that facilitates gluing the print to another surface.

1 lampshade: 4" across top x 8" across bottom x 7" rise (side measurment)
40" flexible flat gold ribbon, 3/16" wide
  Manicure scissors
  Household scissors
1 1" disposable fine-grain foam brush
1 8-ounce jar of Mod Podge Medium, matte finish
  Craft glue, such as Sobo or Welbond
  Cotton swab

1. Cut out a rose with sharp scissors, leaving a 1" black background. Trim edges with manicure scissors, leaving no more than 1/8" border around image. You can cut closer, but be careful not to cut into image.

2. With brush, evenly apply a thin sealing coat of Mod Podge to outside surface of lampshade. Let dry.

3. Apply second coat.

4. While second coat is wet, place cut-out image on lampshade in desired position and smooth down with fingertips to eliminate air pockets and to ensure even adhesion. Pay particular attention to edges.

5. Allow this coat to dry thoroughly, at least 2 hours, but ideally overnight.

6. Evenly apply 6 successive thin coats of Mod Podge, waiting only 15 to 20 minutes between coats. Alternate the direction of brush strokes on each successive coat. Allow to dry overnight.

7. Measure and cut 2 lengths of gold ribbon, 1 for top circumference of lampshade and 1 for bottom circumference, adding 1/4" for overlap. Apply a thin bead of glue on lampshade, inset from rim about 1/8". Apply ribbon over glue, with ends positioned at back of shade; press gently in place. Apply extra dab of glue on ribbon ends to hold in place.

8. Remove any excess glue with a damp cotton swab. ◆

PHOTOGRAPH BY TOM McCAVERA, ILLUSTRATIONS BY LINDA FENNIMORE

Easy-Cut
Decoupage
Rose

Pierre-Joseph Redouté (1759-1840)

Using household scissors, cut out desired rose print leaving a 1" field of black background around the entire image. Using manicure scissors, carefully recut as close as possible to image (leaving no more than ⅛"). Keep in mind that when image is applied to black background, any remaining outline will disappear.

Satin-Leaf Topiary

Satin leaves and a Styrofoam ball make a quick, everlasting centerpiece.

Topiaries can be made from satin leaves, as shown here, or from natural materials such as fresh bay leaves or sheets of moss.

Using satin leaves and a Styrofoam ball, you can make everlasting topiaries that are easily mounted on candlesticks. By making topiaries in different sizes and by varying the height of the candlesticks, you can quickly create a delightful and asymmetrical centerpiece for your table. A group of satin-leaf topiary heads or globes can also be displayed in bowls or used as Christmas ornaments.

Topiaries can also be made from natural materials such as fresh bay leaves, which are applied in overlapping rows using white glue. Hold each leaf in place for a moment with a finger until the glue firms up, or use a pin inserted into the bottom V of the leaf (remove the pin when the glue is dry). Apply a light coat of a glossy acrylic finish when the topiary is completed. You may also use sheets of moss or fresh sage leaves to decorate the topiary heads.

SATIN-LEAF TOPIARY

1 Styrofoam ball, 5" in diameter (or smaller, if desired)
9 packages of satin or velvet leaves (about 110 leaves), 1½" long on wire stems
2 packages of pearl corsage pins (about 65 pins)
½ yard 1" or 1½" wide wire-edge ribbon
  Dark sewing thread
  Floral clay
1 floral spike
1 candlestick of desired height
1 drinking glass, slightly smaller in diameter than Styrofoam ball
  Scissors

1. Push a pearl pin into each of 2 opposite points of Styrofoam ball to mark top and bottom. Tie thread around top pin and guide it all around ball, looping it around bottom pin as you pass it. Repeat with a round of thread perpendicular to the first, so that Styrofoam ball is divided into 4 equal quadrants. Use drinking glass to hold ball steady when working. Trim stems of satin leaves to ½", and bend each stem at a 90° angle to leaf.

2. Place stem of 1 leaf in each quadrant so that tip of leaf touches pin; push stem into ball.

3. Continue to insert stems of leaves into Styrofoam ball, staggering and overlapping each successive round and working toward bottom end of ball. Increase number of leaves in each round as necessary to cover Styrofoam ball completely. Push pearl corsage pins into centers of leaves.

4. Press a wad of floral clay inside candle cup of candlestick. Insert floral spike into clay and push Styrofoam ball onto spike. Tie ribbon around candlestick and cut a V-notch at each end. ◆

Raymond Waites is a designer and creative vice-president of Gear Holdings, Inc., and is the author of *Small Pleasures* (Little, Brown and Company, 1992).

Layering a Topiary, Step-by-Step

1. Divide Styrofoam ball into four quadrants using thread and pearl corsage pins. Bend leaf stems at a 90° angle.

2. Place one leaf in each quadrant, so that tip of leaf touches top pin.

3. Insert additional leaves in staggered and overlapping rows to cover Styrofoam ball completely.

4. Push pearl corsage pins into centers of leaves as shown (use about 65 pins for a 5" ball).

Eight Heirloom Wreaths

From a luxe $300 silk flower wreath to a quick and easy gold-sprayed holly wreath, here are eight heirloom wreaths made with four basic decorating techniques.

The beauty of working with fresh and dried floral materials is that with only a few basic materials and tools, along with an understanding of four elementary decorating techniques, you can make any style wreath you desire, regardless of your level of craft experience.

Though we traditionally associate wreaths with Christmas, you will be able to reinterpret these decorations for year-round display. For example, a plain vine wreath covered in dried tea roses, shiny berries, and foliage can be left bare in winter; add a medallion of grape clusters and eucalyptus leaves in autumn. Because you make the wreaths yourself, you will be able to make them in the size and style appropriate to the season, the settings in which you place them, and the functions you wish them to serve. A wreath of dried roses can be made in miniature and used to decorate a gift package, a table setting, or objects such as candlesticks and clock finials. A fresh evergreen wreath can encircle a hurricane lamp or serve as a holiday centerpiece or it can, of course, be placed on an outside door.

Applying the Decoration

It is best to begin with one floral material at a time, starting with the heavy, larger ingredients and working down to the more delicate, smaller ones to avoid damaging them.

You can apply decorations using a clock for orientation in a 12-4-8 or a 12-3-6-9 configuration. Or, if you prefer, you can work three different sections in sequence, covering the inner edge of the frame first, then the outer edge, finishing with the center surface on the top of the frame. If the arrangement is not an overall design, prepare the background first, then start at the center of the focal point and work outward. Direct all the stems so that leaves and flower heads radiate outward at the sides and the front surfaces. There are no strict rules, only four basic techniques that will allow the design to evolve according to the materials used and your personal taste. Feel free to use more than one technique in a single wreath.

Hot-glue guns are available in either hot-melt or low-melt versions. Low-melt guns use a lower temperature to avoid painful burns usually associated with hot-melt guns. To use, first determine the angle and position of the decoration, as the glue will harden within 10 seconds. Press the trigger to apply a shot of glue to the desired position and place the decoration into the glue. Hot-glue guns are best suited for vine, twig, wire, moss, and all dried materials. Hot glue can melt some foams and plastic; test the glue on a small section first. If hot glue cannot be used, substitute spool wire, string, white glue, or floral picks.

Because it can dispense a superheated stream of liquid glue, a hot-glue gun should always be used with caution. Unplug the gun when it is not in use. Keep a bowl of ice water nearby for accidental burns. Keep children away from the gun.

Wire can be used to attach silk flowers with plastic-coated wire stems. Cut the stems to 6" to 8" lengths using wire cutters. On a vine frame, insert the stem between the vines and through to the back. Bring the stem around to the top and reinsert the stem down between the vines to secure. For flowers and foliage that have weak stems, hold a 6" length of medium-gauge stub wire against the stem, just under the flower head. Beginning at the head, wind fine-gauge spool wire (also referred to as rose wire) around the stem and stub wire, continuing to the end of the stem. Cut the rose wire. To conceal the wires, wrap with floral tape. For small corsages, cut the stems to the same size and bind into a bunch using rose wire. Wrap the ends with floral tape. Wind one end of a medium-gauge stub wire tightly around the bottom of the stems and insert the end into the frame. For pinecones and pods without stems, cut a 6" length of medium-gauge stub wire. Push the end of the wire under the bottom collar of the scales, allowing a 2" length to protrude. Twist the ends tightly around the

scales and bend the ends underneath to form a false stem.

Floral picks can be used to attach any type of material to straw, vine, and foam frames. Simply insert the pick into the wreath frame at a slight angle and secure the decoration to the pick using its attached wire. For vine frames, you may also need a dab of hot glue to secure the decoration.

Use the decorative material itself to attach fresh flowers and foliage to frames made from Oasis (floral foam)

Caring for Your Wreath

To keep your wreath of dried materials looking fresh and beautiful, apply a very light coat of hair spray or acrylic spray. Display it in a dimly lit, dry area because bright sunlight will cause fading and humidity may cause mold. Avoid moving the wreath — it is fragile — and feel free to add new blooms in vivid colors to perk up a tired appearance.

For plastic and silk floral materials, dust lightly with a soft artist's brush. This type of wreath can survive some handling and it can be brought out year after year still looking fresh.

For live plant materials placed in floral foam (Oasis), be sure to saturate foam. Water evaporates quickly when there is a broad surface exposed to air. Fresh arrangements usually do not last more than a few days but their life can be prolonged by making certain the Oasis is wet and the foliage is misted. Add a floral preservative such as Floralife to the water before adding to foam or mister. Wilted flowers and foliage may be replaced as needed.

PRESERVED ROSES AND BERRY CLUSTERS

Preserved roses, white and pink delphinium, Australian daisies, and berry clusters are hot-glued to a vine base.

Eight Wreaths, Four Techniques

Already assembled wreath frames made from vines, foam, straw, or wire are readily available. To complete any of these wreath projects, the dried, fresh, or artificial materials are simply attached to the frame using one of the four methods described in the text (also *see* page 20). Wreaths using dried or artificial plant materials can be hung on a wall or door. Wreaths made with fresh fruits or flowers (Red Roses and Evergreen, Fresh Della Robbia) should be displayed on a flat surface, due to their weight, and with a protective tray underneath to prevent water damage.

AUTUMN BLAZE

This dried flower wreath is made by wiring together small bunches of the same flower and then hot-gluing them to a vine base.

WHITE ROSES AND DOGWOOD

Dried heather is used as a base for preserved white rose blossoms and white dogwood. A French ribbon bow is added for accent.

SILK ROSES AND FRUIT

Silk roses make an everlasting but expensive wreath. For a less expensive decoration, make a smaller version (this wreath measures 36").

TWIG WITH FRUITS AND FLOWERS

A colorful array of dried, artificial, and spray-painted fruits, foliage, and nuts are hot-glued to a twig base.

GOLDEN HOLLY

This wreath is made of fresh holly stems bound to a common wire coat hanger and spray-painted gold. Artificial berry clusters are added as decorative accents.

RED ROSES AND EVERGREEN

This red rose and evergreen design uses an Oasis-filled base to keep the flowers fresh; it is best displayed on a flat surface with a protective tray.

FRESH DELLA ROBBIA

This fresh fruit wreath includes lemons, limes, pears, grapes, cabbage leaves, cloves, and cinnamon sticks. Due to its weight, it should be displayed on a flat surface.

or plastic-covered Oasis. Firm and woody stems are best suited to this method. Simply cut the stems on a sharp angle and insert the stems, one at a time, into the plastic or directly into the Oasis. Remember to water the Oasis at least once a day. Replace wilted flowers when necessary.

Preserved Roses and Berry Clusters

Designed by Galerie Felix Flower
(Finished diameter: 24")

1 16" vine wreath
2 packages green ruscus leaves
2 bunches delphinium, 1 pink, 1 white; dried
1 bunch ixodia or Australian daisies; dried
1 bunch lilac yarrow; dried
10–12 stems poppy; dried
10–12 stems nigella; dried
8–10 clusters pink pepperberries
10–12 clusters deep red berries; artificial
18 roses, 12 pink, 6 ivory; all preserved
    Florist's scissors
    Hot-glue gun and glue sticks
    Wire cutters
    Medium-gauge wire

Cut all stems to 5". On frame, hot-glue green ruscus leaves all around the top and sides. Add material in order listed above. Hot-glue the preserved roses last. Attach hanging loop to back of wreath.

Autumn Blaze

Designed by Galerie Felix Flower
(Finished diameter: 24")

1 16" vine wreath
1 package safflower; dried
1 package golden yarrow; dried
1 package purple statice; dried
1 package blue delphinium; dried
1 package light pink achillea; dried
1 package lona; dried
1 package red celosia cockscomb; dried
1 package deep red hybrid tea roses; dried
2 packages ruscus leaves, 1 hunter green, 1 grass green; dried
    Wire cutters

Hot-glue gun and glue sticks
Florist's scissors
Fine-gauge wire
Medium-gauge wire

Cut flower stems 5" long and use fine-gauge wire to gather into small bunches of the same flower. Insert stems of floral materials into vine frame, hot-gluing to secure. Lay all bunches so that flower heads and leaf tips radiate counterclockwise and slightly outward. Attach hanging loop to back of wreath.

White Roses and Dogwood

Designed by Lauren Adams
(Finished diameter: 28")

1 18" vine wreath
4–5 packages heather; dried
2 yards gray-green French wire-edge ribbon, 2" wide
1 strand faux garnets (costume jewelry necklace)
8 white dogwood blossoms; preserved
10 white rose blossoms, 8 with open blossoms, 2 with closed blossoms; all preserved
    Fine-gauge wire
    Floral picks
    Hot-glue gun and glue sticks
    Wire cutters
    Medium-gauge wire

Cut heather stems to 6". Wire small bunches of heather using rose wire. Cover the entire surface of the frame with bunches of heather wired to floral picks and secured to frame with

Wreath-Decorating Techniques

The eight heirloom wreaths use only four decorating techniques: hot glue, wire, floral picks, and the material itself. Starting with a constructed base of vines, wire, straw, foam, or chicken wire filled with plastic-wrapped Oasis (floral foam used with fresh flowers), the fresh, dried, or artificial materials are easily and quickly attached. Firm or woody stems (e.g. boxwood or hydrangea) can be inserted directly into Oasis (*see* photo 1). Use a hot-glue gun with vine or moss-covered wreaths (photo 2). Wire helps to strengthen weak stems and is best used with a vine wreath (photo 3). Floral picks (not shown) are small picks with an attached wire and are best used with straw and foam wreaths.

1. When working with a wreath frame made from plastic-covered wet Oasis, simply push woody stems through the plastic into the foam. When working with foam or straw frames, floral picks work well.

2. Hot glue can be used to attach flowers and decorations to a wreath base. You can purchase low-melt glue guns that operate at a lower temperature and are therefore safer.

3. Flowers can be wired to a frame. The stem is reinforced with medium-gauge stub wire, which is then wrapped with rose wire and floral tape and attached to the frame with medium-gauge wire.

hot glue. Fan outward in a clockwise direction, overlapping the stems of the preceding bunch with the heads of the next. Make a bow (*see* Quick Tips, page 5) and attach with a separate medium-gauge wire at the 12 o'clock position on the wreath. Hot-glue the strand of garnets beneath bow. Next, hot-glue the largest blossoms of white dogwood and roses, using the photograph as a guide. Hot-glue the remaining smaller blossoms to either side. Attach hanging loop to back of wreath.

Silk Roses and Fruit

Designed by Genevieve A. Sterbenz
(Finished diameter: 36")

1	18" vine wreath
6	mop-headed hydrangea, 1 blue, 2 pink, 3 burgundy; all silk
10	stems of rosebuds, 3 vanilla, 3 white, 4 burgundy; all silk
8	stems open rose blossoms, 4 white, 4 vanilla; all silk
16	peonies, 4 dark pink, 3 light pink, 9 vanilla; all silk
6–7	bunches rose leaves, 3 light green, 2 dark green, 1–2 burgundy-tinged green; all silk
4	bunches grapes, 2 blue, 1 purple, 1 light green; all artificial
2	stems of hops; silk
	Wire cutters
	Medium-gauge wire

Cut stems of each silk flower 6" to 8" long. Begin with flowers, spacing same varieties and colors more or less evenly around frame. Push each stem all the way through the vines and loop around and up to the top; reinsert the stem between the vines to secure. The stems above the frame measure between 2" and 4", giving an undulating appearance. Insert the stems of the rose leaves all around the perimeter of the wreath in the same way, varying color and stem length. Attach the bunches of grapes and stems of hops at the top of the wreath, so they fall into the center space of the wreath when it is hung. Attach hanging loop to back of wreath. Note: This wreath is very expensive to make; each silk flower costs between $1.50 and $4.50. You may wish to use this wreath as a model for a smaller version.

Twig with Fruits and Flowers

Designed by Urte Tuerpe
(Finished size: 36" square)

1	36" square twig base
3	mop-headed hydrangea; dried
6	stems protea; dried
6	stems golden yarrow sprayed gold; dried
5	Australian honeysuckle; dried
4	dryandra; dried
3	globe artichokes; dried
3	cucumbers; dried
3	mushrooms; dried
6	pomegranates; whole and dried
2	green apples; whole and dried
2	lemons; whole and dried
4	kiwi; sliced and dried
6	lemons; sliced and dried
6	apples; sliced and dried
4	oranges; sliced and dried
4	limes; sliced and dried
4	grapefruits; sliced and dried
10	magnolia leaves; dried
10	rose leaves; dried
6	red apples; artificial
3	orange-green squash; artificial
6	bunches of grapes, 3 purple, 3 green; artificial
4	walnuts, sprayed gold
3	pinecones, sprayed gold
2	yards ribbon, 1 burgundy, 1 gold
	Hot-glue gun and glue sticks
	Scissors
	Medium-gauge wire
	Wire cutters
	Gold spray paint

Hot glue the largest ingredients onto the wreath first, using the photograph as a guide. Next, fill in bare spaces with smaller items; finish with the fruit slices and foliage. Stand away from the wreath and assess the distribution of color; add and arrange new items, as desired. Lay gold ribbon over burgundy ribbon and tie a bow (*see* Quick Tips, page 5). Hot-glue in position as desired. Attach hanging loop to back of wreath.

Golden Holly

Designed by Genevieve A. Sterbenz
(Finished diameter: 24")

1	wire coat hanger
180	branchy stems of holly; freshly cut
10	4-berry clusters, dark red with velvet leaves; artificial
	Gold spray paint
	Medium-gauge wire
	Wire cutters
	Kid (calf-skin) or heavy-weight garden gloves

Pull hanger into a hoop measuring 12" to 14" in diameter. Cut off hook with wire cutters. Wear gloves to protect hands from sharp holly leaf tips. Cut holly stems 6" to 7" long and wire into bunches of 6 stems each. Bind small bunches of holly stems to the hanger using wire. Be certain to conceal stems and bare hanger. Spray-paint gold and let dry. Wire berry clusters evenly around wreath for accent. Attach hanging loop to back of wreath.

Red Roses and Evergreen

Designed by Lauren Adams
(Finished diameter: 24")

1	18" molded plastic base
8	red roses; fresh
3	Mercedes or similar Christmas roses; fresh
20	branches balsam, spruce, fir, or other evergreen; fresh
10	stems dusty miller; fresh
6	pine cones (sugar pine or Norway spruce), 4" to 5" long or as desired
2	packages green Oasis (each 8" x 4" x 3")
	Medium-gauge wire
	Florist's scissors
	Wire cutters
	Sharp knife
	Pruning shears
	Florist's adhesive tape

Press foam against base to form cutting template and cut along indentation with knife (*see* "How to Use Floral Foam," steps 1 and 2, page 10). Insert into base to fill. Secure with tape. Trim foam with knife to a height of 1" above base. Trim evergreen to 6" to 8" lengths. Push branches one by one into base, binding in place with tape to secure; use photograph as guide. Trim stems of roses to 4". Insert stems into base. Accent the arrangement with sprigs of dusty miller and wired pinecones (*see* text, page 18). Soak Oasis with water. This wreath should be displayed on a flat surface with a protective tray, due to its weight and water content.

Fresh Della Robbia

Designed by Lauren Adams
(Finished diameter: 20")

1	18" straw frame
2	lemons; fresh
2	limes; fresh
1	orange; fresh
2	green pears; fresh
13	globe artichokes; fresh
5	bunches of grapes, 3 green, 2 purple; fresh
8	cabbage leaves, 4 green, 4 purple; fresh
3	orange slices; dried
4	sunflowers or similarly colored flowers; fresh
40	cloves
12	cinnamon sticks
6	strands raffia
2	packages 6" wooden skewers
	Floral picks
	Sharp knife

1. *To prepare fruit,* insert cloves into orange in a pleasing pattern; bind 3 to 4 cinnamon sticks together to form a log, using raffia to secure; create stripe patterns on limes by cutting skin in bands, just to the white zest, using knife.

2. Arrange lemons, limes, whole orange, pears, and artichokes around the frame using skewers.

3. Use floral picks as follows: secure grapes and any loose items in place; conceal any exposed parts of frame with cabbage leaves; attach sunflowers, cinnamon logs, and dried orange slices as accents. This wreath should be displayed on a flat surface, due to its weight. ◆

How to Wrap a Wine Bottle

Four new ways to wrap the unwrappable.

THE "CHANEL" BAG

These quilted gold-lamé bags can be made in quantity ahead of time for use as gift wrapping.

½ yard prequilted gold-lamé fabric
1 yard copper wire-edge ribbon, 1½" wide
½ yard flat gold trim, ¼" wide
   Small safety pin
   Scissors
   Needle
   Thread
   Ruler
   Grape cluster or artificial grapes (optional)

1. From fabric, cut a rectangle wide enough to encircle bottle plus 3", and long enough to cover height of bottle plus 6".

2. On 1 short side of rectangle, unstitch quilting for 2". Fold back lining and cut away batting. This area will be at bottom of bottle; by eliminating excess bulk, the wrapped wine bottle will be able to stand. At opposite short side, fold fabric 3" to wrong side. Stitch across short side, ½" from raw edge and again ⅜" from first line of stitching, forming a narrow channel.

3. Fold fabric lengthwise, right sides together, and sew along side, leaving a ⅜" seam allowance, and interrupting seam to keep channel ends open. Gather the section of lamé without batting and sew across gather to close bottom. Turn bag right-side out and feed gold trim through channel with safety pin.

4. Insert bottle. Pull ends of gold trim to gather sack; tie in a bow. Wrap ribbon over gather and tie into a bow. Hang a grape cluster (*see* Quick Tips, page 4) or other artificial grapes from the bow knot.

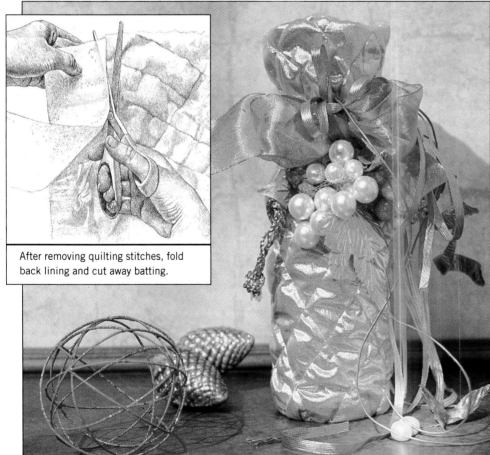

After removing quilting stitches, fold back lining and cut away batting.

These quilted lamé bags can be made ahead of time and used for last-minute gifts. Artificial grapes or other small fruit make a simple decoration.

Spirals of garlands made of metallic stars stand out against the frosted black of a champagne bottle.

THE STAR-STUDDED GARLAND

The monochromatic scheme, silver and crystal against the frosted black of the champagne bottle, makes this garland a sophisticated but simple New Year's party gift.

1 metallic star garland, at least 54"
6 clear plastic teardrops or "crystals"
3 5" lengths of silver-colored beading wire
   Wire cutters
   Ruler

1. Cut 3, 18" lengths from star garland.

2. Wind end of 1 length around cork, twisting to secure, allowing free end to spiral around outside of bottle; repeat with second length.

3. Using third length, wind middle around cork, twisting to secure and allowing free ends to spiral around outside of bottle.

4. Thread 2 "crystals" on beading wire, twisting ends to secure. Repeat with remaining pairs. Hang pairs as desired.

PHOTOGRAPHS BY RICHARD FELBER

Pink silk roses are bound to artificial ivy vine and quickly taped to any wine bottle.

THE FLORAL GARLAND

This quick garland is made with prewired ivy vine interwoven with silk flowers. For best results, bunch flowers of similar color in clusters spaced unevenly along the vine, and fill in the empty spaces in between with tiny flowers. Use rosebuds at the bottom of the vine (not the loop end) so the garland appears to be tapering off naturally.

18" wired ivy vine with leaves of graduating sizes
7 pink silk roses on stems with buds
   Floral tape
   Invisible cellophane tape
   Wire cutters
   Ruler

1. Trim stems of flowers with wire cutters to between 2" and 3". Twist stems around vine, securing with floral tape if necessary.
2. Form a loop from tip of wired vine so it fits snugly around top of bottle. Spiral remainder of vine downward around bottle.

3. Twist leaves and flower heads outward. Use a little clear tape in 3 places to secure garland to bottle. If bottle has been chilled, dry it completely so that tape will stick. Rearrange leaves and/or flowers to cover tape. ◆

Trim rose stems to no more than 3" and wind around main wire of ivy vine.

THE NATURAL WRAP

The use of brown paper and a thin branch is reminiscent of the art of Japanese wrapping. Although the branch forms a "handle," the bottle should be carried from the bottom.

   Branch of curly willow, juniper, or other flexible, woody plant, about 30"–36"
   Small sprig of wire-stemmed berries or leaves
   Medium-gauge spool wire
   Brown paper
   Hemp mesh or burlap, 5" x 14"
   Raffia
   Double-stick tape
   Ruler
   Wire cutters
   Scissors

1. Make a wire armature or "cage" by loosely wrapping center of bottle with a ring of wire. Bring wire under bottle and up opposite side; curve wire ¼ turn around bottle and under, then form another ring closer to bottom. Wrap cage with brown paper and secure with double-stick tape. Wrap brown paper with hemp mesh or burlap and secure with tape.
2. Cut 4, 4" lengths of wire; if branch is dry, soak it in hot water for a few minutes until pliable. Bend branch into a U-shape and "sew" ends to opposite sides of cage, using short lengths of wire as "thread": thread wire through paper and hemp/burlap fibers, bend to catch wire cage, and thread back through both wrappings; twist around branch to secure (*see* photo). Cover wire by wrapping raffia around it and tying ends in a simple knot. Wrap wire-stems of the berries or leaves onto handle. Carry the piece from bottom, so as not to drop bottle.

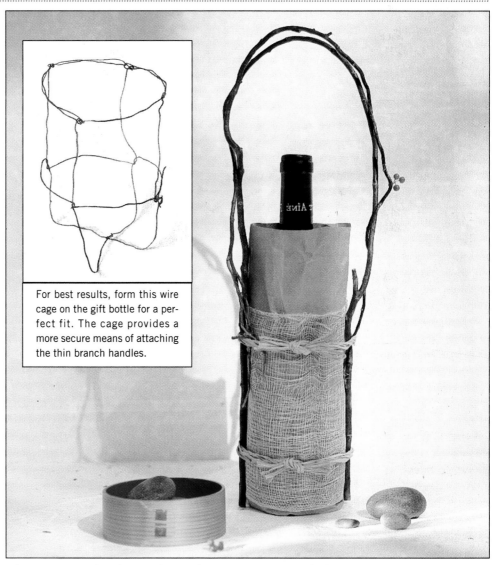

For best results, form this wire cage on the gift bottle for a perfect fit. The cage provides a more secure means of attaching the thin branch handles.

This wrapping is based upon the art of Japanese wrapping, which uses common, natural materials such as brown paper and branches. Texture and simplicity are important elements in this design.

Pastry Cornucopia

*A simple American pie pastry becomes
an edible centerpiece for the holidays.*

This edible centerpiece is as easy as making a large batch of pastry dough. The dough is rolled out, draped over a simple aluminum foil form, and then baked for 35 minutes. Optional pastry decorations are attached with Royal Icing, and then the entire centerpiece is filled with holiday fruits — choose from grapes, kumquats, tiny plums, lady apples, or Seckel pears mixed with dried apples, apricots, pears, or currants — and nuts. At the end of the meal, the fruit and nuts may be eaten along with the pastry cornucopia, which is broken into small pieces. Some cooks prefer to leave the cornucopia itself untouched after the meal, leaving their handiwork on display throughout the holidays.

CORNUCOPIA CENTERPIECE

Pastry decorations should be thin and lightweight, and placed on the cornucopia just before baking. The sides of the cornucopia cannot sustain the weight of additional decoration and therefore they should only be placed on top. If more decorations are desired, bake them separately on a floured cookie sheet or over rolls of aluminum foil to simulate the arch shape of the cornucopia. Attach these additional decorations after they have been baked and cooled, using Royal Icing.

4	cups all-purpose flour
¾	cup cake flour
1	teaspoon salt
2½	tablespoons sugar
1¾	cups (3½ sticks) chilled, unsalted butter
1	egg
½	teaspoon almond extract
	Ice water
1	egg, lightly beaten with 2 teaspoons water, for egg wash
1	egg white, beaten with 1 teaspoon water, for egg-white glaze
2	tablespoons sugar for glaze
	Vegetable oil spray
3	baking sheets
	Heavy-duty aluminum foil
	Fluted pastry wheel or small knife
	Parchment paper
	Plastic wrap
	Small pair of scissors

1. Combine flours, salt, and 2½ tablespoons of sugar in bowl of a food processor. Pulse to combine. Using a large knife, cut butter sticks lengthwise into quarters. Cut butter strips across the width into small ½" pieces. Add butter to flour and process in short bursts until mixture resembles a coarse meal (about 8 to 10 seconds). If you do not have a food processor, cut butter into flour using 2 knives, a pastry blender, or your fingers.

2. In a measuring cup, beat egg lightly. Add almond extract and enough ice water to measure 1¼ cups. With food processor running, add liquid in steady stream until dough holds together in a cohesive ball. If dough is too sticky (it should not stick to the sides of bowl), add flour 1 tablespoon at a time and process in short bursts. Add water in 1 tablespoon increments if dough is too dry. If you do not have a food processor, mix liquid into dough using a fork.

3. Remove dough from processor and form 3 flattened balls. Wrap in plastic and refrigerate for at least 2 hours.

4. To make mold, loosely crumple 8 to 10, 9" squares of foil and form into shape of cornucopia. Tear off a sheet of foil, approximately 20" long, and loosely wrap it around crumpled foil to maintain cornucopia shape. Mold should be about 12" to 14" long and about 5" high at front.

5. Coat form well with vegetable oil spray and set aside.

6. Lightly flour 3 baking sheets and cover with parchment paper. For pastry base, remove 1 ball of dough from refrigerator. On a lightly floured work surface, roll dough out no more than ¼" thick. Put pastry on paper. Place foil form on pastry and cut out a base for cornucopia, making it ½" wider than bottom of foil form. Place pastry base and foil form in refrigerator.

7. On a lightly floured work surface, roll 1 of remaining balls of pastry dough into a rectangle 10" x 14" and ⅛" thick. Using a fluted pastry wheel or a small knife, cut strips of pastry 1" wide and place strips on prepared baking sheets. Repeat with remaining ball of dough, leaving ¼ of dough for decorations that are made separately. Loosely cover all strips with plastic wrap and refrigerate for 1 hour.

8. Remove strips and baking sheet with foil from refrigerator. Brush edge of a pastry strip with egg wash, and beginning with tip of cornucopia, start winding dough onto form in a spiral, sticking egg-washed edge to prior strip, overlapping ¼".

Cover tail completely. Make sure dough is wrapped as closely as possible to foil form. Loose dough can slide and fall off during baking, leaving holes and missing sections.

9. Brush top edge of base with egg wash. Cut pastry strips about 2" longer than necessary to go across form and down each side, touching base. Brush edge with egg wash. Lay strips across top of foil form, overlapping each egg-washed edge over preceding dough about ¼". To seal, gently pinch bottom of strips to base, and trim extra dough at base with a sharp knife. Continue laying strips in same manner until strips come to within 1" of front of cornucopia. Reserve 6 dough strips to be used later as cords.

10. Add a foil arch or crumpled strips of foil under form for additional support. Using a knife, flare front edge of horn upward to make a lip.

11. Brush 2 dough strips with egg wash, fold each in half lengthwise, and press gently to seal. Loosely wind the 2 strips together to make a twisted cord. Brush cord and last strip of dough applied in step 9 with egg wash and lay braid across top of cornucopia, pressing gently to seal.

12. Make 2 more long cords as in step 11. Brush edge of base with egg wash and lay cords along sides, making a decorative spiral at back if desired. Refrigerate cornucopia while making rest of decorations.

13. For decorations, remove remaining ¼ ball of dough from refrigerator. Roll out dough to ⅛" thick. For vine, cut a 1" wide strip using pastry wheel. Place strip on floured surface and roll into a long, smooth rope using flat palms. For grapes, roll small balls of dough in floured palms; for 1 bunch of grapes, roll 6 to 8 balls in varying sizes (from ½" to ¾" in diameter). For leaves, cut out 2 leaves for each bunch of grapes (photocopy leaf below to use as a template). Score leaves with the back of a dull knife.

14. Remove cornucopia from refrigerator and place decorations to get a rough idea of desired design. Remove decorations, brush them with egg wash, and reapply to cornucopia, pressing gently. Refrigerate at least 1 hour. Cornucopia may be made ahead to this point and refrigerated for up to 2 days, or wrapped well

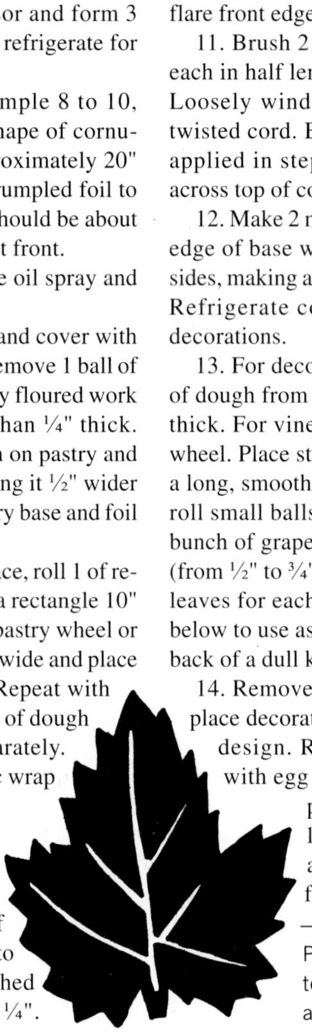

Photocopy leaf and cut out shape as a template. Place on rolled-out dough and trace around shape with a knife.

10-Minute Flower Arrangements

Using the "tripod" construction method, these four arrangements can be assembled in minutes.

The four floral arrangements shown here are easy to arrange using one construction technique based on the inherent stability of a tripod. Formed with the variety of flower that has the thickest stems or multiple stems, the tripod type of base holds the arrangement of flowers together securely. Flowers are added according to their size (large-headed flowers first) with flowers of contrasting color, shape, and texture added thereafter. By placing larger, taller flowers first, you create a supporting framework for the smaller, more delicate blooms. The aim is to create harmony and balance in the overall design.

To form the tripod base, insert three large-blossomed flowers (such as roses, tulips, or stocks) or branchy-stemmed blooms (such as rambling roses, quince, cherry or apple blossoms) into a container, criss-crossing stems just below its rim. You will need to hold the stems in place at first; continue inserting stems into tripod until there is a substantial network of criss-cossing stems to support the remaining flowers. ◆

Paul Bott is a designer and the author of *A Roomful of Flowers* (Harry N. Abrams, 1992) and is currently at work on his second book, *Beautiful Weddings*. **Suzanne Guzzo** is a freelance writer based in New York.

SPRINGTIME IN WINTER
Construct the tripod using pink larkspur. Intersperse lavender freesia, rainbow asters, and apricot beauty tulips, alternating angles and heights of flowers to create contrast.

ALL-WHITE BOUQUET
Construct the tripod using white mountain lilies. Intersperse chamomile and lisianthus by alternating the placement of the flowers to achieve maximum contrast between the longer spikes of lily, the more narrow spikes of lisianthus, and the dotted clusters of chamomile.

PINK AND RED BOUQUET
Construct the tripod using celosia and goblin lilies, keeping celosia close to the rim of the vase since its head is dense and heavy. Intersperse alstromeria.

ARCH OF ROSES
Construct the tripod using red ace rambling roses. Intersperse red velvet roses, inserting them left to right, front and back, heads even with heads of rambling roses, until a soft arch forms.

Artificial Fruits and Berries

New technology, new resins, and new materials have transformed the plastic bananas of the fifties into a highly sophisticated art form.

The artificial fruit and berry industry has come a long way. A spin-off of the artificial flower industry, mass-produced artificial fruit began appearing in the early fifties in response to the public demand for natural-looking fruits and berries for use as decoration. Soon bright red apples, blazing yellow bananas, and translucent green grapes began appearing in profusion. Their appearance, however, was far from real; these artificials were made from molds, in plaster and latex plastic, and enjoyed a bizarre popularity due to their novelty value.

Latex plastic fruit was waxy to the feel, lightweight, and fake-looking. Latex, injected into a mold, provided color; tone and texture had to be added after the molding process. Some fruits, such as peaches, received a coat of flocking, which made them look pretty convincing, although velvet flocking tended to absorb grease and dust and was difficult to keep clean. The shiny, plastic stems added to each plump fruit did little to reinforce its realistic appearance.

Plaster fruit was not much better. Apples and bananas were hard, heavy, and painted with bright acrylic paint. There were no subtle nuances of shading and tone; any critical details were painted by hand. The apple stem was not attached separately, but molded with the apple. Plaster fruit looked dull, unable to effectively reflect any color variations. Prone to chipping, fruits invariably displayed white craterlike holes that further detracted from their appearance.

The Natural Look

However, over the decades manufacturers continued to experiment with other materials — papier-mâché, extruded foam, and, more recently, silks and resins. Artificial fruits and berries are now made with an emphasis on color and on size variations found in nature. Sophisticated materials such as natural resins from Thailand and China are dyed, molded, and textured in multistep processes to imitate the naturally grown items.

The highest-quality fruits or berries are rotocast — thermal plastic is injected into a spinning mold, the heated plastic flies to the sides, and when the plastic cools, it hardens into the shape of the mold. To accentuate the natural color and patina of the fruit or berry, several additional processes can take place that involve applying one or more finishing coats to the molded piece to create frosted, dewy, or variegated patinas.

The most telling evolution of the fruit and berry industry can be seen by comparing the early navy blue, uniform-sized grapes with those available today. Formerly, grapes were held together by bright green stems, at the end of which was a little ball that popped into a hole in the grape. Today's market offers grape clusters (and myriad other bacchanalian choices) that look as if they were just plucked from the arbor. Grapes in graduated sizes are wired, by hand, into cascading bunches of stunningly realistic globes with subtle seasonal hues; embossed, velvet leaves are twisted into place by hand and attached to wrapped stems.

The painstaking care given to the stems is costly but essential — no matter how beautifully orchestrated the fruit, a glaringly unnatural, stiff plastic or wire stem will destroy the finished look of the product. One process, for example, achieves subtle texture variations by adding finely ground particles to the finishing process; adding a fuzzy texture to the stem of a miniature cantaloupe makes the melon look freshly picked. Thorns wrapped meticulously in fine silk turn the stems of raspberries or rose hips into the perfect complement of the fruit or flower. Clusters of berries are accented with carefully dyed, variegated silk leaves and wrapped in silk-covered stems that are underwired for flexibility. Individually wrapped, hand-designed stems increase the price of the product by as much as 30 percent because the work is very labor intensive. The result is a lasting creation that is often a work of art. The emphasis is always on imitating as closely as possible the variety of fruits and berries found in gardens and in the wild.

Bringing the Outside In

The variety of fruits and berries available is overwhelming. Fruits and berries come in all sizes, shapes, colors, and textures. Many types appear in seasonal colors and stages of growth, presenting, in the most intricate detail, particular changes in shape, texture, and palette. Berries that begin as small flowers can be found expressed in plumb berries clinging to long stems and vines. The smallest berries (measuring 4mm to 10mm) come in clusters (i.e., holly, cotoneaster, blueberries, and wild berries), generally cost under $1.00 per package, and are used for accent. Berries that are wired to a stem of 4" to 5" long (fire thorn, spindle, and sweet briar) cost between $1.50 and $3.00, depending on the added details (foliage, floral decoration, or vines). Well suited to table arrangements (and close viewing), they can be used in swags, garlands, and wreaths. Longer vines with berry accents or clusters (bittersweet, raspberries, and pepperberry) are available with stems between 6" and 24" long and on vines up to 48" long. Ranging in price from $2.50 to $5.00, each variety features flexible stems and silk leaves (or leaves of embossed, polymer-coated fabric). Single stems can be intermingled with other dried or silk florals, or mixed with fresh flowers and foliage. Vines can be used as a frame for a wreath, as base wire for a garland, or coiled and placed in a larger arrangement.

Fruits are available individually or in bunches or already wired into arrangements. Ripe fruit, such as apples, oranges, pears, and grapes, can be found in abundance; you can choose plastic, silk, papier-mâché, or the most realistic (and most costly) resin. One piece of fruit made of resin costs $2.50 on average. More esoteric varieties are also sold: crab apple, rose hips, plums, and pomegranate. Needless to say, there are "decorator" versions of each — gold, silver, and glittered versions can be easily found as well.

From a seemingly infinite assortment, you can select the fruits and berries that enhance and integrate natural beauty and interior design. Artificials can be used alone in vases, bowls, and urns (*see* "Victorian Dried Flower Bouquet," page 10); combined with fresh florals and foliage; or mixed with other artificials, silk or dried (*see* "Eight Heirloom Wreaths," page 18). Today's displays are not static, geometric, and symmetrical, but contain elements of movement and surprise. Balance is felt rather than announced. Long branches can arch loosely in a vase, or they can introduce bold splashes of color in otherwise soft florals; simply allowing a vine with seasonal berries to intertwine with other naturals, or with seasonal or even freeze-dried fruits, expands the use of fruits and berries in floral decorations. ◆

Suzanne Guzzo is a freelance writer based in New York.

Field Guide to Artificial Fruits and Berries

1. Pear
2. Dried apple slices
3. Raspberry garland
4. Red apple
5. Rose hips with fall leaves
6. Blueberry
7. Wild grape
8. Currant
9. Coffee bean
10. Garland: apple, peach and cherries
11. Dried orange slice
12. Dried grapefruit slice
13. Spindle berry
14. Coffee bean
15. Mulberry
16. Nandido
17. Rose hips (Primrose)
18. Rose hips (Primrose)
19. Cherry
20. Raspberry
21. Rose hips (Primrose)
22. Mini-grapes
23. Pepperberry
24. Pyrocantha
25. Pomegranate
26. Strawberry
27. Currant
28-30. Antique decorative berries
31. Mountain ash
32. White bruneia
33. Bittersweet
34-41. Grapes
42. Cherry
43. Plum
44-46. Mini-grapes
47. Orange
48. Red apple
49. Green apple
50. Red apple

SOURCES
AND RESOURCES

Most of the materials needed for the projects in this issue are available at your local craft supply, hardware, paint store, garden center, florist, fabric shop, bead and jewelry supply, etc.. Here we have provided you with specific sources for particular items or mail order sources, arranged by project.

Notes from Readers; pages 2-3
Ornamental Dried Fruit: Framed drying screen for $24 from Gilbertie's Herb Gardens (quantities limited). Coats & Clark Knit Cro-sheen crochet cotton for $1.49 per ball and quilting frames starting at $11.95 from The American Needlewoman. *Folk Art Metal Cut-Outs:* Aleene's Tacky Glue for $1.39 for a 4-ounce jar and DecoArt Americana Acrylic Paint for $.99 for a 2-ounce bottle from Craft King. *Caring for Stencils:* Stencils from $.69 to $10.00 from Craft King, Sunshine Crafts, or The Artist's Club. *Eggshell Mosaic:* Brushes and glue from $1.00 from Craft King, Sunshine Crafts, The Artist's Club, and Jerry's Artarama. Delta Gloss Varnish for $3.90 for 8 ounces from Craft King. Village Classic gold spray paint $3.75 for a 6-ounce can and Watermark non-metallic colors for $4.68 for a 12-ounce can from Craft King and Sunshine Crafts. Winsor & Newton Dry Pigments from $5.55 for a 30 ml jar and Coverseal laminate rolls for $22.77 for a 20" x 30" roll from Jerry's Artarama. *Tips on Prolonging the Life of Cut Flowers:* Floralife (cut flower food) for $6.00 for 2 cups from Main Street Nursery. *Reusing Gift Wrap:* Elmer's Rubber Cement for $1.49 for 4.1 ounces from Sunshine Crafts. Krylon Crystal Clear acrylic sealer for $4.20 for a 1-pint can and 3M Spay Adhesive for $8.24 for a 16-ounce can from Jerry's Artarama. Muslin for $2.15 per yard from Newark Dressmaker Supply. *All that Glitters...:* Gold or silver Glitterama for $4 for a 4-ounce can from Chapelle, Ltd. Artists' white tape starting at $2.19 for a 60" roll from Jerry's Artarama. *Heart Baskets:* Excel Knives for $1.49 and an extensive line of art papers in a wide range of prices from Jerry's Artarama. *Floor Cloths:* Stencils from $.69 to $10.00, stencil brushes from $1 to $5, and craft glue from $.99 all from Craft King, Sunshine Crafts, or The Artist's Club. Primed artists' canvas for $34.99 for a 52" x 9" roll and mini paint rollers for $3.29 from Jerry's Artarama.

Quick Tips; pages 4-5
Pearl Grape Cluster Ornament: 4½" side cutters (wire cutters) for $5.79 from Craft King. Gold 34-gauge beading (spool) wire for $1.30 for 24 yards from Newark Dressmaker Supply. Pearls for $3.00 to $12.00 per strand (depends on color, size, and texture) from M & J Trims. *Making a Garland:* Floratape for $1.25 for 90" from Newark Dressmaker Supply. Pinecones for $.20 per cone (size of a tennis ball or larger) from Village Flowers. *Homemade Beeswax Candles:* 10 sheets of 8" x 16¾" beeswax in various colors for $14.99 from S & S Arts and Crafts. Square wick braid for $1.37 (various lengths) and candle wax for $1.59 for 1 pound from Craft King.

How to Create a Verdigris Finish; pages 6-7
Verdigris kit for $25 from Modern Options or from Pottery Barn stores nationwide (call 800-922-5507). Plaster urns for $85-90 (item # T556 for urn in main photo) from Ballard Designs. Fiberglass, terra cotta, and vintage urns can also frequently be found at local garden centers, florist's suppliers, and antique shops. Sponge brushes for $.33 and bristle brushes from $7.50 from Craft King. A full line of wood finishing products for the finish painter from Albert Constantine.

Scented Hanger; pages 8-9
Dried lavender flowers from $1.73 to $2.47 for 4 ounces and lavender oil for $3.30 for 1 ounce from San Francisco Herb Company. Fairfield Polyfil traditional batting for $1.60 for 1 yard, Cintilla satin for $4.40 per yard, ⅝" satin ribbon for $1.35 for 5 yards, Sobo clear-drying glue for $1.85, and a wide variety of thread from $1.65 for 350 yards from Newark Dressmaker Supply. DMC 6 strand cotton embroidery floss for $.33 per skein from The American Needlewoman.

Victorian Dried Flower Bouquet; page 10
Plaster urns from Ballard Designs (item # T276 for urn in main photo). Over 700 varieties of flowers for $8 and up per bunch of about 25 heads, dried fruit for $3-6.50 per bag of about 24 slices, and decorative dried herbs from F/X Floral Express. Gold spray paint for $3.75 for 6 ounces, floral foam for $.85 per block, wood floral picks for $.89 for 60 pieces, medium-gauge (green) wire for $1.09 for 50", Magic Melt Low Temp Glue Gun for $16.70, and low temp glue sticks for $2.99, all from Craft King.

No-Sew Lace Sachets; page 11
All floral ingredients from Cherchez, Ltd. Cotton muslin for $2.15 per yard and various ribbons from $.80 for 5 yards from Newark Dressmaker Supply.

Painted Curly Maple Dresser; pages 12-15
Bjorn chest of 6 drawers 16" x 49½" x 15¼" for about $110 from IKEA which has several stores nationwide (call 516-681-4532 for locations). Grumbacher's Academy Watercolor tube paint for $1.59 for ¼ ounce, T-950 artists' white tape from $2.19, a wide selection of bristle brushes, and foam brushes for $1.19 from Jerry's Artarama. Cheesecloth for $1.10 per yard from Newark Dressmaker Supply. Styrofoam blocks for $1.12 to $1.56 from Craft King.

Candlestick Lampshade with Rose Decoupage; page 16
Finely sanded basswood boxes in various shapes and sizes for $7-9, Mod Podge medium for $3.20 for 8 ounces, a wide variety of brushes, and Liquitex acrylic gel medium for $5.35 for 8 ounces all from Pearl Paint. An extensive line of books full of copy-right free designs, many in full color, that can be used by decoupers from Dover Publications. A good selection of shades in various sizes and materials (item # E-6421 for $19.50 for shade from project) from Home Decorator's Collection. Sobo clear-drying glue for $1.85 and a variety of ribbon from Newark Dressmaker Supply.

Satin-Leaf Topiary, page 17
Styrofoam balls for $1.39 for a 5" ball and green floral clay for $1.28 for 5 ounces from Craft King. Single satin leaves from Pany Flowers. Wire-edge ribbon from $1.65 to $2.00 per yard and a wide variety of thread from Newark Dressmaker Supply.

Heirloom Wreaths; pages 18-21
Silica gel for $20 for 4 pounds from Lauren Adams. Wreath frames and 600 different kinds and sizes of silk flowers from $1.00 to $10.00 from Pany Flowers.

How to Wrap a Wine Bottle; pages 22-23
New "natural" wrapping materials such as raffia cord for $4 for a bundle containing several dozen 3" strands, in natural and dyed colors and exotic Japanese and European papers from Kate's Paperie. Floral tape for $1.61 for 60 yards, medium-gauge wire for $1.09 for 50", a wide variety of beads, and metallic star garland for $1.54 for 9" from Craft King. Wire-edge ribbon for $1.65 to $2.00 per yard, 34 gauge beading (spool) wire for $1.30 for 24 yards, and a wide variety of thread and trim from Newark Dressmaker Supply. Ivy vines for $12.00 to $15.00 for 6" and silk flowers from Pany Flowers.

The Secrets of Quick Gilding; pages 26-28
Composition leaf for $4.10 for a "book" of 25 sheets, 5½" square, Rolco Quick-Dry Synthetic Gold Size for $2.90 for a ¼ pint (enough for at least 50 fruit), and various pigment powders (on pears, Cres-lite #20, $3.75 for 10 gram vial, enough for 50 fruit), pearl essence, and graphite powder all from Pearl Paint. Plastic fruit from Woolworth's. Sponge brushes for $.33 and bristle brushes from $7.50 from Craft King.

Quick Projects; inside back cover
8" x 6¼" frames for $4 from Woolworth's or 8" x 6" frames for $5 from The American Needlewoman. Over 100 selections of metallic trims for $.50 to $12.00 yard (depends on width and material) from M & J Trims.

The following is a list of the companies mentioned in the listings above. Contact them individually for complete information and for their price list or catalog.

Albert Constantine and Sons Inc., 2050 Eastchester Road, Bronx, NY 10461; 800-223-8087

The American Needlewoman, P.O. Box 6472, Fort Worth, TX 76115; 800-433-2231

The Artist's Club, 5750 N.E. Hassalo, Portland, OR 97213; 800-845-6507

Ballard Designs, 1670 DeFoor Ave. NW, Atlanta, GA 30318; 404-351-5099

Chapelle, Ltd., P.O. Box 9252, Ogden, UT 84409; 801-621-2777

Cherchez, Ltd., P.O. Box 550, Front Street, Millbrook, NY 12545; 800-422-1744

Craft King Discount Craft Supply, P.O. Box 90637, Lakeland, FL 33804; 813-686-9600

Dover Publications, Inc., 31 East 2nd Street, Mineola, NY 11501; 516-294-7000

F/X Floral Express, 239 South Main Street, Caribou, ME 04736; 800-392-7417

Gilbertie's Herb Gardens, 7 Sylvan Lane, Westport, CT 06880; 203-227-4175

Home Decorator's Collection, 2025 Concourse Drive, St. Louis, MO 63146; 800-245-2217

Jerry's Artarama, P.O. Box 1105, New Hyde Park, NY 11040; 800-U-ARTIST

Kate's Paperie, 8 West 13th Street, New York, NY 10011; 212-633-0570

Lauren Adams, 347 Sea Cliff Ave., Sea Cliff, NY 11578; 516-759-6542

M & J Trims, 1008 6th Ave., New York, NY 10018; 212-391-9072

Main Street Nursery, 475 W. Main St., Huntington, NY 11743; 516-549-4515

Modern Options, 2325 Third Street, #339, San Francisco, CA 94107; 415-252-5580

Newark Dressmaker Supply, P.O. Box 20730, Lehigh Valley, PA 18002; 215-837-7500

Pany Silk Flowers, 146 W. 28th St., New York, NY 10001; 212-645-9526

Pearl Paint Co., Inc., 308 Canal Street, New York, NY 10013; 800-221-6845 ext. 2297

S & S Arts and Crafts, Box 513, Colchester, CT 06413-0513; 800-243-9232

San Francisco Herb Company, 250 14th St., San Francisco, CA 94103; 800-227-4530

Sunshine Discount Crafts, 1280 N. Missouri Ave., Largo, FL 34640; 813-581-1153

Village Flowers, 297 Main St., Huntington, NY 11743; 516-427-0996

Credits
Front cover — photo by Tom McCavera. **Page 2** — *American Country Folk Crafts* by Carol Endler Sterbenz (Harry N. Abrams, 1987), photo by Beth Galton. **Page 3** — *The Decorated Tree* by Carol Endler Sterbenz (Harry N. Abrams, 1989); *Decorating with Giftwraps* by Carol Endler Sterbenz (Harry N. Abrams, 1989). **Page 10** — design for Victorian Dried Flower Bouquet © 1992 by Raymond Waites author of *Small Pleasures* (Bulfinch Press, 1992). **Page 17, 26,** and **back cover** — design for gilded pear, satin-leaf topiary, and red-velvet Christmas ornament inspired by originals featured in *Small Pleasures* (Bulfinch Press, 1992) by Raymond Waites. **Page 18** — silica gel information derived from *Dried Flowers* by Malcolm Hillier and Colin Hilton (Simon and Schuster, 1986). ◆

Quick Projects

Plain frame

Weathered wood

Gold filigree

Every once in a while I come upon a craft project that is so satisfying to the spirit and the eye that I am inspired to make several more versions. Decorating these frames was a case in point and I soon began to experiment with unconventional decorative treatments. I bought four medium-size, inexpensive frames and disassembled them so that I could work on the frames only. Although you may find it easier to work on flat frames, I chose frames with beveled molding to guide the placement of the decorative material. Here are some treatments I recommend:

Gold filigree — spray-paint the frame gold. Measure and cut lengths of metallic trims — cord, lace, and filigree — and hot-glue in parallel lines along the top and side surfaces of the frame, gluing scalloped trims along the frame's perimeter. Conceal frayed miters with gold bugle beads or trim.

Verdigris — paint the entire surface of the frame using a store-bought verdigris kit (*see* "How to Create a Verdigris Finish," page 6, for complete instructions).

Weathered wood — spray-paint the frame white. Measure and cut four narrow strips of weathered wood or molding using the frame as a guide. Hot-glue the strips to the top surface of the frame.

Brass buttons — spray-paint the frame gold; when dry, hot-glue small brass buttons (8mm to 14mm) that you find in your button box or purchase at flea markets onto the top surface of the frame; cluster the buttons, varying sizes and heights. Accent with swags of beaded chain using hot-glue.

Brass buttons

The possibilities for decorating these simple frames are limitless — let your imagination run free. Make several and give some as gifts. Find some great snapshots or pretty prints or postcards and slip them into the frames. Personal gifts are always appreciated.

Verdigris

Red Velvet Christmas Ornament

Lay a 12" to 14" square of crushed velvet, wrong side up, on work surface. Make ½" folds to conceal raw edges and cement with a glue gun or iron-on hem adhesive. Crush a sheet of newspaper into a ball. Place ball in center of fabric square. Bring fabric corners up around ball of newspaper and bind with a 9" length of florists' wire. Tuck fabric edges into center hole formed by wire collar. Conceal wire by wrapping with ribbon and tie a bow. Spray-paint pinecones with gold enamel. When dry, wrap florists' wire around bottom tier of scales and tuck ends into wire collar. Add silk roses, velvet leaves, or other embellishments as desired. Finished Christmas ornament is 4" in diameter.

NUMBER TWO

JULY/AUGUST 1994

HANDCRAFT
~ ILLUSTRATED ~

HOW TO MAKE HEIRLOOM BOOKS

New Folded-Paper Method Streamlines Bookbinding

Art Nouveau Watermelon

Transform a Watermelon into an Elegant Carved Tureen

Slip-On Chair Cover

Easy-Sew Slipcovers Transform Folding Chairs

The Art of Trompe L'oeil

Paint 3-D Decorations in Minutes

HOW TO "WEATHER" FURNITURE

•

THE SECRETS OF SPONGE PAINTING

•

SPECIAL INSERT:
8 COLOR COPIER BOOKPLATES

$4.00 U.S./$4.95 CANADA

TABLE
OF CONTENTS

**ART NOUVEAU
WATERMELON**
page 6

SLIP-ON CHAIR COVER
page 8

**HOW TO PAINT
A TUSCAN WALL**
page 10

TROMPE L'OEIL APPLES
page 14

**SIMPLE WEATHERING
TECHNIQUES**
page 18

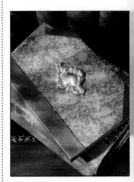

**HEIRLOOM
BOOKS**
page 24

HANDCRAFT
~ILLUSTRATED~

Editor
CAROL ENDLER STERBENZ

Executive Editor
BARBARA BOURASSA

Senior Editor
MICHIO RYAN

Managing Editor
MAURA LYONS

Directions Editors
CANDIE FRANKEL
SUSAN WILSON

Editorial Assistant
KIM RUSSELLO

Art Director
MEG BIRNBAUM

Publisher and Founder
CHRISTOPHER KIMBALL

Editorial Consultant
RAYMOND WAITES

Circulation Director
ADRIENNE KIMBALL

Publicity Director
CAROL ROSEN KAGAN

Circulation Assistant
JENNIFER KEENE

Production Director
JAMES MCCORMACK

Treasurer
JANET CARLSON

Office Manager
JENNY THORNBURY

Customer Service
CONNIE FORBES

Handcraft Illustrated (ISSN 1072-0529) is published bimonthly by Natural Health Limited Partners, 17 Station Street, Box 509, Brookline, MA 02147. Copyright 1994 Natural Health Limited Partners. Application to mail at second-class postage rates is pending at Boston, MA, and additional mailing offices. Editorial office: 17 Station Street, Box 509, Brookline, MA 02147; (617) 232-1000, FAX (617) 232-1572. Editorial contributions should be sent to: Editor, *Handcraft Illustrated*, 17 Station Street, Brookline, MA 02147. We cannot assume responsibility for manuscripts submitted to us. Submissions will be returned only if accompanied by a large self-addressed stamped envelope. Subscription rates: $24.95 for one year; $45 for two years; $65 for three years. (Canada: add $3 per year; all other foreign add $12 per year.) Postmaster: Send all new orders, subscription inquiries, and change of address notices to *Handcraft Illustrated*, P.O. Box 51383, Boulder, CO 80322-1383. Single copies: $4 in U.S., $4.95 in Canada and foreign. Back issues available for $5 each. PRINTED IN THE U.S.A.

EDITORIAL

CAROL ENDLER STERBENZ

Few seasons hold the attraction that summer does for me. One of the most evocative images of summer is one of a painted wooden cupboard with chips of honey-brown wood showing through the old layers of milky-blue and chalky-white paint. Standing imperfectly in the morning light, its appearance takes me back to my childhood. In an instant, I am reminded of the weekends when my family and I piled into a '39 Ford coupe for a ride to Hopewell Junction, New York. My parents had "borrowed" a plot of land from some friends who opted to leave the city in favor of the country. Only an hour or so north out of the city and you were offered *real* summer — a place where the air always seemed warm; a place where the air was filled with the fragrance of damp earth, blossoming roses, and tomatoes ripening on the vine.

One weekend we were busy with hoes, rakes, and twine for trellises, while the next we were watching tender green sprouts poke up through the brown soil. By midsummer we were marching in single file between the rows of beans, spinach, lettuce, beets, and tomatoes. Ah, the tomatoes! Being no taller than the vines ourselves, we could pick the plump fruit right from the vine. The little hairs on the stems would prick my fingers, and the smell of tomatoes would stick to my hands, but there was such quiet pleasure in biting into a warm tomato right there in the garden. When we had filled a small basket, my father would carry it into the house and set it on the first shelf of an open cupboard, just like the one on page 18.

The cupboard we've pictured in this issue is not the cupboard of my childhood, though I wish it were. This cupboard belongs to a friend who lives in a beautiful old home on Long Island. She discovered it in a nearby barn, where it served as disorderly storage space for garden tools and assorted rusty junk. It was structurally sound, simply in need of a good dusting. She brought it home. Before long she had filled it with folded linen and nested crockery bowls.

In the past, this cupboard probably wouldn't have been treasured for its well-worn finish. It might have been salvaged, but most likely stripped of its old paint and repainted to look brand new. Fortunately, returning furniture to its original appearance is not as popular today.

We've come to appreciate the patina that age and use can endow on furniture, and we often find ourselves searching for pieces which show their honest history — chips, dirt, flaking paint, and all. When that search isn't successful or feasible, however, we can simulate such an aged look on new wood. The intention, of course, is not to fool the eye and confer an air of antiquity, but rather to enhance the decorative effect of a piece already possessing aesthetic substance, appealing geometry, and structural soundness.

My interest in finding a cupboard of my own inevitably led to a search for ways to age new wood and recreate the period finishes found on the cupboard we've pictured. I was delighted to find, on close inspection, that the cupboard possessed several distinct surface finishes: milky wash (reminiscent of liming), chipping and flaking, and distressing. With the "real" thing so close at hand, we studied the weathered looks and practiced several techniques until we were certain that we'd developed the best methods, using everyday materials, for artificially aging any piece of unfinished furniture. We offer the results of our efforts on page 18.

Our straightforward methods and practical step-by-step directions can be applied to a large piece of furniture, like the cupboard, or a smaller, unfinished piece such as a chair or even a box. Naturally, the results will vary a little from one piece of furniture to another, and that's part of the charm behind do-it-yourself decorative finishes. Whatever your chosen piece, you'll discover the joy of transforming unfinished wood into woodwork that appears softly aged.

Lee Bailey, a noted cook and gardener, once said, "I wish I could more often be the person I sometimes am — and I am most often that person in the garden." It comes as no surprise to me that I am most often my best self when I'm making something by hand, and that a simple farmhouse cupboard should bring me back to myself. My love of cupboards has stayed with me ever since those hot, quiet afternoons in the garden at Hopewell Junction. I can be back there in a second — all I need is some paint and a tomato.

Carol Endler Sterbenz

NOTES FROM READERS

LEMON PEEL ICE CUBES

Do you know of any simple decorations for ice cubes? As much as I'd love to freeze rose petals or other flowers in ice cubes, it's not always practical. What can you suggest?

LONNIE JONES
Bernardsville, NJ

For pretty ice cubes, especially in ice tea, use lemon peel. Simply peel the skin off the lemon, scraping away as much of the white zest as possible without piercing the peel. On a cutting board, flatten the sections of peel with the heel of your hand. With a very sharp knife, cut the sections into very narrow sticks of varying lengths. Place three or four in crisscross patterns in the bottom of each ice cube tray cup. Pour in water and freeze.

SIMPLE WILD GRASS ARRANGEMENTS

Can you suggest a simple and elegant way to use wild grasses in summer arrangements?

BETH DANGE
Topsfield, MA

Bind bouquets of flowering weeds and wild grasses with thin wire onto a length of twine and drape from a doorway or window. The graceful turns of grass as it dries, in combination with flowering weeds, make fresh and natural accents in a summer house setting. Specific varieties to look for include long-blade grasses, reeds, clubrush, timothy, and rough bristle grass.

DRYING ROSES FROM YOUR GARDEN

What's the best method for drying roses from my own garden?

MARY GENTRY
Rochester, NY

Roses are very easy to dry at home. Cut them at their peak, before the blossoms open completely. If you want to dry purchased roses, take them out of the water just as they are beginning to droop. (Full-bloom roses do not dry well, as their petals fall off as they dry.) Lay them on a sheet of newspaper and remove the leaves at the bottom of each stem to prevent them from rotting. Wrap a rubber band around 6 to 8 stems (it will contract as the stems dry and shrink) and hang the roses upside down in a dry, dimly lit place. The roses should dry in a week or so, depending on the humidity. When dry, the stems will be stiff and the petals will feel dry, like paper. Be aware that roses do change color as they dry. Some varieties, such as pale yellow and pink, lose their color quickly. Red roses darken significantly as they dry; they often appear reddish black when completely dry.

QUICK-RIP TABLECLOTHS

For quick summer entertaining I still prefer a cloth tablecloth and napkins to paper. Is there a fast, inexpensive way I can make a set for use on a small table without using a sewing machine?

ROBERTA CARLSON
Lancaster, PA

From 1⅔ yards of flat-woven cotton fabric, 36" wide, tear a square section measuring 36" x 36"; this will be the tablecloth. Tear two strips across the remainder of fabric, each measuring 12" x 36". Tear each strip in thirds again. These squares will be the napkins, each measuring 12" x 12". Ravel the edges of all the fabrics by pulling the threads until a fringe forms.

USING WALLPAPER PASTE IN GARDENING

I recently heard of an interesting crossover technique between home decorating and gardening called liquid sowing. Just what is this, and how is it used?

TRACY SMITH
Tampa, FL

Liquid sowing involves using wallpaper paste (one without a fungicide) to help sow pregerminated seeds. The paste suspends the tender seedlings, protecting them and giving the gardener an easy means of distributing them across a row.

Pregerminate your seeds on paper towels or some other absorbent paper. Wash the seeds off the seed-covered paper and into a fine-hole colander using cold running water. Transfer the seeds from the colander into a plastic bag half-filled with wallpaper paste. (You can mix the paste yourself or purchase premixed paste. Either should have a medium-stiff consistency.) Distribute the seeds in the wallpaper paste by swooshing your hand in the paste, taking care not to damage the seedlings' tender roots. Knot the top of the bag to close. After preparing the soil, cut off a corner of the plastic bag and gently squeeze the mixture down the row, much as you would squeeze out icing. Cover the row with soil and water immediately to prevent the wallpaper paste from hardening.

QUILT BATTING FROM NATURAL FIBERS

I've been using polyester batting for my quilts but would prefer a batting that drapes more softly, one made of natural fibers. Do you know of one?

KATHY PETERS
Chicago, IL

There is a new soft batting made from 100-percent cotton fiber called Warm & Natural. The batting does not contain glue to bond the fibers together but is made by punching cotton fibers through a thin scrim. The natural cotton, produced by Warm Products, Inc., of Woodinville, Washington, is washable and does not tear or shift. Because there is no glue used in the manufacturing process, your quilting needle will glide through the batting with ease.

DYES VERSUS STAINS

What is the difference between dyes and stains when used in woodworking finishes?

SANDRA HELM
Rockingham, NH

Stains and dyes are both used to introduce permanent color into wood, such as floors and furniture. Inexpensive woods such as pine can be colored to resemble rarer woods, and imperfections of grain can be leveled out by using darker-colored stain or dye. Conventional stains often simulate natural wood colors such as oak, walnut, or mahogany, although colored stains (i.e., blue, green, and burgundy) have recently become available.

Aniline dyes, unlike stains, do not rely on minute particles of pigment to color the topmost layer of the wood, but rather on a dye, which penetrates the wood fibers. As a result, dyes produce much more transparent color. While dyes are less useful for covering up defects, they allow the grain of beautiful woods to show through. In addition to the usual range of natural wood colors found in stains, aniline dyes can produce brilliant shades of red, orange, blue, and yellow, among others.

Preparations are available that are soluble in water, alcohol, or oil.

CHARTER ISSUE FEEDBACK

I have just finished reading (literally, from start to finish) the charter issue of Handcraft Illustrated. *I was so thoroughly impressed that I called my friend to tell her that "there is finally a craft magazine for us." It is so exciting to find a craft magazine with classy, professional-looking projects. I have sent for my subscription and one for my friend. We'll look forward to each beautiful issue!*

JACKIE BELLIZZI
Woodinville, WA

*C*ongratulations on the first issue of Handcraft Illustrated. *It's absolutely gorgeous! The elegant design, excellent instructions, and quality projects make this magazine stand out from the crowd. How refreshing, considering the glut of crafty magazines out there.*

JODIE DAVIS
Gainesville, VA

*W*hat a refreshingly different magazine you have produced, full of interesting projects and beautifully presented. May I draw your attention to the fact that to prolong the life of cut flowers and foliage (see Notes from Readers, Charter issue, page 2), hard, woody stems should never be smashed or hammered. You should not make a vertical cut up the stem and the bark should never be scraped away. European research over the last five years has proven categorically that doing this damages the cells. Damaged cells are quickly attacked by bacteria, thus shortening the life of the cut flowers or foliage. Bleach can be added to the water, but must be done in conjunction with a little sugar as food.*

JUDITH BLACKLOCK
London, England

BUILD-YOUR-OWN MODEL CARS

*A*lthough it may sound old-fashioned, I am very interested in model-building, especially plastic model kits of antique cars. Can you recommend a source that has a wide variety of such kits?*

BILL DUNKLE
New York, NY

Contact Lou Babiak, owner of Ace Hobbies, Inc., in New York. The store offers a wide range of kits and also has a model-building club. If you don't find exactly what you are looking for, Ace Hobbies will try to locate what you want and order it for you.

DRYING YOUR OWN HERBS

*I*love the look of herbs tied in bundles hanging in the kitchen. Although I don't have an herb garden of my own, I visit nearby farm stands that offer a great variety of fresh herbs. Are some herbs better for drying than others? Is there a faster way to dry them than the traditional method of tying the stems and hanging them upside down in a dry, dark place? That takes a few weeks and some herbs, especially basil, rot before they dry.*

SUSAN COSTELLO
San Mateo, CA

The best herbs for drying in bunches are those that grow on thinner, stalkier stems such as oregano, rosemary, sage, anise, hyssop, chamomile, cilantro, dill, and thyme. Heavily-leafed herbs such as mint and basil can be dried by the traditional hanging method; try stripping off the leaves at the section of stem that is going to be bundled closely together. Use a rubber band to hold them together, since the stems will shrink as they dry.

You can also dry heavily-leafed herbs in a microwave oven. Place the stems on a paper towel; cover the herbs with a second paper towel. Use high heat for 1 to 1½ minutes (or longer if the leaves and stems are particularly thick and succulent). Remove the herbs from the oven and hang, or carefully snip off the leaves and store them in a clean jar with a tight cover.

QUICK CHANGES FOR OLDER CURTAIN RODS

*I*have a pair of wooden rods for drapes that I would like to use again, this time with a different, more dressy fabric. Is there a way I can recycle these rods? I don't want to buy another set.*

LAURA SMITH
Albuquerque, NM

One inexpensive means of achieving a new look is to paint a faux finish on your wooden rods, such as verdigris or brushed gold. Modern Options and Pottery Barn, both of San Francisco, California, offer a variety of kits that include everything you need to create these finishes yourself. Any abrading areas should be sealed properly to prevent flaking.

CLEANING FOUND SHELLS

*I*have a collection of shells from the beach that I'd like to display. What do I need to do to clean them properly?*

BETH ZIMMERMAN
Richmond, VA

Clean shells by washing them in warm, soapy water. Scrub off any sand or mud with a stiff brush,

drain thoroughly, and dry overnight. If the shells are stained, soak them in a solution of 1 part household bleach to 5 parts water. Keep a watchful eye on the soaking shells, as oversoaking will cause the shells to lose their lustre or color.

Snail and clam shells may need to be pretreated. If the shells are closed or have an occupant, you'll need to open and/or empty them before cleaning. For snail shells, you can soak the shells in fresh water overnight, followed by an alcohol soak for 4 to 5 days and removal of the snail. Or, place the shells in cold water and gradually bringing the water to a boil. When the shells are still warm, remove snails using a nut pick. For clam shells, place the shells in fresh water and when open (about 3 hours), remove and discard the clam. Scrub the interior with a stiff brush.

PREVENTING CORD FROM UNRAVELING

*W*hen I cut twisted cording, the cut ends unravel quickly. Once unraveled, the ends are impossible to twist back to their original tightness. What can I do?*

CAROLYN TISCHLER
Sandy Hook, NJ

Your best bet is to prevent the unraveling altogether. Before you cut the twisted cord, wrap a piece of clear tape around the cording, centering it over the place where you'll cut the cord in two pieces. Cut through the tape and cording at the midpoint of the tape. Do not remove the tape, even when you apply it to your sewing project; if needed, hide the taped ends in a seam.

SPONGE PAINTING FOR BEGINNERS

*I*love the look of sponging as a decorative finish, especially on walls. I have heard that it is quick and easy to do, even with no previous experience. How do I start?*

BETSY FREEDMAN
Los Angeles, CA

The world of sponging techniques is a vast one. There are an infinite number of effects possible, depending on the type of sponge you use, the way you manipulate it, and the number and order of colors you apply. None of this even begins to address variables involved with the wall, such as its original texture, color, or the desired style.

You can experiment easily, however, using an everyday sponge and a still-wet painted wall. The technique is called "sponging off." In principle, you use a clean damp sponge to mottle the wet surface, pressing the sponge in an overlapping, dabbing motion across the entire painted surface. The effect will be an overall pattern of light and subtle shadows. For another sponging technique, *see* "How to Paint a Tuscan Wall," page 10. ◆

Quick Tips

Re-Covering a Picture Mat

Use this technique to re-cover a new picture mat to match your decorating scheme or to rejuvenate an older picture mat. You'll need a picture mat, a piece of wallpaper or giftwrap at least 3" larger than the dimensions of the mat, rubber cement, a ruler, a pencil, an X-Acto knife, scissors, and a cutting board or a scrap piece of cardboard.

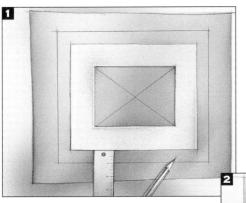

1. Lay the mat face down on the wrong side of the wallpaper or giftwrap. Using a pencil and ruler, mark a line 1" beyond the edge of the mat around all 4 sides. Mark 2 diagonal lines that cross in the center of the mat's cut-out section.

2. Cover the work surface with the cutting board or cardboard. Cut along all the marked lines (outside border and inside "x") using an X-Acto knife held against a ruler.

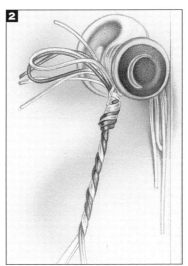

3. Lay the mat face down on the wrong side of the paper aligning the "x" cut within the mat's inner section. Fold back the triangular paper flaps against the mat's inner edges and press them with your fingers to crease. Using the scissors, trim the triangular portion of the flaps, leaving approximately ½" of paper. Glue remaining paper to the backside of the mat using rubber cement. To miter the outside corners, trim the excess paper at each corner by making a slightly curved cut that passes ⁵⁄₁₆" from the corner of the mat.

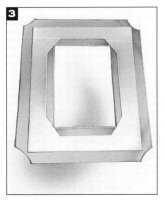

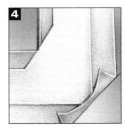

4. Fold the paper onto the mat at the corners and glue it in place.

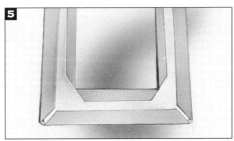

5. Fold the side, top, and bottom flaps to the backside of the mat and glue them in place.

Twisting Decorative Cord

This twisted cord is perfect for decorating the edge of a pillow, or you can use it as a tieback for a curtain. The benefit to making your own cord is that you can match or combine any colors you wish. To make approximately 2' of twisted cord, you'll need two 20' pieces of different-colored nylon cord, scissors, and a 12" piece of twine.

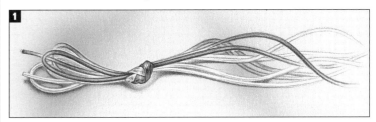

1. Fold each 20' piece of cord in half once and in half again. Put the cords together, holding the looped ends of the cord. You should have 8 strands, each measuring 5'. Tie a knot about 2" from an end of the cord using all strands.

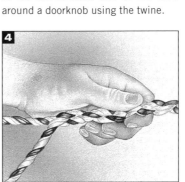

2. Tie the knotted end of the cord around a doorknob using the twine.

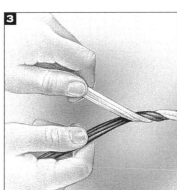

3. Gather the strands of one color in 1 hand and the other color in the other hand. Twist the cord tightly by exchanging the cords from hand to hand, wrapping the cords around each other. Make sure they are tightly twisted throughout.

4. Pull the twisted cord tight. Find the middle and fold over at that point. The cord should start twisting around itself.

5. When the full length is twisted, hold the twisted cords together and cut the twine to remove the knotted end from the doorknob. Secure the twist by tying a knot using all strands. Snip the twine off the end of the cord.

ILLUSTRATIONS BY HARRY DAVIS

Decorative Citronella Candle

These candle covers help conceal and beautify traditional citronella candles. You'll need a glass-enclosed citronella candle measuring 3" x 5", a 12" lace doily, a jar of Mod Podge, ½ yard of 1" wire-edged ribbon, a full 1-liter soda bottle, a small bowl, and a rubber band.

1. Fill the bowl with Mod Podge. Dip the doily into the bowl until it is fully saturated.

2. Center the candle upside down over the top of the soda bottle (this allows for easy application of the doily). Shape the doily around the candle using cupped hands, gathering the doily at the neck of the candle bowl. Smooth out any bubbles or large wrinkles.

3. Secure the doily with a rubber band. Allow to dry 1 to 2 hours.

4. Accent with wire-edged ribbon.

Lace Appliqué Pillowcase

If you're looking for an inexpensive way to decorate your plain pillowcases, add elegance to a bedroom, or design your own gift for a bridal or wedding shower, consider the lace appliqué pillowcase. You'll need a plain pillowcase, a lace appliqué, a sewing machine with a zigzag or machine appliqué stitch, embroidery or manicure scissors, pins, a needle, thread to match the appliqué, contrasting basting thread, and an iron.

1. Lay the pillowcase on a flat surface with the hemmed opening at the bottom. Center the appliqué along the hemmed edge; pin it in place. Hand-baste using broad (½") stitches across the entire surface of the appliqué; remove the pins.

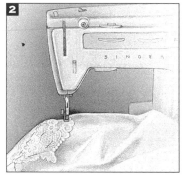

2. Set the sewing machine for machine appliqué or a closely spaced zigzag stitch. Starting at the edge of the pillowcase, sew around the top edge of the appliqué, following the curves and contours and centering your stitches over the edge of the appliqué.

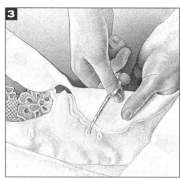

3. Turn the pillowcase inside out. Trim away the excess pillowcase fabric from behind the appliqué. Stay close to and follow your stitches, taking care not to cut into the stitches or the appliqué.

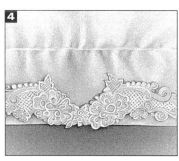

4. Press lightly with the iron from the wrong side, then turn it right side out.

Decal Gift Soaps

Decal soaps are easy to make and may be decorated to suit your personal taste. To make a decal soap you will need a bar of soap with a flat surface, a package of paraffin wax, a cutout of a pattern or a picture taken from wrapping paper, manicure scissors, a double boiler and stove, a cup of water, and 1 yard of ½" ribbon (optional).

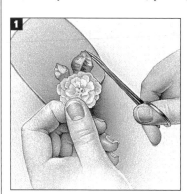

1. Cut out an image from the wrapping paper with the manicure scissors.

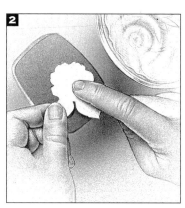

2. Wet the surface of the image and the soap with a drop of water; rub the soap with your finger. Place the cutout image on the soap and smooth it down. It should affix easily.

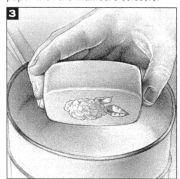

3. Melt the wax in the double boiler. The wax will melt to a clear liquid. Dip the soap (decal side down) ⅛" into the melted wax. The wax will dry almost instantly. Set aside for 5 minutes to dry completely.

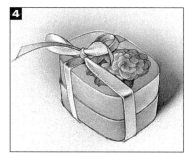

4. Stack 2 bars of soap and tie with a ribbon for further decoration, if desired.

Art Nouveau Watermelon

*Transform an ordinary watermelon into a carved tureen
filled with champagne fruit compote.*

Watermelon is the ultimate summer fruit, and a melon that doubles as a tasteful tureen is twice as refreshing. Using the art nouveau pattern we've provided and ordinary kitchen tools, you can turn an everyday melon into an elegant serving bowl in less than an hour. Add the fresh fruit and champagne compote created by Chef Guy Reuge, owner of the Restaurant Mirabelle in St. James, New York, and you'll have a dessert fit for any summer occasion.

A seedless watermelon is preferable for this project, as the skin is easier to pierce. You can use a watermelon with seeds, but the skin may be tougher to work with.

ART NOUVEAU WATERMELON

1 10–12 pound seedless watermelon
   Melon baller
   Long serrated kitchen knife
   Paring knife with blunt blade
   Serving spoon
   Plastic wrap
   Sponge
   Swivel pounce wheel or straight pin with
     ball top
1 sheet 9" x 12" tracing paper
   Pencil
   Masking tape
   X-Acto knife with ⅞" slanted blade
   Tape measure
   Access to standard photocopy machine

Making the Pattern

Measure watermelon from stem to tip on both sides; divide larger measurement in half. Enlarge pattern (page 7) on photocopier to match half measurement. Fold tracing paper in half crosswise and lay over pattern, matching folded edge of paper to dashed line on pattern. Using pencil, trace leaves, flower, berries, and leaf veins. Turn tracing paper over (without unfolding) and lay on plain surface. Retrace along marked lines onto other side of tracing paper. Open up tracing paper to complete petal that overlaps dashed line.

Carving the Melon

1. Set melon on flat surface and roll gently to examine skin for blemishes. The side that rested on the ground when the watermelon was growing may be flatter or lighter in color. Position melon so it doesn't wobble and skin on sides is green, smooth, and blemish-free.

2. Using serrated knife, cut out top ¼ of melon, from stem to tip. Remove wedge. Using melon baller, scoop out flesh from wedge and remaining melon. Place balls in a container. Using serving spoon, scrape final bits of flesh from melon until white rind shows. Place in separate container. Scoop or pour out remaining juice into another container. Cover all containers with plastic wrap and refrigerate. Discard wedge rind.

3. Center tracing paper pattern on 1 side of melon, aligning tips of leaves on pattern with cut edge of melon. Tape in place at sides. Mark pattern shapes and lines by pricking with swivel pounce wheel or pin about every ⅛", piercing through paper and rind. Pierce lines of entire pattern onto surface of melon. Note: pin-pierced pattern may be difficult to see once you remove tracing paper. Refer to tracing-paper pattern as needed for cutting.

4. Repeat step 3 on opposite side of melon.

5. Once entire pattern has been pierced, begin carving using X-Acto knife. Cut contoured leaves along top rim. To make smooth edges, cut from top of rim down into crevices and corners, rocking blade gently to maneuver it around curves.

6. (Omit this step if you want to fill melon to a higher level with compote.) Cut leaves marked cut out on pattern from point to point in same way, pushing cut-out section into melon to remove it.

7. For flowers and cherries, wrap masking tape 1" up from tip of paring knife blade to protect fingers. Holding taped portion of knife between fingers, use flat edge to scrape away green rind inside flower and cherry outlines. Wipe off scrap-

The carved watermelon tureen, filled with fruit and champagne compote and topped with sorbet, is elegant enough to use as a centerpiece.

ings with damp sponge.

8. With masking tape still affixed, use knife point to scribe veins of contoured leaves. Add freehand swirls and curlicues as desired. Cover with plastic wrap and chill until ready to serve. (The melon can be carved a day ahead of time and refrigerated; be sure to cover cut melon edges with wet paper or cloth towels and cover melon with damp towels.)

CHAMPAGNE FRUIT COMPOTE

5 medium to large peaches
1 750 ml bottle of champagne
1 cup sugar
1 bunch fresh mint
1 large cantaloupe
   Refrigerated watermelon flesh and balls
     (from above)
1 pint blueberries or huckleberries
1 pint blackberries or raspberries

1. Bring 2 quarts of water to boil in large pot. Plunge peaches one by one into boiling water for about 30 seconds. Remove using strainer; place in ice cold water. With paring knife, peel off loosened skin.

2. Uncork and pour champagne into deep-sided skillet. Add sugar and a few stems of mint. Bring mixture to boil.

3. Set peaches in mixture, cover, and reduce to slow-rolling boil. Cook until tender, about 10 to 12 minutes. Remove peaches and chill. Measure 1 cup of cooked champagne syrup and set aside for use in sorbet (optional); set aside remaining champagne syrup. Let both batches cool to room temperature.

4. Cut or peel skin from cantaloupe using sharp knife. Cut in half and remove seeds. Cut flesh into julienne strips (¼" x 1" to 2") to yield 2 cups. Set aside remaining melon flesh for sorbet (optional).

5. Cut 4 peaches in half and remove pits; then quarter each half, yielding 8 pieces per peach. Refrigerate remaining peach until ready to serve compote.

6. In food processor or blender, puree scraps of watermelon flesh. Strain into large bowl.

7. Remove mint stems from champagne syrup; add syrup to watermelon puree. Wash berries in strainer. Add sliced peaches, watermelon balls, berries, and julienned cantaloupe to syrup mixture; refrigerate until ready to serve. Yields 3 to 4 quarts. (For a juicier compote, add reserved watermelon juice).

8. To serve, fill melon with fruit compote. Garnish with fresh mint leaves, remaining whole peach, and sorbet (optional).
Makes 12–16 cups.

CHAMPAGNE SORBET (optional)

Reserved cantaloupe flesh (from above)
1 cup champagne syrup (from above)
Ice-cream maker

1. In food processor or blender, puree cantaloupe flesh and strain into medium bowl. Add reserved champagne syrup and mix well.

2. Freeze mixture in ice-cream maker, following manufacturer's instructions. Store, covered, in freezer until ready to serve.
Makes 1 pint. ◆

CARVING PATTERN

T o transfer this pattern to your watermelon, start by measuring the melon from stem to tip on both sides. Divide the larger measurement in half; enlarge the pattern to match this half measurement. Fold the tracing paper in half crosswise and lay it over the pattern, matching the folded edge of the paper to the dashed line on the pattern. Trace the entire pattern. Turn the tracing paper over (without unfolding) and lay it on a plain surface. Retrace the pattern (through the tracing paper) along the marked lines onto the other side of the tracing paper. Open up the tracing paper to complete the petal that overlaps the dashed line.

½ PATTERN

CUT OUT

Carving the Watermelon

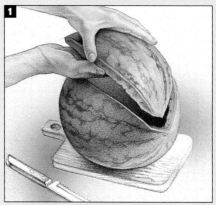

1. Using a serrated knife, cut out ¼ of the melon in a wedge shape.

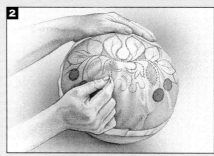

2. Center the pattern on one side of the melon and tape in place. Using a straight pin or swivel pounce wheel, prick the entire pattern onto the melon.

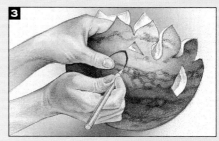

3. Cut out both the contoured leaves along the top rim of the melon and the leaves marked cut out on the pattern using an X-Acto knife.

4. To scribe the flowers and the cherries, hold the taped portion of the paring knife between your fingers and scrape away the melon's green rind.

Slip-On Chair Cover

Loose-fitting, easy-sew slipcovers transform inexpensive folding chairs.

⋙ BY MARY FRAZIER ⋙

In need of extra seating with a touch of class? Consider this slip-on chair cover, which transforms ordinary folding chairs into elegant seating. In a day's time, you can stitch up either slipcover: the more formal indoor version, or the informal patio or porch look. Although previous sewing experience is not mandatory for this project, familiarity with sewing terms and procedures is helpful.

Fabric selection is a critical part of the project, as certain fabrics are designed for home decorating. The fibers that make up these fabrics have usually been treated with Scotchguard (or a similar process) so that they resist stains, wrinkles, and fading. In addition, upholstery fabric typically features thicker threads than the fabric used in dressmaking, making it more resistant to wear and tear.

Rich-looking fabrics, such as damasks and moirés, work well in a classic, formal setting. (For the indoor view pictured here, Granville/9705 Garnet, at $10.39 per yard, was used.) For a country look, try a miniature print. For an outdoor design, look for bright, splashy florals, such as the Daybreak/Willow

fabric pictured at right, at $18.99 per yard. If this is your first attempt at making slipcovers, it's a good idea to choose a plain fabric or a fabric with an allover design.

Upholstery fabrics typically come in 54" or 60" widths; this pattern can use either. We designed it for a folding chair with the following measurements: back, 16½" on all sides; seat, 13" deep x 14" wide; height from seat to floor, 17".

SLIP-ON CHAIR COVER

Straight pins
2 yards 54" or 60" fabric
1 large spool of thread to match fabric
Fabric pencil
Sewing machine
Scissors
Iron
Ruler

For the formal version:
2 yards rope fringe

For the informal version:
2¼ yards strong, narrow cord for drawstring
1 yard 54" or 60" fabric for ruffle (same fabric as chair cover, or complementary fabric)
1 large safety pin or paper clip

1. Follow steps outlined in "Enlarging the Pattern," page 9.

2. Pin pattern pieces on wrong side of fabric following cutting diagram on page 9; cut out each piece. Locate dots, notches, and stay-stitch lines on pattern pieces; turn up outside edges of pattern slightly in order to mark dots, notches, and lines with fabric pencil on wrong side of fabric. Remove all pattern pieces and pins from fabric.

3. Stay-stitch backrest along stay-stitch line between dots. Cut out marked notches from edge of fabric to within ⅛" of stay-stitch line. (This will allow the fabric to ease around edges of chair seat, so skirt will fall

The more formal chair cover (left) was sewn using a rich, cranberry-colored damask. The floral fabric used on the design at right is better suited for an informal setting, such as on a patio or porch.

evenly without pulling around edges.)

4. Pin backrest to seat, with right sides facing and dots matching. Stitch together along seam line (½" from edge). Using iron, press seam toward seat.

5. Fold a tie piece in half along fold line with right sides together. Stitch long and angled sides along seam line. Turn right side out and press. Repeat with other tie.

6. Lay back right side up on flat surface. With right sides together, pin unfinished end of tie to back where indicated on pattern. Stitch approximately ¼" from raw edge. Repeat with other tie.

7. On skirt, stay-stitch between dots. Cut out marked notches from edge of fabric to stay-stitch line.

8. With right sides together, pin skirt to seat and backrest sections. Stitch together along seam lines.

9. With right sides together, match back to skirt, seat, and backrest. Pin and stitch together.

To finish slipcover with fringe:
1. Turn slipcover right side out and try it on chair; mark or pin up

hem so edge meets floor. Remove from chair. Make a double hem by folding fabric under approximately 1" and pressing. Fold again and press or pin in place. Stitch hem along inside edge.

2. Pin fringe to right side of skirt bottom, making sure tips of fringe and bottom of skirt are even. Turn under unfinished ends of trim and stitch in place.

3. Place slipcover on chair and tie a bow with sashes at back.

To finish slipcover with ruffle:
1. Cut 3 strips of fabric 54" or 60" wide by 11" long. (Cut 11" length along fabric selvage.)

2. With right sides together, stitch 2 strips together at short ends. Stitch remaining piece to both ends of combined piece to make a continuous loop of fabric.

3. Turn up ½" hem on bottom edge of fabric and stitch in place. Turn up a 2½" hem on top edge of fabric; press. Stitch raw edge, leaving a 2" gap unstitched for insertion of cord in next step. Stitch another row ¾" inside raw edge stitch.

4. Pierce cord with safety pin or

paper clip. Feed cord into channel between 2½" hem and seam ¾" above hem. Insert safety pin into gap; push safety pin along, pulling cord through at same time.

5. Continue threading until you return to 2" gap. Tie both ends of cord together in square knot and trim extra. Even out gathered fabric over cord to create ruffle. (You should

have approximately 2 yards of ruffle). Set aside.

6. Try slipcover on chair and measure 7" up from floor. Mark with fabric pencil at several points. Remove from chair and press skirt under at marked points to create creased line. Line up crease and ruffle so that top edge of ruffle extends 1" above crease. Stitch ruffle to skirt

½" from top edge taking care not to stitch over cord. Remove cord if desired. Turn slipcover inside out and trim extra skirt fabric to 1" from seam line.

7. Place slipcover on chair and tie a bow with sashes in back. ◆

Mary Frazier is a professional seamstress based in New York.

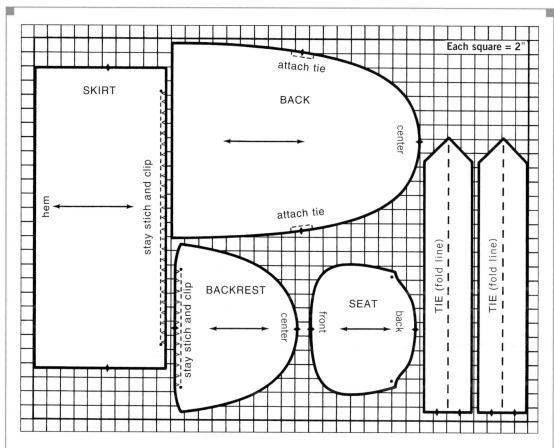

Each square = 2"

SKIRT

hem

stay stich and clip

attach tie

BACK

center

attach tie

BACKREST

stay stich and clip

center

SEAT

front

back

TIE (fold line)

TIE (fold line)

ENLARGING THE PATTERN

The chair cover pattern pictured above must be enlarged before use. To enlarge the pattern you can photocopy it yourself, have a copy shop photocopy it, or enlarge the pattern by hand. Because the resulting pattern is quite large, allow at least 1 hour for any of the methods.

Yardstick (if needed)
1 30" roll brown wrapping or butcher paper (if needed)
Scissors
Scotch tape (if needed)
Ruler
2 felt-tip markers of different colors (if needed)
Access to copy machine (if

needed)
Fabric pencil

If using a photocopy machine, make a copy of the above pattern and cut out each piece. Enlarge each piece individually until the grid squares measure 2" square. (You may need to tape some pieces together between enlargements.) When done, lay the enlarged pattern pieces on a large, flat surface; line up the enlarged grids and pattern lines and tape in place. Trim off any excess paper.

To enlarge the pattern by hand, tape together brown wrapping or butcher paper to create a large sheet measuring 58" x 76". Starting

from the corner point, mark off every 2" along all 4 sides of the paper using a felt-tip marker. Using a yardstick, connect the corresponding 2" measurements to create a grid. In principle, you're creating an enlarged version of the pattern grid on the brown paper. Working block by block, transfer the pattern to the paper using the fabric pencil. Transfer the pattern lines from the grid into each 2" square, enlarging the lines to fit the larger grid blocks. When you have transferred the entire pattern, trace around the lines with the other color felt-tip marker, reinforcing and straightening the enlarged pattern lines where necessary. Cut out pattern pieces.

3-D VIEW OF THE CHAIRCOVER

To assist you in assembling the pattern, here is a 3-dimensional view of the chair cover in progress.

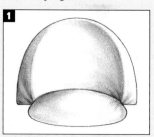

1. Here, the seat has been attached to the backrest.

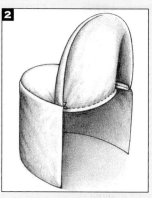

2. In this view, the skirt has been attached to the pieces pictured above. What's missing: the back and ties.

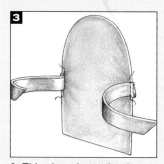

3. This view shows the ties attached to the back.

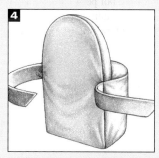

4. This view shows all pieces attached: the back, the ties, the skirt, the seat, and the backrest.

How to Paint a Tuscan Wall

Create a mottled, sixteenth-century look using latex paint and sponges.

≈ BY CHRIS ALTSCHULER ≈

This mottled, Tuscan look was achieved using the warm tones shown on page 11. For alternative color choices, see *page 12.*

Admiring the look of aged stucco walls no longer means traveling to the central region of Italy. Using standard latex paint and sponges, you can create the look of mottled Tuscan plaster in two days' time for an average-size room.

Stucco walls were a common feature of Tuscan farmhouses and villas built during the fourteenth, fifteenth, and sixteenth centuries. Color was applied using one of several methods: Fresco (Italian for fresh) involved mixing paint pigment with water and applying the mixture onto wet plaster. Fresco *secco* (Italian for dry) applied the same mixture to dry plaster. Colorwashing, also popular, involved washing a plaster wall with a mixture of pigment, powdered chalk, and water.

Today, creating the look of aged plaster no longer requires replastering walls or hand-mixing pigments. The concept behind this project is a simple one: apply a base coat of latex paint over the entire wall and accent that underlying layer by sponging on two additional colors, which creates a mottled finish.

If your walls are in good condition, you'll need only to prepare your room for painting before starting. However, if your walls are in need of more serious preparation, such as priming oil paint or filling major holes or cracks, be sure to start with the instructions outlined in "Preparing the Wall Surface" on page 12.

TUSCAN WALL FINISH

1 or more gallons latex paint in color 1 (*see* colors on page 11)
1 quart latex paint in color 2 (same sheen as color 1; *see* colors on page 11)
1 quart latex paint in color 3 (same sheen as color 1; *see* colors on page 11)
1 roll 2" low-tack painter's masking tape (to protect ceiling)
1 roll 1" standard masking tape (to protect woodwork)
1 5-gallon bucket
1 9" wide roller screen
1 9" paint roller
1 medium-nap roller cover
1 paint roller extension handle or broom handle with screw threads
1 2"–3" high-quality synthetic-bristle brush
1 large rectangular household sponge
2 empty 1-quart plastic bottles with screw caps
2 disposable plastic or heavy paper plates
  Drop cloths for covering furniture
  Drop cloths, rosin paper, or newspapers for covering floor
  Screwdriver
  Pail of warm water
  Stepladder (if needed)
  Sticks for stirring paint
  Funnel
  Latex gloves
  Hammer
  Nail, any size

Preparing the Room for Painting

1. Move furniture into center of room and cover with drop cloths. Cover exposed floor with drop cloths, newspaper, or rosin paper. Take down all window treatments, mirrors, pictures, and associated hardware. Unscrew and remove switch plates, outlet covers, and light fixtures.

2. Apply 2" tape around perimeter of ceiling and 1" tape to edges of window and door trim, baseboards, built-in cupboards, chair rails, etc. Tape over outlets and switches with either tape.

Applying the Base Coat

1. Open windows and keep room well-ventilated throughout painting and drying periods.

2. Slip on gloves. Using screwdriver, pry open lid on color 1 paint can. Before pouring paint, hammer nail holes 1" apart around entire lip of can, so paint in rim can drip back into can. Stir paint with stick in brisk figure-8 motion. Pour paint into plastic bucket to a height no deeper than ½ brush bristle length.

3. To load brush with paint, dip bristles into paint until halfway coated, lift handle straight up, and slap bristles back and forth against inside of bucket once or twice to shake off excess paint. Beginning at ceiling and working down toward floor, brush edges and corners of each wall surface. Outline door and window trim, following tape guidelines. Aim for smooth, even strokes about 2' long. Avoid dabbing with brush; instead, work in a smooth, easy rhythm.

4. Assemble roller and roller cover. Fill ⅓ of bucket with paint. Hang screen on edge of bucket;

PHOTOGRAPHS BY STEVEN MAYS

The 3 Colors of the Tuscan Wall

To create the Tuscan wall shown on the previous page, you need to purchase paint in each of the colors pictured here. The easiest approach: take this issue to a paint store and find matching paint samples. This method allows you to choose the specific brand and price range of paint you prefer.

1. Cover entire wall surface with color 1 (above).

2. Sponge color 2 (above) over color 1.

3. Sponge color 3 (above) over colors 1 and 2.

dip roller in paint and roll off extra paint onto screen. Roll an M shape onto wall over a 5' square area, then spread paint around wall by back-rolling in different directions. The more you back-roll, the smoother the finish.

5. Attach extension or broom handle to roller. Use extension handle (and stepladder if needed) to reach up to ceiling and down to baseboard. Cover entire surface with smooth, even strokes. Let dry overnight.

Applying the Tuscan Finish Coats

1. Repeat steps 1 and 2 from "Applying the Base Coat" on page 10 with color 2.

2. Using a funnel, pour paint from can into quart container until about ½ full. Add tap water to bring level to approximately ⅝ full. Screw on cap tightly and shake vigorously to thin paint.

3. Submerge sponge in pail of warm water, then squeeze out excess until sponge is damp enough to glide easily over wall surface without dripping.

4. Pour a small amount of thinned paint onto plastic plate, enough to coat surface of sponge. Set large, flat surface of damp sponge into paint. Using a light, delicate touch, wipe sponge across wall in a sweeping, back-and-forth motion. Start in an inconspicuous place in the room in case you don't like your first attempt. The goal is to create a nondirectional, fairly even texture without applying color to the entire wall. Use minimal pressure for a thin, transparent glaze of color. Don't try to blend strokes, but allow patchy shapes that emerge to become part of overall texture. Proceed from top of wall down to floor all the way around the room, going back for more paint as necessary. If you have difficulty manipulating the sponge in corners and near edges, stab color into these areas using a paintbrush and smear over using sponge.

5. After sponging the entire room, step back

4 STEPS TO CREATING THE TUSCAN FINISH

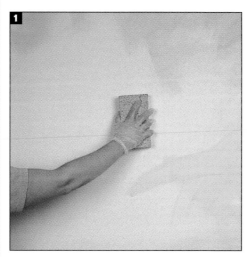

1. Sponge on color 2 over the base coat using a sweeping, back-and-forth motion.

2. Don't try to blend your strokes; allow patchy shapes to emerge.

3. Re-sponge any areas that appear light or off-balance using color 2.

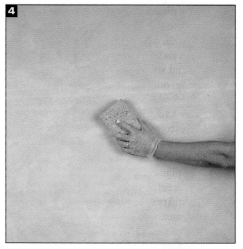

4. Sponge on color 3 more sparingly to fill in random areas or to accent naturally ocurring patterns.

and evaluate your work. Re-sponge any areas that appear light or off-balance. Strive for a pleasing overall effect rather than focusing on (and overworking) specific areas. When finished, rinse out sponge thoroughly in warm water. (Because paint is so thin, it will dry in 1 to 2 minutes. If third color is applied before second coat is dry, however, it shouldn't affect outcome.)

6. Follow steps 1 and 2 from "Applying the Tuscan Finish Coats" on page 11 with color 3. Pour a small amount of thinned paint onto plastic plate, enough to coat surface of sponge. Remoisten sponge and apply new color over wall surface in same manner as before, only more sparingly, to fill in random areas or to accent naturally emerging patterns. To mimic an old wall, concentrate paint near ceiling and trim edges.

7. When finished, clean up all paint supplies in warm, soapy water. ◆

Chris Altschuler is a decorative painter and wallpaper maker living in Chicago.

Choosing a Sheen

When purchasing paint, you'll need to choose between the major categories of sheen: flat, eggshell, and glossy. Flat paint hides imperfections in the walls, but tends to be less durable and washable. Glossy paint is more durable and can have a nice effect, but it shows every fault in the wall. Eggshell is a nice compromise.

PREPARING THE WALL SURFACE

If your walls are not smooth and blemish-free, start by filling holes or cracks with Spackle or other patching compound. Once you've completed that process and sanded down any rough surfaces, you can proceed with the base coat of latex paint.

If your walls are covered with glossy latex or oil-based/alkyd paint, you'll need to apply a coat of 100-percent acrylic primer before painting.

1 quart ready-mixed
    Spackle or patching
    compound
1 or more gallons 100-
    percent acrylic primer
    (if needed)
1 2" paintbrush
¼ cup base coat color (color
    1) for spot-priming
Medium (100- or 120-
    grit) sandpaper
Paint scraper
Putty knife with wide
    blade

Spackling trowel
Sanding block (if needed)
Screwdriver
Hammer

1. To fill cracks, dents, or other imperfections, tap along cracks with a screwdriver, using tip to work free any loose or chipping plaster. Widen thin cracks to receive Spackle more easily. Brush away dust particles with dry paintbrush. Tap down nail pops and nail holes that pucker outward with hammer, denting surface inward. Scrape off any loose paint chips with paint scraper.

2. Using trowel or putty knife, spread Spackle or patching compound over all cracks, holes, and dents, filling evenly. Run blade across surface of wall to scrape off excess. Let dry 1 hour or more, depending on humidity and depth of holes; consult container for specific recommendations.

3. When Spackle is dry,

use 100- or 120-grit sandpaper to sand off excess. If compound filling large holes has shrunk beneath the surface during drying, repeat steps 1 to 3. To sand broad areas easily, wrap paper around sanding block.

4. Spot-prime walls by brushing paint over all spackled areas. Since dry Spackle absorbs paint more readily than surrounding wall surface, this ensures even roller coverage later on.

5. If your walls have been previously painted with a glossy latex or oil-based/alkyd paint, follow the instructions on page 10 for "Preparing the Room for Painting." Before applying base coat, apply a 100-percent acrylic primer coat (such as Muralo or Benjamin Moore) over entire wall surface. Follow steps 1 to 5 of "Applying the Base Coat" on page 10, using primer; let dry to touch (3 to 4 hours). Apply secondary colors as outlined on pages 10 and 11.

VARIATIONS ON THE TUSCAN WALL

1. This Tuscan finish uses a darker, orangy hue for highlights.

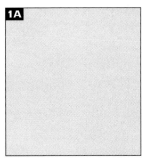

1a. Color 1 (base coat).

1b. Color 2 (sponge on over base coat).

1c. Color 3 (applied over colors 1 and 2).

2. This cooler Tuscan finish resembles a stone wall.

2a. Color 1 (base coat).

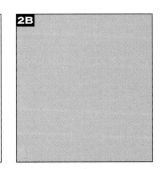

2b. Color 2 (sponge on over base coat).

2c. Color 3 (applied over colors 1 and 2).

Edwardian Hearth Arrangement

An antiqued container, boxwood, and dried flowers dress up a summer fireplace.

BY CHRISTOPHER BASSETT

The green boxwood and preserved foliage in this arrangement will dress up any fireplace.

Your fireplace needn't stay cold and empty all summer long. Using a combination of boxwood and colorful dried flowers, you can create an Edwardian arrangement that dresses up this oft-forgotten space.

For this project we used a decorative terra-cotta container, but one made from wood, metal, or other material would work equally well. In putting together the materials list, we've estimated the amount and types of foliage you'll need to create the dense arrangement pictured. Be aware that foliage quantities vary considerably by supplier. If you prefer a looser look for your arrangement, start with half the amounts listed in the materials list and go from there. Of course, you're free to leave out particular varieties, add other types as desired, or make substitutions if certain varieties are not available.

EDWARDIAN HEARTH ARRANGEMENT

- 1 solid container with an opening 10" or more in diameter
- 1 10" Styrofoam ball
- 1 12" x 12" x 2" sheet of Styrofoam or 2 bricks floral foam, 4½" x 9" x 2"
- 4 thin wooden picks or dowels, 5" long
- 2 floral picks (if needed)
- 1 12"–15" thin wooden pick or dowel
- 1 can matte black spray enamel
- 1 can dark green spray enamel
  - Sharp 10"–12" scalloped bread knife
  - Scissors
  - Latex gloves
- 10-15 sheets newspaper for covering paint surface and for wadding
  - Wooden block slightly smaller than base measurement of container
- 1 36" curtain tieback with fringe or 1 yard silk cord with make-your-own tassel (*see* Charter Issue, page 5)
  - Hot-glue gun and glue sticks
- 4 packages (20 branches) green boxwood
- 6 cranberry pin oak twigs with multiple leaves
- 5 copper beech twigs with multiple leaves
- 4 mallee eucalyptus stems
- 4 holly stems
- 8 ruscus leaf stems
- 10 stems rough bristle grass
- 5 stems common quaking grass
- 10 stems timothy grass
- 1 lotus pod
- 4 string bean pods
- 6 preserved pink roses, large-head variety
- 20 strawflower stems, 4 each in cream, magenta, pink, rust, and orange; all with multiple flowers
- 3 cranberry heather stems
- 6 purple statice stems
- 11 lavender stems: 3 gray sea, 8 purple
- 10 melaleuca stems
- 6 pink mullein stems
  - Plant mister
- ½ package sphagnum moss, pulled into 6 wisps

1. Place wooden block on laid-out newspaper. Position container on top of block in order to spray slightly under bottom lip of pot for complete coverage. Always wear gloves and work in well-ventilated area when using spray paint.

2. Hold can of black spray paint about 10" from container and spray a light, even coat until outside of container is completely covered. Repeat if necessary. (The inside will not need to be painted.) Let dry 1 to 2 hours, or until dry to the touch. Follow manufacturer's instructions for specific drying times.

3. Push long wooden pick or dowel into 10"

Styrofoam ball. Hold stake and spray-paint ball with dark green spray paint as outlined in step 2. Let dry. When dry, remove pick.

4. When container is completely dry, drape curtain tieback or cord with tassel around container. Hot-glue in place.

5. Fill container to within 3" to 4" of top rim with tightly wadded newspaper. Place block of Styrofoam or floral foam on top of container; press firmly to form indentation in foam. (If foam is not large enough to cover mouth of container, connect 2 foam bricks by inserting floral picks in between.) Using knife, slice along indentation made by rim; round and taper foam edges to fit container just below rim. Wedge into top of container with palms of hands. (*See* "How to Use Floral Foam," Charter Issue, page 10, for illustrations.)

6. Apply hot glue at end of a 5" pick or dowel and push 1" into Styrofoam ball. Repeat with 3 other sticks, creating 4 legs for ball. Hot-glue opposite ends of 4 picks and push into foam-filled container. Base of ball should be centered in container and even with rim of pot.

7. Cut boxwood into 2" to 2½" twigs with scissors.

8. Insert boxwood twigs into ball, creating green base. Cover front half of ball completely.

9. Using photograph as guide, insert other foliage into ball, followed by dried flowers, to cover front half of ball. Insert preserved roses last. Vary the length and groupings of flowers by snipping stalks with scissors and pushing stems deeper into Styrofoam ball. Clip statice to about 5" to add depth to arrangement. Periodically check arrangement's size to ensure a good fit in fireplace.

10. Mist moss lightly for easier handling. Arrange and trim moss around base of arrangement, concealing Styrofoam. ◆

Christopher Bassett is a professional floral artist specializing in fresh and dried arrangements.

Trompe L'oeil Apples

Create the illusion of three-dimensional fruit in an hour.

BY FRANCIS DEARDEN

The French phrase *trompe l'oeil,* which translates to trick of the eye, refers to a style of painting that employs light, shade, and perspective to give flat images a 3-dimensional, lifelike appearance. Although perfected by the Baroque painters of the late seventeenth century, trompe l'oeil effects have long been used as decorative elements in homes and dwellings. The Egyptians painted their ceilings to resemble skies, while the Greeks and Romans created elaborate, illusionary gardens and vistas on the walls of their homes. In both cases, creating the illusion of an open window or ceiling using paint is easier, quicker, and less expensive than constructing the desired item.

While the Greek and Roman trompe l'oeil masters covered entire rooms with their illusory patios and gardens, this project will create a smaller version of the same effect using water-based acrylic paint and the apple template provided on page 15. In about an hour's time, even beginner painters can create the illusion of fresh fruit situated on a wall, shelf, kitchen back splash, or lintel.

Walls or surfaces made of plaster, Sheetrock, or other smooth material make the best foundation for this project. Be sure to consider how much traffic the area gets, since paintings near a light switch, for example, may wear off in time.

TROMPE L'OEIL APPLES

1 2-fluid-ounce tube each of Liquitex (water-based) acrylic paint in permanent green light, cadmium yellow lemon, black, and white
1 #3 long-handled artist's paintbrush
1 #1 artist's paintbrush
1 water-filled jar (for cleaning brushes)
1 sheet 220- or 240-grit sandpaper (if working on oil-paint or enamel surfaces)
   Sponge or rag
   Cheesecloth or rag (if necessary)
   Liquid detergent (if necessary)
   Sharp pencil
   Pencil sharpener (if necessary)
   Scissors
   Scrap paper
   Access to photocopy machine
   Plastic plates for mixing paint
   Acrylic spray sealer (optional)

Francis Dearden, a professional artist based in Lloyd Harbor, New York, specializes in decorative art.

These trompe l'oeil apples work well in a kitchen. Paint them on a shelf, chair rail, or chair back or above a back splash.

Dry-Brush Techniques

This project uses 2 basic dry-brush techniques: a heavier dry brush, found on the gray-green shading, and a lighter technique, which is used in applying the white and yellow highlights. Be sure to practice both methods on scrap paper before working on the actual project.

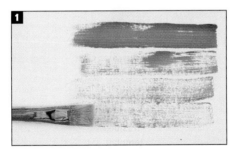

1. & 2. For a heavier dry-brush, load the brush with a small amount of gray-green paint. Dab the flat side of the brush on clean scrap paper, then gently brush the bristles over the scrap paper to achieve a light, feathery texture.

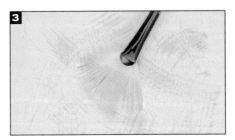

3. & 4. For a lighter dry-brush, load the brush with a small amount of yellow (or white) paint. Dab the flat side of the brush on the scrap paper, then brush the bristles over the paper to acheive a wispy texture. Add a second stroke which crosses over the first to create a cross-hatching effect.

PHOTOGRAPHS BY STEVEN MAYS

PAINTING THE APPLES

1. Prepare the site by removing any grime or dust with liquid detergent and a sponge or rag. Wipe with a clean, damp sponge and let dry. If the paint on the site is oil-based or high gloss, rub the site with sandpaper to create a tooth for the water-based acrylic paint. Wipe with a damp cheesecloth or rag to remove any sanding dust.

Mix or lay out the paint on the plastic plates as follows, using the #3 brush:

(a) Base color of the apple: Mix equal blobs (i.e., ¼" squeeze from the paint tube) of green, yellow, and white.

(b) Shading on the apple and stem: Make a second batch of the base color and add a dab of black. Start with a ¹⁄₁₆" squeeze from the black paint tube and add more as needed.

(c) Shadow on the wall: Combine a dab of black with a blob of white.

(d) Outline: Use pure black.

(e) White highlights: Use pure white.

(f) Yellow highlights: Use pure yellow.

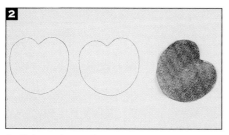

2. Enlarge the apple template at right, using a photocopy machine, to a width of 3¾". Cut out the enlarged apple. Place the template on the site and trace, using a sharp pencil. Move the template to the next position and trace it again; repeat for the third apple.

3. Using the #3 brush, fill in the apple shapes with the base color (a) from step 1 above. Apply the paint in even, smooth strokes, be-

ing careful to stay within the pencil lines. Let the paint dry completely (10 minutes is typical, thicker coats of paint may take a few minutes longer). Clean the brush in the water jar.

4. Using the photograph as a guide, paint the shading on the apples using the gray-green paint (b) from step 1, the #1 brush, and a heavier dry-brush technique (*see* "Dry-Brush Techniques," page 14). Step back from your work to assess the natural appearance and 3-dimensionality. Continue painting the shading on the remaining apples.

5. When done with the shading, freehand paint the stems using the gray-green (b) paint and the #1 brush. Let the paint dry completely (10 minutes) and clean the brush in the water jar.

6. To create the illusion of a shadow behind the apples, offset the template approximately ½" to the right of the apple. Using a pencil, trace the shadow outline on all 3 apples.

7. To fill in the shadow portion, use the #1 brush with the light-gray paint (c) from step 1. Freehand paint the shadow of the stems. Let the paint dry 10 minutes. Clean the brush in the water jar.

8. Paint a thin black line between the apple and shadow using the pure black paint (d) from step 1 and the #1 brush. Accent the stems with black paint as desired. Let the paint dry completely (10 minutes). Clean the brush in the water jar.

9. Add the white highlights to the shoulder and edge of the apple using the #1 brush, pure white paint (e) from step 1, and a lighter dry-brush technique. Let the paint dry completely (10 minutes). Clean the brush in the water jar.

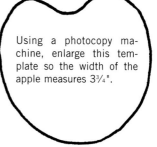

10. Add the yellow highlights to the midsection of the apple using the #1 brush, pure yellow paint (f) from step 1, and a lighter dry-brush technique. Let the image dry 10 minutes. Clean the brush in the water jar. If desired, spray acrylic sealer over the entire painted surface to fix the image.

Using a photocopy machine, enlarge this template so the width of the apple measures 3¾".

Hand-Tinted Bookplates

Use the images printed in this issue to produce your own hand-colored bookplates.

BY SUZANNE GUZZO AND NANCY JOHNSON

Bookplates, also known by their Latin name of *ex libris,* for "from the library of," originated hundreds of years ago. In those earlier times, artists, printers, and engravers were commissioned to create unique plates for their wealthy patrons. Today, creating and mass-producing hand-colored, customized bookplates for yourself or to give as gifts requires only a set of colored pencils or watercolors and access to a color copier.

HAND-TINTED BOOKPLATES

Black-and-white bookplate (*see* special insert, following pages)
Colored pencils, watercolor pencils (such as Rembrandt by Lyra), or watercolor paints (such as Winsor & Newton)
Assorted watercolor paintbrushes (if needed)
Plastic or metal watercolor palette (if needed)
Scrap paper
Pencil sharpener (if needed)
Calligraphy pen or fine-line permanent marking pen
Scissors or metal-edge ruler and X-Acto knife
Rubber cement
Access to black-and-white and color copy machines with reduction/enlargement features

1. Choose bookplate from designs included in this issue, or find 1 in an older book or antique print shop.

2. Make a black and white photocopy of bookplate that is 200 percent larger than original. If lines in photocopy appear too feathery or disappear when enlarged, adjust photocopier to a darker setting or a slightly smaller enlargement — no smaller than 180 percent — and try again until image is clear and lines are sharp.

3. Color the enlarged photocopy with colored pencils, watercolor pencils, or watercolor paints. Avoid using very light pastel colors, which tend to appear washed out when photocopied, or very dark colors, which will obliterate dark lines of the drawing. (Remember that image is a double-size copy. When image is reduced, colors will intensify.) *When using 2 colors side by side,* try to vary their relative lightness or darkness for maximum contrast. For most dramatic contrast, choose several colors that are opposite on the color wheel (i.e., yellow-green and red-violet). *If using colored pencils,* be sure to keep pencil points sharp and press down firmly, especially with lighter colors. *If using watercolor pencils,* be sure to practice on scrap paper. Try coloring with pencils, then brushing with a moist (not wet) brush to blend pencil strokes. *If using tube watercolor paints,* squeeze 1 drop of each color and 1 drop of water into individual palette wells. Dip tip of brush into water, then into paint. Blend on a flat section or in a clean palette well. Brush across a scrap of paper to blend and thin color and to shed excess water drops. Black copy lines will help contain the color and keep it from running. Do not wet paper before painting.

4. If using watercolor pencils or watercolor paints, paper may be slightly damp once coloring is finished. Lay paper on a flat surface away from heat to dry. Do not be concerned if paper buckles slightly; it will be compressed flat by lid of photocopier and will not affect final image.

5. Using a color photocopier set at 50 percent reduction (45 percent if your enlargement in step 2 was only 180 percent), photocopy handcolored image to return it to original size. If personally operating photocopier, try varying color buttons to intensify either warm (i.e., yellow) or cool (i.e., cyan) colors to give bookplate different looks. (*See*

Using a single bookplate image and a variety of colored pencils or watercolors, you can create a library of bookplates to give as gifts.

"How to Be Creative with a Color Photocopier," page 17.) *One note of caution:* Experimenting with a color photocopier can be expensive, as color photocopies are significantly more expensive than standard photocopies. (At a shop we contacted, making anywhere from 1 to 10 photocopies of 1 original image costs $2.70 each; making more than 10 photocopies of 1 original costs $1.50 each.) This expense can be reduced by grouping images for photocopying. After reducing hand-colored images once, place several images together on a sheet of 8½" x 11" paper and then make multiple photocopies.

6. To personalize bookplate, use calligraphy pen or fine-line marker with permanent ink to inscribe appropriate name on blank area of bookplate. Practice writing on scrap paper first. (If making set of book-plates for one person only, write person's name on 200 percent enlargement. When image is reduced, flaws will be minimized and finished bookplates will look professionally printed.)

7. To dry-mount bookplate, trim any extra paper from around image using scissors or a metal-edge ruler and X-Acto knife. Brush back of bookplate with rubber cement and let dry 1 to 2 minutes. Brush an area the size of bookplate on front inside cover of book with rubber cement and let dry 1 to 2 minutes. Place bookplate onto this area and press bookplate and front cover together for a permanent bond. ◆

Suzanne Guzzo is a free-lance writer based in New York. **Nancy Johnson** is a full-time artist specializing in painting, pottery, and silversmithing.

PHOTOGRAPHS BY STEVEN MAYS

Color Your Own Bookplates

Ex Libris

EX LIBRIS

U sing a black-and-white photocopy machine, enlarge the images presented here by 200 percent. Color the images using colored pencils, watercolor pencils, or watercolor paints, then reduce the image by 50 percent (returning the image to its original size) on a color photocopier. To save expense when running off additional color photocopies, group colored images together on a single sheet and make photocopies of that sheet.

From The Collection Of

Ex Libris

Ex Libris

Ex Libris

From The Library Of

EX LIBRIS

Color Development

1. To develop the final hand-colored bookplate, the colors are added in stages. In our samples, the first step involved coloring parts of the sky with a light blue pencil.

2. For the farmhouse roof, the artist used a brown pencil.

3. Next, the artist colored the trees, the grass, and all the foliage, using a light green pencil.

4. Finally, the artist highlighted small areas throughout the image, using a purple pencil.

HOW TO BE CREATIVE WITH A COLOR PHOTOCOPIER

Most color photocopiers use varying proportions of 4 colors — magenta (red), yellow, cyan (blue), and black — to create color photocopies. By varying the intensity of any of the colors or a combination of colors, you can give your hand-colored bookplate a different feel.

3. In this image, the magenta was maximized and the other colors were minimized. The resulting picture appears as though seen through rose-colored glasses.

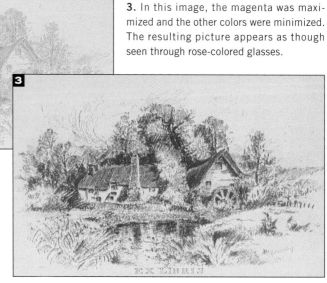

2. For this image, the yellow was maximized and the other colors were reduced, giving the scene a tropical feel.

1. In this image, the cyan on the photocopier was maximized, and the other colors were minimized. The resulting blue image has a cool, wintry feel.

3 Simple Techniques for Weathering Furniture

Replicate aged finishes using paint, sandpaper, and Vaseline.

BY CHRIS ALTSCHULER

The techniques outlined in this article are designed to replicate the aged finishes found on the cupboard's door, drawer, and side section.

The weathered finishes found on this aged, antique cupboard can be reproduced on any unfinished wood, from armoires, chairs, and tables to mantels, chair rails, or crates.

Searching for that great antique find can take years. With the 3 simple weathering techniques outlined in this project, however, you can create your own aged pieces in 2 days' time.

The cupboard pictured is unusual in that it features a number of different weathered finishes. This project outlines how to replicate 3 of those distinct looks. The first technique, called "Paint and Sand," replicates the look of paint that has faded due to prolonged exposure to light. The second technique, "2-Coat Paint and Sand," simulates how a piece with 2 different layers of paint looks as it ages. The third technique, "Paint and Rub," uses Vaseline, applied between 2 layers of paint, to simulate the look of chipped or flaking paint.

If you study the cupboard closely, you'll notice that the different finishes are interspersed. In weathering your furniture, you can mix the 3 methods, use 1 technique over an entire piece, or combine 2 or more methods on a specific section or feature of the piece.

If you decide to combine methods, you may find yourself moving back and forth between 2 types of paint: oil-based/alkyd and latex. In general, oil-based/alkyd paint is easier to sand off than latex, hence the reason you'll use it for particular situations. Due to local laws, however, oil-based/alkyd paints are not available in all areas. If this is the case in your area, simply substitute latex paint, but be aware that it will take more effort to achieve the same sanding effects. (If you opt for oil-based/alkyd paints, be sure to read "Cleaning Up Oil-Based/Alkyd Paints," page 20. Latex paint cleans up easily with warm water.)

All 3 weathering techniques (and both types of paint) work equally well on any type of unfinished furniture, though results may differ slightly between pine and oak, for instance. (Unfinished raw wood is the easiest surface to work on because it requires very little preparation.) Look in the yellow pages for stores that sell unfinished furniture to locate suitable pieces, such as tables, chairs, hutches, corner cupboards, armoires, benches, dressers, or chests. The weathering methods will also work on other wooden pieces, such as mantels, mirrors or picture frames, doors, banisters, wainscoting, chair rails, shelves, boxes, or crates.

WEATHERED FURNITURE

Getting Ready to Paint

Unfinished cupboard or other furniture
Drop cloth
Painter's masking tape, any width
Latex gloves
Screwdriver
Hammer
Nail, any size
Sticks for stirring paint
Plastic bucket

1. Choose a work area that is well-ventilated and dust-free; lay down drop cloth. Remove drawers (if any) and set aside; these will be painted separately. Place cupboard on drop cloth.

2. Remove knobs, hinges, and other hardware; set aside in safe place. (To age hardware, *see* "Aging Knobs and Handles," page 20.) Tape edges of areas you want to keep free of paint, such as inside of drawer front or glass windows.

3. Slip on latex gloves. Using screwdriver, pry open lid of appropriate paint (depending on finishing method being used). Hammer nail holes 1" apart around lip of can so paint that gets into rim can drip back down into can. Stir paint with stick in a brisk figure-8 motion. Pour paint into plastic bucket to a height no deeper than ½ brush bristle length.

Paint and Sand

In principle, this method involves applying paint and sanding it off. The sanding lightens and wears off the base coat color, simulating natural wear and tear. This finish is shown on the door of the cupboard and in photo 1 at right.

1 quart satin-finish blue oil-based/alkyd paint
1 1½"–2" paintbrush with synthetic bristles
Medium (100- to 120-grit) sandpaper
Dust mask
Cheesecloth or rags
Sanding block (if needed)
Paint thinner (if needed for cleanup)

1. Cover cupboard (or desired section of piece) with base coat of blue paint following the recommendations in "Painting Tips," page 20. (Apply paint more thinly in areas that you plan to sand.) Clean up following tips in "Cleaning Up Oil-Based/Alkyd Paints," page 20. Let dry overnight.

2. Slip on particle mask. Sand edges of doors and drawers, around handles, and near moldings and other trims to simulate wear. Sand other sections as desired. To sand broad, flat areas easily, wrap sandpaper around sanding block.

3. When finished sanding, wipe all surfaces gently with damp cheesecloth or rag to remove sanding dust.

WEATHERING TECHNIQUES

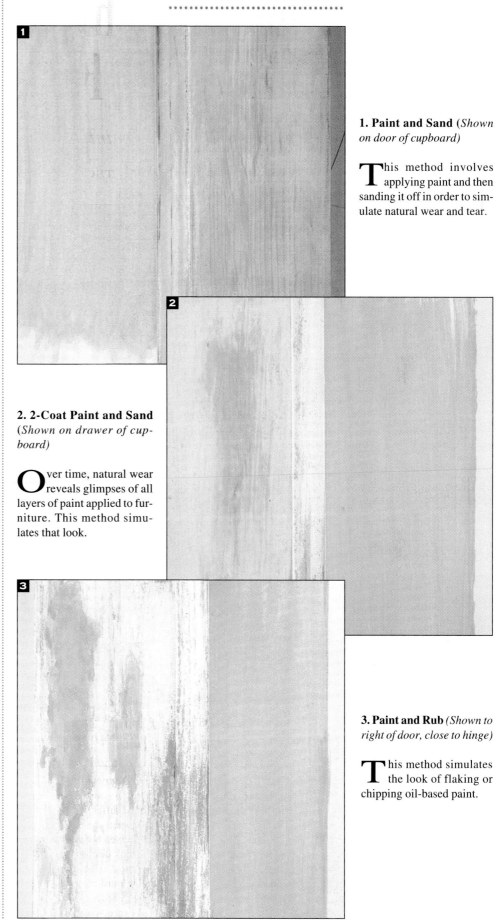

1. Paint and Sand (*Shown on door of cupboard*)

This method involves applying paint and then sanding it off in order to simulate natural wear and tear.

2. 2-Coat Paint and Sand (*Shown on drawer of cupboard*)

Over time, natural wear reveals glimpses of all layers of paint applied to furniture. This method simulates that look.

3. Paint and Rub (*Shown to right of door, close to hinge*)

This method simulates the look of flaking or chipping oil-based paint.

Painting Tips

To load the paintbrush, dip the bristles into the paint until it is halfway coated. Lift the handle straight up, then slap the bristles back and forth against the inside of the bucket once or twice to shake off any excess droplets. (This method allows the interior bristles to hold the maximum amount of paint and reduces the excess liquid on the outer bristles, which will drip down and ruin your work.)

To paint the wood surface, brush on the paint going with the grain, then move the brush back and forth against the grain to coax the paint in between the wood fibers. For a smooth finish free of brush strokes — especially desirable for a worn-paint finish — brush over the wet surface once again with the grain, barely touching the bristles to the surface. For best results, paint the cupboard or furniture from the top down. Paint the moldings and any other details first and then move to the flatter surfaces. Paint the drawers last.

2-Coat Paint and Sand

If a piece of furniture has had 2 coats of paint applied to it, natural wear over time will reveal the coat beneath the top coat. This method, shown on the drawer of the cupboard and in photo 2 on page 19, simulates this wearing-away process.

1 quart satin-finish dusty mauve latex paint for base coat
1 quart satin-finish white oil-based/alkyd paint for second coat
1 1½"–2" paintbrush with synthetic bristles
   Medium (100- to 120-grit) sandpaper
   Dust mask
   Cheesecloth or rags
   Sanding block (if needed)
   Paint thinner (if needed)

1. Cover cupboard (or desired section of piece) with base coat of mauve paint following "Painting Tips," above. Let dry overnight.

2. Cover cupboard (or desired section) with thin layer of white paint using paintbrush, or wipe on thin coat of paint using clean rag. Clean up oil-based/alkyd paint materials following tips in "Cleaning Up Oil-based/Alkyd Paints," below.

Let dry overnight.

3. Slip on particle mask. Sand through white paint layer to reveal mauve color underneath in selected areas. To sand broad, flat areas easily, wrap sandpaper around sanding block.

4. If desired, soften effect of sanding by rubbing a small amount of white paint onto areas where mauve undercoat is revealed using clean cheesecloth or rag.

Paint and Rub

This method is designed to simulate the look of flaking oil paint. In the past, oil-based paints were used to cover furniture. When exposed to moisture (such as the humidity of a kitchen or bathroom), oil-based paint tends to flake off. Using this method, you can cause paint to flake off by applying Vaseline between the layers of paint. Be sure to practice on a piece of scrap wood before trying the real thing. The effects of "Paint and Rub" are shown to the right of the cupboard door and in photo 3 on page 19.

1 quart satin-finish ochre latex paint for base coat
1 quart satin-finish off-white latex paint
1 quart satin-finish white latex paint (optional)
1 1½"–2" paintbrush with synthetic bristles
1 jar Vaseline
   Clean rag (for applying Vaseline)
   Cheesecloth or rags
   Scrap wood

1. Cover cupboard (or desired section of piece) with ochre base coat following "Painting Tips," above. When dry to touch, smear a thin coat of Vaseline randomly over selected areas with rag.

2. Cover cupboard (or desired section of piece) with coat of off-white paint following "Painting Tips," above. Be sure to paint over greased areas. Clean up paint materials using warm water. Let dry overnight.

3. Using clean rag, rub greased spots. Paint should flake off easily, creating a chipped look. Wipe off remaining Vaseline with a clean rag.

4. If desired, rub a small amount of white paint onto wood using clean cheesecloth or rag to soften effect. ◆

Chris Altschuler is a decorative painter and wallpaper maker living in Chicago.

AGING KNOBS AND HANDLES

If you want truly authentic looking aged furniture, you'll want to weather the piece's knobs, handles, hinges, or other hardware. The following are aging methods for metal.

Start by roughing up the shiny surface of the hardware by sanding with any grade of steel wool. If the surface of the hardware is naturally rough, you can skip this step.

1. OIL-BASED WOOD STAIN

For this method, you'll need a clean rag, brown wood stain, and hand cleaner. Using a corner of the rag, wipe the wood stain over the entire piece of hardware. When dry (approximately 2 hours), apply a second coat, concentrating the stain in the crevices and on the edges. Let dry completely (5 to 6 hours) before reattaching the hardware. To clean up, discard the rag and use hand cleaner to clean any stain off your hands.

2. RUSTED BLACK PAINT

For this method, you'll need a 2-ounce tube of black water-based acrylic artist's paint, a 2-ounce tube of ochre yellow or earthy orange acrylic paint, a #3 artist's paintbrush, and a clean rag. Using the paintbrush, cover the hardware with black paint. Let dry (10 to 20 minutes). Using a corner of the rag, dab on the yellow- or orange-colored paint in small patches to create the look of rust spots. Focus on the crevices and edges rather than on covering the entire piece. Let dry completely (1 to 2 hours) before reattaching the hardware. Clean up using warm water.

3. PATINA

For this technique, you'll need a 2-ounce tube of dark green water-based artist's acrylic paint, a 2-ounce tube of white acrylic paint, two clean rags, a plastic plate, a #3 artist's paintbrush, and a cup of water. Squeeze three ½" blobs of dark green paint onto a plastic plate. Using a corner of the rag, cover the entire piece of hardware with dark green paint. Let dry (10 to 20 minutes).

Using a paintbrush, mix a small amount of white paint into the second green blob to create a middle shade of green; clean the brush in a cup of water. Mix a small amount of white paint into the third green blob to create an even lighter shade of green. Moisten a rag with water. Dip the wet rag into all 3 shades of green paint at once, allowing the 3 colors to blend and bleed. Dab the 3 shades of paint onto the hardware, letting the wet rag soften the edges between the shades of green. Let dry completely (1 to 2 hours) before reattaching the hardware. Clean up using warm water.

CLEANING UP OIL-BASED/ALKYD PAINTS

Unlike latex paint, which cleans up easily with warm water, you must use paint thinner to clean up when using oil-based/alkyd paints. Pour a small amount of thinner into a glass jar or old coffee can and rinse the paintbrush. When done cleaning, pour the thinner back into its original container for storage. *Do not* pour it down the drain. (Some people opt to wear a dust mask during cleanup. It's not mandatory, however.)

After a week or 2, all the paint remnants will settle to the bottom of the paint thinner container and solidify. At that time, you can pour off the unused thinner and reuse it.

Re-Cover a Chair Seat in 30 Minutes

This quick reupholstering project transforms chair seats without sewing.

➤ BY MARY FRAZIER ➤

RE-COVERING THE SEAT

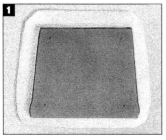

1. Lay chair seat topside down on batting and draw a cutting line 4" from seat's perimeter using felt-tip pen and ruler. Remove chair seat and cut batting. Lay chair seat topside down on batting once again.

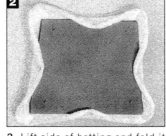

2. Lift side of batting and fold it over seat. Staple or thumbtack in place at the midpoint. Repeat same process at opposite side, making sure not to pull batting too tight. Continue stapling or tacking at center of each remaining side.

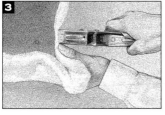

3. Lift and fold batting in same manner 2" on both sides of each corner and staple or tack in place.

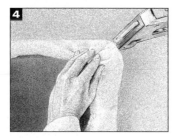

4. Ease batting around corners, stapling or tacking at ½" intervals to reduce number of wrinkles.

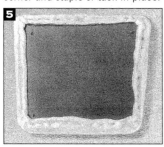

5. Staple or tack along sides at ½" intervals.

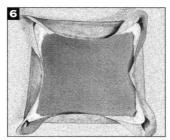

6. Repeat step 1 with fabric. Be sure to center fabric pleasingly if you are using patterned fabric. If using striped fabric, make sure stripes are straight.

7. To staple seat-cover fabric, repeat steps 2 to 5, working carefully to keep fabric smooth and taut but not so tight that it pulls. Flip chair seat over periodically to check.

In half an hour's time you can update a chair seat to match a new decorating scheme or replace an older seat. Unlike traditional reupholstering, which requires precise measuring and fitting, this project uses a staple gun or thumbtacks to attach cut-to-fit fabric.

RE-COVERING A CHAIR SEAT

Chair with removable seat
1 yard batting 1" thick, any width (if needed)
1 yard fabric of choice, any width
1 yard solid fabric, any width, for underside (optional)
5/16" staple gun and staples or 2 packages thumbtacks
Staple pull, pliers, or hammer
Screwdriver (if needed)
Felt-tip pen
Scissors
Straight pins (if needed)
Iron (if needed)
Ruler

1. To prepare seat for re-covering, lift seat from chair frame. If seat does not come away from chair easily, do not force it, as seat may be screwed into frame of chair. Turn chair upside down. Find screws and remove using screwdriver.

2. Place seat topside down and remove tacks or staples attaching original cover to seat with staple pull, pliers, or claw of hammer. Lift original fabric off seat. Check condition of original batting to determine if it needs to be replaced or added to. A fresh layer of batting will enhance the finished results by softening edges and adding loft.

3. Follow instructions at left to enhance batting and re-cover seat.

4. If desired, follow instructions below to line underside of seat.

5. Replace seat and secure with screws if necessary. ◆

Mary Frazier is a professional seamstress based in New York.

This project is designed for chairs with removable seats.

Lining the Chair Seat

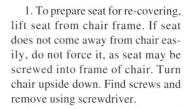

1. To cover raw edges of seat cover on underside of seat, lay seat face up on wrong side of solid fabric and trace around it. Cut fabric. To create hem, fold fabric in approximately ¾" on all sides, wrong sides facing, and pin in place. Press. Remove pins.

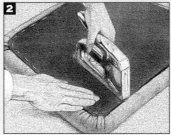

2. Lay fabric on underside of seat, with pressed hem side down. Arrange fabric carefully to cover all raw edges of fabric and batting. Staple or tack along sides at ½" intervals.

French Silk Purses

Miniature purses made from ribbon are perfect for holding jewelry, decorating place settings, or doubling as elegant giftwrap.

These silk-ribbon purses, made of wire-edged ribbon instead of fabric, can serve as wrapping for small gifts, favors on a dinner table, pouches for potpourri, or a place for storing jewelry. Assembly is as simple as gluing strips of ribbon together, attaching a ribbon ruffle, and, if desired, accenting with a handmade ribbon rose.

For this project, wire-edged silk ribbon has certain advantages over ordinary ribbon. Although wire-edged ribbon is not a new invention, it has gained popularity in the last 5 years. The primary reason: The concealed wire edge makes it easy to add 3-dimensionality or shape to such decorative items as ruffles and flowers.

Silk ribbon, like the silk used in dressmaking, adds a certain luxuriousness to any project. The use of silk dates back to at least 2640 B.C., and the fabric has long been associated with nobility. This may be, in part, because the process of producing, processing, and weaving what is essentially the byproduct of silkworms is both costly and labor-intensive. Though silk may appear delicate, due to its fine fibers, it is actually very strong and durable, making it a good choice for purses such as these.

Fill these silk-ribbon purses with your favorite collectibles, such as potpourri or candy, or use them as giftwrapping at bridal or baby showers.

FRENCH SILK PURSE

½ yard 1½"-wide silk wire-edged ribbon, any color (Ribbon A)
1⅓ yard 1½"-wide silk wire-edged ribbon in matching or contrasting color (Ribbon B)
½ yard 1"-wide silk wire-edged ribbon in matching or contrasting color (Ribbon C) for tying purse closed
Hot-glue gun and glue sticks
Scissors
Ribbon rose (optional; *see* directions below)
Needle (if making rose)

Thread to match ribbon rose (if needed)

1. Cut two 9" lengths of Ribbon A and two 9" lengths of Ribbon B.

2. Lay length of Ribbon A on flat surface. With glue gun, apply line of glue along 1 long edge of ribbon. Quickly overlap edge of long side of Ribbon B on top of glue and tap with fingers to allow glue to adhere.

3. Repeat gluing and overlapping from step 2 with remaining 2 lengths of ribbon, alternating colors. Set aside 4-ribbon rectangle.

4. To make ruffles, cut remaining length (2½') of Ribbon B in half. Use 1 cut length of ribbon and slide ribbon along 1 wire until 1" of wire is exposed. Bend wire over end of ribbon and twist to keep ribbon from sliding off wire as you gather. Slide ribbon from other end toward bent-wire end until it is evenly and tightly gathered across wire and measures approximately 6". Bend over second end of wire and cut to 1" with scissors. Repeat for second ruffle.

5. Lay 4-ribbon rectangle on flat surface with short side at top. Apply line of glue along short edge; quickly place gathered side of ruffle onto glue and tap with fingers until glue adheres. Repeat with second ruffle on other short side. Snip off ends of twisted wire.

6. To form pouch, fold rectangle in half, right sides together and raw sides of ruffle even. Hot-glue in place along both sides of bag, from ruffle edge to fold.

7. Turn pouch right side out. Tie Ribbon C around neck of pouch to close. Accent with ribbon rose (*see* below), if desired, by hand stitching in place using threaded needle.

SILK-RIBBON ROSE

1 yard 1½"-wide variegated silk wire-edged ribbon
Fine-gauge spool wire
Scissors
3½" green ribbon, 1" wide, for leaf (optional)

1. Lay ribbon on flat surface. Working with 1 end, fold corner of end down to form a right triangle. This forms center portion of rose.

2. To form bud, wrap ribbon 3 times around first fold to make a cone shape. Pinch base of bud with fingers and bind tightly with wire.

3. Holding base of bud, twist free end of ribbon at base of bud and wrap outward over finger. Pinch ribbon to base of bud to create first petal. Bind petal at base with wire.

4. Turn bud and first petal counterclockwise and create second petal by wrapping free end of ribbon outward over finger, and then returning to base of bud. Bind petal at base with wire.

5. Continue turning, folding, and wiring folds until rose reaches desired fullness of approximately 8 petals.

6. Secure all petals at base by binding tightly with wire.

7. Shape petals by folding down edges of petals at corners and curving them to create a cupped appearance. Overlap adjacent petals.

8. To make leaf, twist green ribbon at its center and fold over. Wire free ends to base of flower and pinch into shape. ◆

MAKING A SILK-RIBBON ROSE

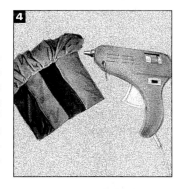

1. Fold a corner of the ribbon down to form a triangle.

2. Wrap the end of the ribbon 3 times around the first fold to make the center bud. Bind the base of the bud with wire.

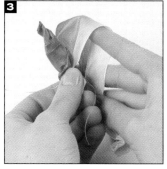

3. Holding the bound bud, wrap the ribbon over your finger. Pinch the ribbon to the base of the bud to form the first petal; bind to the bud with wire.

4. Turn the bud and the first petal counterclockwise; continue forming 7 additional petals using the method outlined in step 3. Wire each petal to the base of the bud.

5. Curve the petals to create a cupped appearance. Overlap the adjacent petals.

Making the Silk Purse

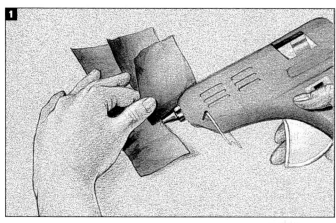

1. Apply a line of glue along a long edge of the ribbon using the glue gun. Try to apply the glue in a thin, consistent stream for better adhesion. If you're having difficulty, practice on scrap paper. When tapping the ribbon lengths together to adhere the glue, avoid burns by taking care not to touch the hot glue with your fingertips.

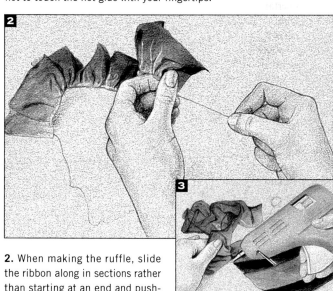

2. When making the ruffle, slide the ribbon along in sections rather than starting at an end and pushing all the ribbon along the wire. The sectional approach will allow more even spacing of the ruffle along the ribbon. Pushing a section at a time is also easier than attempting to push all the ribbon at once.

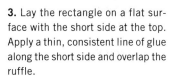

3. Lay the rectangle on a flat surface with the short side at the top. Apply a thin, consistent line of glue along the short side and overlap the ruffle.

4. To form the pouch, fold the rectangle in half with the right sides together. Line up the edges of the ruffles. Hot-glue in place along the sides of the pouch and the edges of the ruffle. To finish, turn the purse right side out. Tie 1/2 yard of contrasting ribbon around the neck to close.

How to Make Heirloom Books

Create hand-bound books at home using a simple pamphlet stitch.

BY LLOYD TRAINOR

A hand-bound book, filled with special photographs, mementos, or poetry, makes a truly unique gift. You can even make multiple books for the same person, as changing the book's look and feel is as easy as selecting different paper.

1 17" x 6½" sheet of medium- to heavy-weight cover stock
1 12" x 12" sheet of medium-weight stock for endsheets
1 10" x 10" sheet of stiff, medium-weight paper for spine cover and corner accents
1 8" x 10" sheet of 2-ply bristol board or stiff paper for stiffening spine
1 25" x 38" sheet of text-weight paper for book pages
1 spool waxed linen thread, heavyweight thread, or thin string
Stiff #5 or #6 flat-bristle paintbrush
Adhesive (i.e., Elmer's Glue)
X-Acto or utility knife
24" or 36" metal straightedge or ruler
Awl
Chipboard (large enough to cut paper on)
#20 large-eyed needlepoint needle
1" diameter wooden dowel (8" long) or burnisher
Scissors
Hammer
Pencil
Small pliers (optional)
Brass cartouche or medallion for finishing book (optional)

Lloyd Trainor is an artist and bookbinder living in Greene, Rhode Island. He has lectured extensively on book arts and sold his fine handmade books at craft fairs throughout the Northeast.

DETERMINING PAPER GRAIN

All machine-made paper has a grain direction along 1 dimension of the sheet. Bound paper should be oriented with its grain along the spine or the height of the book. Note: handmade paper has no grain. It can be used in either direction. The following are methods for determining the grain direction of machine-made paper:

1. **Tear Test.** In general, paper tears in a straight line when torn *with* the grain.

2. **Wet Test.** Cut a small square out of a corner of the paper. (Be sure to mark it to identify its original orientation to the full sheet.) Wet 1 side of the paper only. The stock will curl with the grain.

Why create a hand-bound book? Not solely for its personal feel, but also for its ultimate usefulness. You can create your own address books, guest books, wedding books, photo albums, and journals. Or take a page from the Victorian age and create a common book. Over time, such books were filled with important notes, photographs, quotations, poetry, clippings, and drawings, giving the keeper a personalized record of things that mattered or items that shaped their thoughts and lives. When constructed and decorated by the user, books such as these offer an added level of personal significance.

Unlike traditional hand-bound books, which require extensive use of adhesive, this project relies on a basic sewing technique — the pamphlet stitch. Although some glue is used in our project, the amount is minute compared to traditional bookbinding techniques.

Using such traditional techniques, taking a hand-bound book from start to finish might have taken several days. In less than a day's time, however, you can create the 4¼" x 6¾" book pictured here using the paper of your choice. (*See* "Paper Recommendations," page 26, for specific suggestions.)

HEIRLOOM BOOK

For all steps involving an X-Acto or utility knife, be sure to protect your work surface with chipboard.

1 17" x 6½" sheet of marbled paper for decorative cover

Cutting the Book Pages

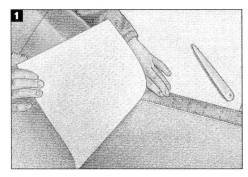

1. Find a clean, flat surface to work on. Place 25" x 38" sheet of page paper flat. Measure and cut or tear 18 sheets, each measuring 8" x 6". Make sure 6" measurement goes *with* grain of paper. (*See* "Determining Paper Grain," page 24.) To simulate rough edge of handmade paper, tear sheets toward you, dragging paper against metal straightedge or ruler. For clean-cut edge on pages, draw X-Acto knife against edge of straightedge or ruler.

2. Stack 3 groups of 6 sheets evenly; fold each group in half to make 4" x 6" pages. These groupings are called signatures and will be sewn separately into the book binding. Run dowel or burnisher over crease of each signature.

Cutting the Decorative Endsheets

3. Place 12" x 12" endsheet paper on flat surface. Measure and mark two 4¼" x 6" sheets, making sure 6" length goes *with* grain. Tear or cut following step 1. Place a signature evenly on top of an endsheet, with extra ¼" of endsheet projecting out at folded edge of signature. Holding signature in place, fold extra ¼" around folded edge of signature; crease lightly with dowel or burnisher. Repeat for second endsheet. (Endsheets will become first and last pages of book. You will have 1 signature without an endsheet which will fill middle of book). Set signatures and endsheets aside.

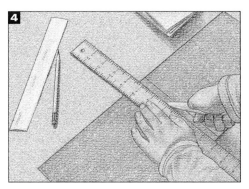

Measuring and Creating the Book Cover

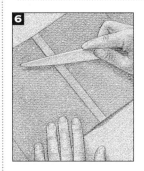

4. Lay 17" x 6½" medium- to heavy-weight cover stock on flat surface. Measure and cut one 15¾" x 6¼" sheet, with 6¼" length going *with* grain. Draw 4 lines parallel to short (6¼") side of cover stock at following distances from either edge: 3½", 7⅝", 8⅛", and 12¼". Score each line by dragging unsharpened tip of scissors blade or edge of burnisher gently along straightedge or ruler at each measurement. Take care not to tear paper.

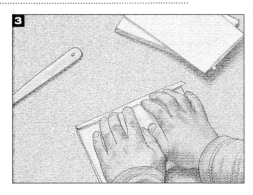

5. Fold 2 center lines (7⅝" and 8⅛") inward to create spine. Roll dowel or burnisher over each crease to firm up folds. (Take note of these inward creases, as they identify the inside cover from this point on.) Flatten paper and flip over. Fold creases at outer edges (3½" and 12¼") toward center of cover. Firm up creases with dowel or burnisher.

Stiffening the Spine

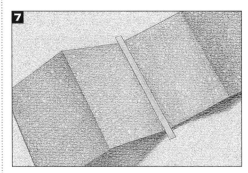

6. Using 8" x 10" sheet of stiff paper or 2-ply board, measure and cut two ½" x 6¼" pieces. Grain should run *with* 6¼" measurement. (One piece will be glued to outside of spine; the other will be used as a piercing guide in step 8.) Spread a thin layer of glue on 1 side of a ½" x 6¼" strip with paintbrush. Attach to outside of spine. After positioning, press firmly with dowel or burnisher along entire glued portion.

7. Using leftover endsheet paper, cut one ⁷⁄₁₆" x 7" piece. Grain should run *with* 7" measurement. Paint on thin layer of glue and attach to inside of spine, with extra paper projecting evenly at top and bottom of spine. Fold extra portion over to outside of spine and over stiff spine strip attached in step 6. Press firmly with dowel or burnisher.

Creating the Piercing Guide

To prepare the book for binding, sewing holes must be pierced through the 3 signatures, the endsheets, and the spine. To aid with this process, the remaining ½" x 6¼" piece of stiff paper from step 6 will be made into a piercing guide.

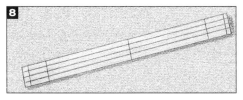

8. Lay strip flat in vertical orientation. Using straightedge or ruler and pencil, draw 3 straight lines along length of strip: 1 line down center, and the other 2 evenly spaced on either side of center line. Turn strip to horizontal position for drawing lines across width of strip. Measure ⅛" in from each end and draw a line at both points. Measure ½" in from each end and draw a line at both points. The fifth line should be drawn in the exact center of strip. (When complete, guide should have 5 lines across width and 3 lines down length of strip.)

Piercing the Sewing Holes

9. Work on chipboard for steps 9 to 11. Place guide inside signature with accompanying endsheet, running guide alongside crease. Line up ⅛" top and bottom marks on guide with top and bottom of signature. Holding guide alongside crease with 1 hand, use other hand and awl to pierce a hole *next to* guide and through crease at ½" horizontal mark. Pierce through entire signature and endsheet. Repeat process at opposite ½" horizontal mark and at center horizontal mark. Repeat entire process on remaining signatures. (When finished, each signature should have 3 pierced holes.)

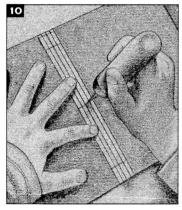

10. Lay cover, inside portion face up, on flat surface. Position piercing guide along spine, lining up tops of guide and cover. Push awl through guide at intersection of each ½" and center horizontal lines with 3 vertical lines. (A total of 9 holes). Push awl through guide, making hole marks in, but not piercing, spine.

11. Remove guide. Pierce holes through spine fully by tapping lightly on awl with hammer at each of 9 hole marks. Pierce just enough to create holes large enough to sew through. (If necessary, push needle through hole to test hole size.)

Sewing Signatures into Book Cover

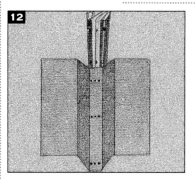

12. Hold cover, inside portion face up. Signature with endsheet as its first page will be sewn into far-left set of pierced holes; signature without endsheet will be sewn into middle set of holes; and signature with endsheet as its last page will be sewn into far-right set of holes. Note: this illustration is designed for reference only. Signatures of your book will not extend above the book as shown.

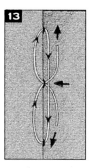

13. Start with signature that contains endsheet as its first page. Place signature in cover with endsheet facing inside front cover. Cut a 19" piece of waxed thread. Thread needle and push through center hole of signature from inside of signature. If needed, use pliers to pull needle through hole. Push needle through corresponding center hole in endsheet and in cover. Pull thread to leave 3" tail inside signature. Push needle back through corresponding top ½" hole of cover, endsheet, and signature. Pull thread snug. From inside of signature, push needle back out through corresponding lower ½" hole of signature, endsheet, and cover. Pull thread snug, drawing signature and cover tightly together. Push needle back to inside of signature through corresponding center hole of cover, endsheet, and signature. As needle comes back inside signature, guide it to other side of center thread, opposite tail. Slip needle off thread. Pull string ends snug and tie square knot over center thread, catching center thread inside knot. Pull knot tight; trim ends to about ⅜". Repeat steps 12 and 13 for second signature (without an endsheet), using middle set of pierced holes, and for third signature, using far-right set of pierced holes. On third signature, endsheet should face inside back cover.

Paper Recommendations

While the paper you choose for your book will depend in large part on personal taste, certain weights of paper are better suited for specific parts of a book than others.

One means of measuring paper weight is by grams per square meter (g/m^2), meaning a square meter of paper weighs so many grams. If purchasing paper through mail order, this measurement will give you a feel for the paper's relative thickness. The main advantage to the g/m^2 measurement is that you can compare any paper, regardless of sheet size.

Generally, most text-weight papers fall in the 80 to 120 g/m^2 range. Medium- to heavy-weight stock ranges from 150 to 250 g/m^2. Cover stocks will generally fall in the 250 g/m^2 range; on the other end of the spectrum, handmade tissue paper falls in the 10 to 40 g/m^2 range.

Most paper is sold in sheets; prices vary considerably, depending on whether the paper is machine-made or handmade, text-weight or cover stock, and so on. In general, handmade paper is more expensive than machine-made. (In all cases, the larger the quantity of paper you buy, the lower the cost per sheet.) Most art supply stores should have a good selection, but mail order in general offers greater variety.

When ordering by mail, consider purchasing paper samples to get a feel for texture, weight, and color. If you're ordering a small amount of paper (i.e., 1 to 2 sheets), you may end up paying more for shipping than for the paper itself. It's best to order larger quantities.

1. **Text pages.** Some suitable papers to consider for text pages: Mohawk Superfine, Strathmore Drawing, Frankfurt, Lana Laid, Rives Lightweight, and Arches Text.

2. **Endsheets.** Endsheets can be fashioned from light, handmade paper such as Fabriano Roma (130 g/m^2; comes in 8 colors) or machine-made paper such as Strathmore Charcoal or Fabriano Ingres Antique.

3. **Cover stock.** For the semisoft book covers in this project, a stronger, heavier stock is preferable, around 250 g/m^2. Consider the variety of handmade Indian sheets for a natural look or Duchene (such as the Larroque Mouchettes) and Dieu Donne papers for an elegant traditional or contemporary look. Many heavier machine-made papers, such as Ingres Cover or the Japanese Wynstone papers, are also appropriate for small books.

4. **Marbled paper.** Marbled paper is available in a variety of colors. Prices vary considerably, depending on whether you purchase printed paper ($1 to $2 per sheet) or hand-marbled paper ($18 per sheet). We don't recommend the latter for this project, as it is too delicate.

5. **Spine and corner accents.** In general, text-weight paper (80 to 100 g/m^2) will work well for the corner accents. Spine covers should be medium- to heavy-weight stock (150 to 250 g/m^2).

6. **Spine stiffener.** Just about any 2-ply bristol board or stiff paper will work. Murillo, a mold-made paper by Fabriano, is a good choice. It comes in about a half dozen neutral shades.

Cutting and Applying Spine Cover

14. Lay 10" x 10" sheet of spine cover paper flat. Measure and cut a 2½" x 6¼" piece from edge of sheet. (Remaining paper will be used in steps 19 to 21.) Grain should run *with* 6¼" measurement. Measure in 1" and 1½" from long side of paper; draw and score 2 lines parallel to long side of paper at those points. Check fit of spine cover by placing it over book spine. Adjust if necessary. Once fit has been confirmed, firm up folds with dowel. Open spine cover and lay flat. Apply ⅛" line of glue to both inside long edges of spine cover. With cover closed, place spine cover over spine. Keeping spine straight, press with fingers along glue lines until glue begins to set. When set, run dowel or burnisher along glued edges. Let glue dry ½ hour before proceeding.

Applying Marbled Paper to Book Cover

15. Lay sheet of marbled paper on flat surface. Cut two 6½" x 8" pieces (grain should run *with* 6½" measurement); set 1 aside. Lay cover flat with inside facing up. With marbled side of paper down, brush a ⅛" line of glue along one 6½" side. Turn marbled paper over (marbled side up) and position glued edge along spine crease of inside front cover. Before gluing in place, make sure edges of marbled paper and cover are lined up. Press glued edge with fingers until glue begins to set; set glue more securely by pressing dowel or burnisher over glued areas.

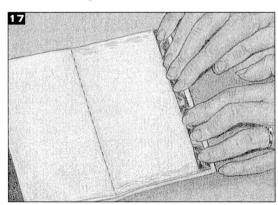

17. Brush glue on nonmarbled side of extra paper; adhere to backside of cover by pressing lightly with fingers. Set glue more securely by pressing dowel or burnisher over glued areas. Lay cover flat, marbled side down. Begin with outermost portion of 1 side of cover. Apply ⅛" line of glue around outside 3 edges of cover section.

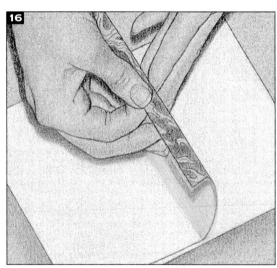

16. Fold cover and marbled paper back toward spine; then fold extra marbled paper over outermost edge of cover. Press fold with fingers along entire edge to create crease.

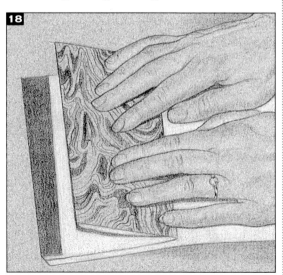

18. Fold cover inwards toward spine so marbled side shows; press glued edges firmly with fingers to set glue. Once glue is set, press firmly with dowel or burnisher. Repeat steps 15 to 18 with back cover.

Adding Corner Accents

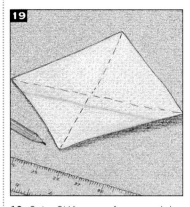

19. Cut a 2½" square from remaining spine cover paper. Fold in half to form triangle. Fold in half again to form 4 equal triangles. Unfold flat. Draw a parallel line ½" away from either crease.

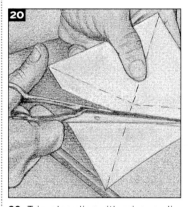

20. Trim along line with scissors; discard smaller triangle.

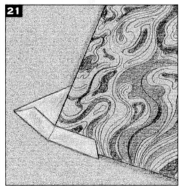

21. Start with front cover. With cover closed, fit accent on lower righthand corner with creases and edges of book lining up. Glue portion overlapping cover in place. Open cover. Fold ½" bottom edge of accent upward; glue in place. Fold over remaining side of accent, line up edges, and glue in place. Repeat steps 19 to 21 for each corner of front and back cover. If desired, glue brass cartouche or medallion on front cover.

English Cottage Tapestry Pillow

Create the look of antique needlepoint pillows using precut fabric and Velcro.

BY MARY FRAZIER

No need for buttonholes or zippers on this pillow: a strip of Velcro serves as the closure.

It's easy to re-create the look of English cottage tapestry pillows without spending a fortune on fabric. The key: a precut, finished square of tapestry that serves as your pillow front. With a minimum of sewing, backing fabric of your choice, and a Velcro closure that replaces a zipper, you can create a fringed pillow in half a day's time.

ENGLISH COTTAGE PILLOW

1 precut 18" square piece of tapestry
½ yard 45"-wide wool (or similar non-nap fabric) in coordinating solid color for back of pillow
16" ¾"-wide Velcro hook and loop fastener tape
2 yards sew-on 1¼"-wide fringe in coordinating color
1 18" square pillow form
   Thread to match Velcro tape, backing fabric, and fringe (up to 3 spools, depending on colors)
   Sewing machine with size 12 or 14 needle
   Ruler or yardstick
   Scissors
   Straight pins
   Iron

1. Using iron, press backing fabric on wrong side to remove wrinkles. Place backing fabric on smooth surface. Measure and cut a 14" x 18" rectangle and a 9" x 18" rectangle.

2. Fold one 18" edge of each piece of backing 1" to wrong side and press. Fold each of these same edges over another 1" and press again to make a double-fold pressed edge on each piece of fabric.

3. Lay smaller rectangle right side up on flat surface with pressed edge at bottom. Separate Velcro into 2 pieces. Center looped half of tape across hemmed edge of fabric, fuzzy side up and bottom edges matching. Using sewing machine, stitch along all tape edges through all layers of fabric, using thread to match Velcro.

4. Open out pressed folds of larger rectangle and lay it right side up on flat surface with folds at bottom. Center hooked tape portion of Velcro, rough side up, across area between 2 folds so that lower tape edge rests on lower fold line; pin in place. Stitch along all tape edges. Refold along pressed lines and pin from right side. Load machine with spool of thread matching color of backing fabric. Topstitch ⅞" from folded edge through all layers. Overlap larger piece over smaller piece by 1" to reattach Velcro halves. Finished pillow back should measure 18" square.

5. Lay tapestry square right side up on flat surface. Center pillow back on top of tapestry, right side down, with smaller rectangle at bottom. Pin together along edges of back piece. If necessary, use back piece as pattern and cut tapestry fabric to match, making sure corners are square. Pin all edges together. Using matching thread, sew around entire pillow (½" from edge) through all layers, rounding corners. Using scissors, trim corners diagonally ⅛" from stitching. Turn pillow cover right side out through back opening, and poke out corners from inside with your index finger. Roll seam between your fingers to make a neat edge, pinning or hand-basting as you go. Press lightly, then remove pins or basting.

6. To attach fringe, pin it to front of pillow, overlapping ½". Load sewing machine with thread on spool to match fringe and thread on bobbin to match pillow back. Before sewing, turn under starting and ending edges of fringe slightly. Topstitch fringe to pillow, stitching through all layers. Compress pillow form and insert it into cover through back opening. Manipulate form into corners before pressing Velcro closed. Plump up finished pillow from right side. ◆

Mary Frazier is a professional seamstress based in New York.

Assembling the Pillow

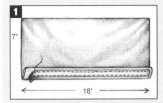

1. Center the looped half of the Velcro tape (fuzzy side up) across the hemmed edge of the smaller pillow back rectangle; stitch in place.

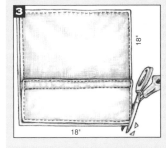

Refold bottom edge and topstich

2. Open out the pressed folds of the larger pillow back rectangle; center the hooked half of the Velcro tape (rough side up) across the area between the 2 folds. Stitch in place. Refold along the pressed lines and pin from the right side; stitch in place.

3. After stitching the back and the front pieces together, trim the corners diagonally ⅛" from the stitching.

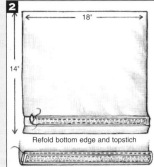

4. Turn under the starting and the ending edges of the fringe to prevent fraying. Stitch the finge to the pillow front.

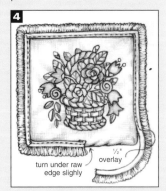

turn under raw edge slightly
½" overlay

ILLUSTRATIONS BY JUDITH LOVE, PHOTOGRAPH BY STEVEN MAYS

How to Make a 2-Tiered Topiary

Majestic 2-tiered topiaries are perfect accents for patios and doorways.

BY MADI HELLER AND FELIX BLUME

The topiary as we know it today evolved from the Romans, who added interest to gardens that normally contained few flowers by clipping and training trees and shrubs into ornamental shapes and figures. Modern topiaries are more easily assembled using dried foliage and Styrofoam and they require little to no upkeep. This 41" two-tiered topiary is a perfect accent for a screen porch, patio, or doorway.

TWO-TIERED TOPIARY

- 1 terra-cotta pot, 9"–11" tall, 10"–11" in diameter
- 1 37" dowel or straight natural wood stem, 1"–1½" in diameter
- 2 bricks dried floral foam measuring 8" x 4" x 3"
- 1 6" Styrofoam ball
- 1 8" Styrofoam ball
- 6 6" floral picks or thin dowels
- 4 pounds (one package) plaster of Paris
- 18–20 packages (4 branches/pkg.) boxwood
- 4 packages (5 berry clusters/pkg.) pink pepperberries
- 1–2 packages sheet moss or Spanish moss
- 2 pairs latex gloves
- Metal knitting needle or other pointed device
- Scissors
- Hot-glue gun and glue sticks
- 2"-wide postal-grade sealing tape
- Long-blade serrated kitchen knife
- 24" ruler
- Wood paint stick
- Plastic bucket
- Clean rag
- Green acrylic enamel spray paint
- Dark brown acrylic enamel spray paint (if needed)
- Newspaper

Preparing the Container

1. Be sure to work in a well-ventilated area when using spray paint. Cover work area with newspapers and pull on latex gloves. Insert 3 floral picks or thin dowels into base of 6" Styrofoam ball. Holding 1 stick in 1 hand, spray-paint entire ball green using other hand. Set ball on tripod to dry. Repeat process with 8" ball. Let balls dry completely, then remove picks. (Follow spray paint manufacturer's specific drying times.)

2. If using dowel, spray paint 1 side of dowel using brown paint; let dry thoroughly before rolling over and painting other side. Let dry. If using wood stem, skip this step.

3. Wipe inside of terra-cotta pot with clean, damp rag. Cut 2 pieces of tape about 3" to 4" long and criss-cross. Press into inside bottom of pot to seal off drainage hole.

4. Turn pot upside down and measure bottom diameter; use knife to cut a foam brick into a circle 2" larger in diameter than pot. Push foam brick down into base of pot. With both hands and using force, push wood stem or dowel straight down into center of foam until it reaches bottom of pot. Do not twist stem, and take care not to break tape seal. Dry foam should hold stem secure and upright. Reinforce joint with hot glue around base of stem or dowel.

5. To form a cushion between pot and plaster of Paris, cut other foam brick into 8" x 2" x 1" pieces. Using illustration as reference, hot-glue foam pieces around inside of pot at 1" to 2" intervals; trim 1" to 2" below rim of pot.

6. Slip on latex gloves. In plastic bucket, mix approximately 2 pounds (½ package) plaster of Paris following package directions. Pour wet plaster into terra-cotta pot, covering foam in bottom of pot completely. If plaster does not completely cover foam, immediately mix another pound of plaster and pour it on top. Use clean, damp rag to wipe up any spatters from inside rim of pot before they set. Let pot sit undisturbed until plaster is cool and hard to the touch, about ½ hour. As plaster cures it expands, but lining will prevent plaster from cracking pot. (Outside of pot will remain moist for up to several days, depending on humidity.)

7. Use knitting needle to pierce a starter hole clear through center of each Styrofoam ball. Work needle to increase hole's diameter until it is slightly smaller than stem or long dowel.

8. Impale larger ball on stem by pushing it straight down with firm, even pressure until 15" of stick emerges above ball. Impale smaller ball on stem until its top is even with top of stem.

9. Turn pot on its side and rest rim on edge of a table. With pot in this position, apply hot glue

Just 2 types of foliage—green boxwood and pink pepperberries—are used to create this simple 2-tiered topiary.

to underside of each ball-stem joint. Turn pot upright and hot-glue top of each joint. Wipe off foam dust from stem before proceeding.

Creating the Topiary

1. Using scissors, cut stems of boxwood to 3" to 4".

2. To decorate bottom globe, insert boxwood into ball, pushing gently to prevent stems from breaking. Cover all sides, angling stems so they radiate from center of ball. Use forked stems first to help establish shape, turning pot as you work so that you can view it from different angles. Continue cutting and inserting stems until globe is full. Final shape should measure 14" to 15" in diameter.

3. To form top-level globe, repeat process outlined in step 1. Finished globe should measure 12" to 13" in diameter.

4. Randomly hot-glue pink pepperberry clusters to interior branches on both globes, nestling bunches so pink color shows on outer leafy surface.

5. Arrange and trim moss around dowel or base of tree stem, concealing plaster. ◆

Madi Heller and **Felix Blume** are founders of the American Association for the Dried and Preserved Floral Industry, a nonprofit organization dedicated to promoting the use of dried and preserved flowers.

1. Hot-glue foam pieces around inside of pot and fill with plaster of Paris.

2. Cover globes completely with 3" to 4" boxwood stems.

Field Guide to Preserved Foliage

The 21 varieties of preserved foliage pictured here are well-suited for any of the projects in this issue calling for preserved flowers or foliage. (*See* pages 13 and 29.) If you don't recognize all the varieties, don't be surprised — the majority are new additions to the market.

Each of the varieties shown is easy to work with, although some are better suited for primary coverage than others. Those varieties ideal for primary coverage include boxwood, miniature oak, ming fern, surry bush, salignum, and luca foliage. (Any of these varieties could also replace the boxwood in the 2-Tiered Topiary project on page 29.) The others are better suited for use as decorative accents, but it's all a matter of personal taste.

Typical prices range from $9 to $12 a bunch, although the definition of a bunch varies considerably from source to source.

Row 1 (*left to right*)

1. Salal
2. Myrtle
3. Black spruce
4. Tree fern
5. Needle fern
6. Salignum

Row 2 (*left to right*)

1. Springerii
2. Foxtail
3. Plumosa
4. Princess pine
5. Luca foliage

Row 3 (*left to right*)

1. Boxwood
2. Wild eucalyptus
3. Fraser fir
4. Cattail
5. Buck foliage

Row 4 (*left to right*)

1. Mahonia
2. Miniature oak
3. Ming fern
4. Surry bush
5. Leatherleaf

SOURCES AND RESOURCES

Most of the materials needed for the projects in this issue are available at your local craft supply, hardware, or paint store, garden center, florist, or fabric shop, bead and jewelry supply, and so on. Following are specific sources for particular items or mail order sources, arranged by project.

Notes from Readers; pages 2–3
Simple Wild Grass Arrangements: Variety of wild grasses for $2.25 per bunch or $35 per case from F/X Floral Express. Jute twine for $1.39 for 400' from Sunshine Discount Crafts. *Drying Roses from Your Garden:* Large selection of rose bushes from $10.95 per bush from White Flower Farm. *Quick-Rip Tablecloths:* Cotton fabric from $4.25 per yard from Newark Dressmaker Supply. *Using Wallpaper Paste in Gardening:* Wide variety of vegetable and flower seeds from $1.50 per packet from Shepherd's Garden Seeds. *Quilt Batting from Natural Fibers:* Hobbs Heirloom Cotton Batt with all natural fiber for $15.85 for queen size, 90" x 108", from Nancy's Motions. *Dyes versus Stains:* Wide variety of stains, dyes, and other finishing products from Pearl Paint. *Build-Your-Own Model Cars:* Wide range of modeling kits from $5 from Ace Hobbies. *Drying Your Own Herbs:* Large selection of herb seeds from $1.60 per packet from Shepherd's Garden Seeds. Variety of microwave ovens from $100 from Service Merchandise. *Quick Changes for Older Curtain Rods:* Variety of faux finish kits from $25 from Pottery Barn and Modern Options. *Preventing Cord from Unraveling:* ½" transparent tape for $1.16 for 36 yards from Co-op Artists' Materials. 8" bent stainless steel scissors for $7.25 from Reliable. *Sponge Painting for Beginners:* Miracle Sponges for $3.19 per package of 6 from Jerry's Artarama.

Quick Tips; pages 4–5
Re-Covering a Picture Mat: Wide variety of wallpapers, no minimum charge, from Peerless Wallpaper and Blind Depot. Surgrip Utility (X-Acto) retractable knife in plastic for $3.75 or metal for $4.75 and 12" stainless steel corkback rulers for $3.80 from Co-op Artists' Materials. Precut mat boards for $1.99 for 9" x 12" (also available in larger sizes) from Maplewood Crafts. Wide selection of giftwrap for $2.95 for 4 sheets from Dover Publications. Rubber cement for $1.49 for 4.1 ounces from Sunshine Discount Crafts. 8" bent stainless steel scissors for $7.25 from Reliable. *Twisting Decorative Cord:* Multicolored craft cords for $2.85 for 27 yards from Craft King Discount Craft Supply. Jute twine for $1.39 for 400' from Sunshine Discount Crafts. 8" bent stainless steel scissors for $7.25 from Reliable. *Decorative Citronella Candle:* Citronella candles and craft doily available at Woolworth's. 12" lace doily for $3.75 and 1½" wire-edged ribbon for $2 per yard from Newark Dressmaker Supply. Mod Podge for $1.99 for 4 ounces from Sunshine Discount Crafts. *Lace Appliqué Pillowcase:* Pillowcases from $15 for 2 from Coming Home. Thread from $1.60 for 164 yards, lace appliqués from $9.50, embroidery scissors for $13, large selection of pins from $1.65 for a box of 30, needles from $.70, and 100 percent cotton thread for $3.15 for 200 yards, all from Newark Dressmaker Supply. Selection of sewing machines from $140 and irons from $12 from Service Merchandise. *Decal Gift Soaps:* Wide selection of giftwrap for $2.95 for 4 sheets from Dover Publications. Candle wax for $1.59 for 1 pound from Craft King Discount Craft Supply. Ribbon starting at $1 per yard and embroidery scissors for $13 from Newark Dressmaker Supply.

Art Nouveau Watermelon; pages 6–7
Watermelons and large selection of other produce from Frieda's. Two-sided melon baller for $14.50 from La Cuisine Kitchenware. Swivel pounce wheels from $3.60 and Surgrip Utility (X-Acto) retractable knife in plastic for $3.75 or metal for $4.75 from Co-op Artists' Materials. 9" x 12" parchment tracing pad for $4.56 for 100 sheets and 1" standard masking tape for $1.99 for 60 yards from Jerry's Artarama. Donvier Premier Ice Cream Maker for $50 from Williams-Sonoma. Ball-top pins for $1.55 for 150 and ⅝" wide and 60" long tape measure for $1.25 from Newark Dressmaker Supply.

Slip-On Chair Cover; pages 8–9
Large selection of decorator fabrics and trims from $8.99 per yard from Calico Corners. Large selection of fabrics from $3 per yard, fringes from $3.75 for 4 yards, cotton piping cord for $.70 for 10 yards, fabric pencil for $.95, needle-steel pins for $2.10 for 300, and sewing thread for $1.55 for 300 yards, all from Newark Dressmaker Supply. 36" roll brown wrapping paper for $48.35 and 8" bent stainless steel scissors for $7.25 from Reliable. ½" transparent tape for $1.16 for 36 yards, extra fine felt-tip marker for $.82 and 12" stainless steel corkback ruler for $3.80, all from Co-op Artists' Materials. Selection of sewing machines from $140 and irons from $12 from Service Merchandise. ¼" thick yardstick for $3.50 from G Street Fabrics.

How to Paint a Tuscan Wall; pages 10–12
9" Roller Kit containing plastic tray, 9" cover, extra cover and roller frame, for $4.02, extension poles starting at $3.13, and 2" nylon bristle brush for $1.13 from Torrington Brushes. Ready-made custom colored Latex paint ranges from $18 to $35 for 1 gallon and $5 to $15 for 1 quart, 2" low-tack painter's tape for $3 for 40 yards, drop cloths starting at $.69 for 9" x 12" plastic cloth, spackle starting at $2.50, acrylic primer for $14.98 for 1 gallon, paint scrapers starting at $.78, and 2" x 5" sanding block for $3.19, all from Pearl Paint. Standard trowel knife with 3" long blade for $3.89, Miracle Sponges for $3.19 per package of 6, and 1" standard masking tape for $1.95, all from Jerry's Artarama. Rubber gloves for $1.23 for 5 pairs and sandpaper sheets for $1.55 for two 4½" x 5½" sheets from Craft King Discount Craft Supply. Hammer for $11.97 and 6-piece screwdriver set for $9.97 from Service Merchandise.

Edwardian Hearth Arrangement; page 13
Set of 3 terra-cotta pots and tray starting at $14 from Pottery Barn. More than 700 varieties of flowers for $8 and up per bunch of about 25 heads from F/X Floral Express, J & T Dried Flowers Imports, or Pany Silk Flowers. You can also order boxwood from your local florist. Magic Melt Low Temp Glue Gun for $16.70, low temp glue sticks for $2.99, floral foam for $.85 per block, green and black Watermark acrylic enamel for $4.68 for 12 ounces, 2½" wood floral picks for $1.09 for 60 pieces, and rubber gloves for $1.23 for 5 pairs, all from Craft King Discount Craft Supply. Curtain tieback fringe starting at $3.75 for 4 yards from Newark Dressmaker Supply. Wood picks, blocks, or dowels available at local lumberyard. Spray bottle for $2.19 from Jerry's Artarama. 8" bent stainless steel scissors for $7.25 from Reliable. 10" styrofoam ball for $15 from Industrial Plastics.

Trompe L'oeil Apples; pages 14–15
4 ounce tubes of Liquitex acrylics available in permanent green light for $4.45, cadium lemon yellow for $5.18, black for $3.25, and white for $4.45, ½" long-handled acrylic paintbrush for $1.60, variety of thin paintbrushes in brights, flats, or rounds starting at $2.96, all from Co-op Artists' Materials. Acrylic sealer for $2.99 for 12 ounces from Sunshine Discount Crafts. 4½" x 5½" sheets of sandpaper for $1.55 for 2 from Craft King Discount Craft Supply. Miracle Sponges for $3.19 per package of 6 from Jerry's Artarama. 8" stainless steel scissors for $7.25 from Reliable. Pencil sharpeners from $.59 from Ott's Discount Art Supply. Cheesecloth for $1.10 per yard from Newark Dressmaker Supply.

Hand-Tinted Bookplates; pages 16–17
Large selection of watercolor pencils from $8.99 for 12, large selection of watercolor paints from $13.49 for 12 from Jerry's Artarama. Variety of watercolor paintbrushes starting at $2.26, calligraphy pen for $12.20, calligraphy markers for $.78, watercolor palette for $3.40, paper cement for $3.37 for 8 ounces, Surgrip Utility (X-Acto) retractable knife in plastic for $3.75 or metal for $4.75, metal-edged rulers from $4.80, and Prismacolor Art Pencil Set for $11.40 for 12-color set, all from Co-op Artists' Materials. Pencil sharpeners from $.59 from Ott's Discount Art Supply. 8" bent stainless steel scissors for $7.25 from Reliable.

3 Simple Techniques for Weathering Furniture; pages 18–20
Particle masks starting at $.30, 9" x 12" plastic drop cloths starting at $.69, 2" x 5" sanding block for $3.19, alkyd paints ranging from $6 to $18 for 1 quart, and paint thinner for $2.20 for 1 quart from Pearl Paint. 1" wide T-12 artist masking tape for $1.95 and 1½" synthetic paintbrush for $12.99 from Jerry's Artarama. Sandpaper for $1.55 for two 4½" x 5½" sheets and rubber gloves for $1.23 for 5 pairs from Craft King Discount Craft Supply. Cheesecloth for $1.10 per yard from Newark Dressmaker Supply. Hammer for $11.97 and 6-piece screwdriver set for $9.97 from Service Merchandise. Ready-made custom colored latex paint ranging from $5 to $15 for 1 quart, Minwax wood stain for $4.44 for ½ pint, Handcleaner for $2.04 for 16 ounces, cotton rags for $2.69 for 8 ounces or cheesecloth for $2.69, all from Pearl Paint. Windsor & Newton Yellow Ochre Acrylic Paint for $1.97, Mars Black for $1.97, Permanent Green Deep for $2.30, Iridescent White for $2.82 (all 2 ounces) and #3 Winsor & Newton Series 505 paintbrush for $3.33 from Jerry's Artarama.

Re-Cover a Chair Seat in 30 Minutes; page 21
Extra thick (1" plus) polyester batting for $4 per yard, cotton-blend fabric for $3.40 per yard, needle-steel pins for $2.10 for box of 300 and Quilter's Large Thumb Tacks for $3.05 for package of 100, all from Newark Dressmaker Supply. Swingline 101 Staple Gun for $14.99 and 5/16" staples for $2.19 for 1,000 from Jerry's Artarama. Staple remover for $.79 and 8" bent stainless steel scissors for $7.25 from Reliable. 12" stainless steel corkback rulers for $3.80 from Co-op Artists' Materials. Large selection of irons from $12, 3-piece plier set for $16.83, hammer for $11.97, and 6-piece screwdriver set for $9.97 from Service Merchandise.

French Silk Purses; pages 22–23
1½" wire-edged ribbon for $2 per yard, 1" wide solid-colored ribbons for $1.75 for 5 yards, 34 gauge beading (spool) wire for $1.30 for 24 yards, wide variety of thread from $1.65 for 350 yards, and hand sewing needles for $.70 for 20, all from Newark Dressmaker Supply. 1" to 3" wired-edged ribbon in a variety of colors starting at

$1.10 per yard from G Street Fabrics. Magic Melt Low Temp Glue Gun for $16.70 and low temp glue sticks for $2.99 from Craft King Discount Craft Supply.

Folded-Paper Bookbinding; pages 24–27
Large selection of papers from Daniel Smith, Bookbinder's Warehouse, and New York Central Art Supply. French marble and other decorative papers priced by quantity (sample pack for reference for $15), 24" ruler for $5.80, 24" straightedge for $19.95, Surgrip Utility (X-Acto) retractable knife in plastic for $3.75 or metal for $4.75, 20" x 30" illustration boards for $1.69, and 1" wide paintbrushes from $1.50, all from Co-Op Artists' Materials. 8" bent stainless steel scissors for $7.25 and LePages White Glue for $.89 for 5 ounces from Reliable. Extra heavy duty thread for $2.25 for 250 yards, awl for $2.15, and large-eye needle for $.90, all from Newark Dressmaker Supply. Hammer for $11.97 and 3-piece plier set for $16.83 from Service Merchandise. Burnish starting at $1.84 from Pearl Paint. Brass Filigrees in various sizes and shapes from Craft King Discount Craft Supply.

English Cottage Tapestry Pillow; page 28
18" x 18" square pillow form for $5.29 from The American Needlewoman. Precut tapestry starting at $8.99 from Calico Corners. Tapestry fabric starting at $25 per yard and ¼" thick yardstick for $3.50 from G Street Fabrics. Velcro nylon closure (hook and loop) for $4.25 for 2 yards and $47.50 for 25 yards, variety of fringes from $3.75 for 4 yards, variety of scissors from $10.25, wool blend/fusible fabric for $2.20 per yard, steel pins for $2.10 for 300, variety of thread from $1.65 for 350 yards, and #14 sewing machine needles (as part of an assortment of 5) for $2.50, all from Newark Dressmaker Supply. Selection of sewing machines from $140 and irons from $12 from Service Merchandise.

How to Make a 2-Tiered Topiary; page 29
Boxwood for $5.90 for 20 bunches of 6 ounces, pink pepperberries for $4.05 for 20 bunches of 4 ounces, sheet moss or Spanish moss from $4.75 per pound, and a large selection of other preserved foliage from J & T Dried Flowers Imports, Mills Floral, or F/X Floral Express. Plaster of Paris for $5.26 for 5 pounds, 6" Styrofoam ball for $2.31, floral foam for $.85, wood floral picks for $.89, Magic Melt Low Temp Glue Gun for $16.70, low temp glue sticks for $2.99, green and brown acrylic enamel spray paint for $4.68 for 12 ounces, rubber gloves for $1.23 for 5 pairs, all from Craft King Discount Craft Supply. Wood dowels available at local lumberyard. Set of 3 terra-cotta pots and tray starting at $14 from Pottery Barn. PlasTerra pots starting at $1.49 from Akro-Mils Specialty Products.

2" wide J-Lar Crystal Clear tape for $19.49 for 72 yards from Jerry's Artarama. 24" ruler for $5.80 from Co-op Artists' Materials. 8" bent stainless steel scissors for $7.25 from Reliable. Knitting needles starting at $3.09 from The American Needlewoman. 8" styrofoam ball for $8.40 from Industrial Plastics.

Field Guide to Preserved Foliage; page 30
Large selection of dried foliage sold in pieces or bunches for $4.25 to $12 per bunch from J & T Dried Flowers Imports and F/X Floral Express.

Quick Projects; page 33
Variety of switch plates starting at $3.29 from The Antique Hardware Store. *Victorian Filigree:* gold spray paint for $3.75 for 6 ounces, Magic Melt Low Temp Glue Gun for $16.70, and low temp glue sticks for $2.99 from Craft King Discount Craft Supply. Variety of embroidered appliques from $.20 from Newark Dressmaker Supply. Surgrip Utility (X-Acto) retractable knife in plastic for $3.75 or metal for $4.75 from Co-op Artists' Materials. *Gold-Leaf Plastic:* 8" bent stainless steel scissors for $7.25 from Reliable. Knitting needles starting at $3.09 from The American Needlewoman. Friendly Plastic for $.75 per stick from Craft King Discount Craft Supply. Surgrip Utility (X-Acto) retractable knife in plastic for $3.75 or metal for $4.75 and 12" stainless steel cork back ruler for $3.80 from Co-op Artists' Materials. *Dutch Still Life:* Wide selection of giftwrap for $2.95 for 4 sheets from Dover Publications. Large squeeze bottle of Sobo glue for $1.85 from Newark Dressmaker Supply. 8" bent stainless steel scissors for $7.25 from Reliable. Knitting needles starting at $3.09 from The American Needlewoman. 12" stainless steel cork back ruler for $3.80 and Surgrip Utility (X-Acto) retractable knife in plastic for $3.75 or metal for $4.75 from Co-op Artists' Materials. *Starry Night:* 3-piece plier set for $16.83 from Service Merchandise. Blue acrylic enamel for $4.68, brass stars from $1.19 for 24 smalls, Magic Melt Low Temp Glue Gun for $16.70, and low temp glue sticks for $2.99 from Craft King Discount Craft Supply. *Concentric Cord:* braided cord for $1.25 for 10 yards and snow white cable cord for $1.90 for 10 yards from Newark Dressmaker Supply. Metallic cord in various colors for $1.99 for 27 yards from Sunshine Discount Crafts. Transparent Tape for $1.16 for ½" x 36 yards and 12" stainless steel cork back ruler for $3.80 from Co-op Artists' Materials. 8" bent stainless steel scissors for $7.25 from Reliable. Magic Melt Low Temp Glue Gun for $16.70 and low temp glue sticks for $2.99 from Craft King Discount Craft Supply.

Dried Rose Bouquet; back cover
Set of 3 terra-cotta pots and tray starting

at $14 from Pottery Barn. PlasTerra pots starting at $1.49 from Akro-Mils Specialty Products. 8" cube of styrofoam for $6.94 from Pearl Paint. Dried roses ranging from $5.18 to $8.65 for 1 dozen and spanish moss for $.40 for 4" square from F/X Floral Express. 1" wire-edged ribbon for $1.10 per yard from G Street Fabrics.

The following companies are mentioned in the listings above. Contact each individually for a price list or catalog.

Ace Hobbies, 35 West 31st Street, New York, NY 10001; 212-268-4151
Akro-Mils Specialty Products, 1293 South Main Street, Akron, OH, 44301; 216-253-5592
The Antique Hardware Store, 9730 Easton Road, Route 611, Kintnersville, PA 18930; 800-422-9982
The American Needlewoman, P.O. Box 6472, Fort Worth, TX 76115; 800-433-2231
Bookbinder's Warehouse, 31 Division Street, Keyport, NJ 07735; 908-264-0306
Coming Home, One Land's End Lane, Dodgeville, WI 53595; 800-345-3696
Co-op Artists' Materials, P.O. Box 53097, Atlanta, GA 30355; 800-877-3242
Craft King Discount Craft Supply, P.O. Box 90637, Lakeland, FL 33804; 800-769-9494
Daniel Smith, P.O. Box 84268, Seattle, WA 98124-5568; 800-426-6740
Dover Publications, 31 East 2nd Street, Mineola, NY 11501; (telephone orders not accepted)
Frieda's, P.O. Box 58488, Los Angeles, CA 90058; 213-627-2981
F/X Floral Express, 239 South Main Street, Caribou, ME 04736; 800-392-7417
G Street Fabrics, 12240 Wilkins Avenue, Rockville, MD 20852; 800-333-9191
Industrial Plastics, 309 Canal Street, New York, NY 10013; 212-226-2010 (They will UPS items if you send a check in advance).
Jerry's Artarama, P.O. Box 1105, New Hyde Park, NY 11040; 800-U-Artist
J & T Dried Flowers Imports, 143 S. Cedros Avenue, P.O. Box 642, Solano Beach, CA 92075; 619-481-9781 (Will ship orders of a $50 minimum)
La Cuisine Kitchenware, 323 Cameron Street, Alexandria, VA 22314; 800-521-1176
Maplewood Crafts, Humboldt Industrial Park, 1 Maplewood Drive, P.O. Box 2010, Hazleton, PA 18201-0676; 800-899-0134
Mills Floral, 4550 Peachtree Lakes Drive, Duluth, GA 30136; 800-762-7939
Modern Options, 2325 Third Street, #339, San Francisco, CA 94107;

415-252-5580
Nancy's Motions, 333 Beichl Avenue, P.O. Box 683 Beaver Dam, WI 53916-0683; 800-833-0690
Newark Dressmaker Supply, 6473 Ruch Road, P.O. Box 20730, Lehigh Valley, PA 18002-0730; 800-736-6783
New York Central Art Supply, 130 East Twelve Street, New York, NY 10003; 800-950-6111
Ott's Discount Art Supply, 102 Hungate Drive, Greenville, NC 27858; 800-356-3289
Pany Silk Flowers, 146 W. 28th Street, New York, NY 10001; 212-645-9526
Pearl Paint, 308 Canal Street, New York, NY 10013; 800-221-6845 ext. 2297
Peerless Wallpaper and Blind Depot, 39500 14 Mile Road, Walled Lake, MI 48390; 800-999-0898
Pottery Barn, 100 N. Point Street, San Francisco, CA 94133; 800-922-9934
Reliable, 101 W. Van Buren, Chicago, IL, 60607; 800-735-4000
Service Merchandise, P.O. Box 25130, Nashville, TN 37202-5130; 800-251-1212
Shepherd's Garden Seeds, 30 Irene Street, Torrington, CT 06790; 203-482-3638
Sunshine Discount Crafts, P.O. Box 301, Largo, FL 34649; 813-581-1153
Torrington Brushes, P.O. Box 56, Torrington, CT 06790; 800-262-7874 or 800-525-1416
White Flower Farm, P.O. Box 50, Litchfield, CT 06759-0050; 203-496-9600
Williams-Sonoma, P.O. Box 7456, San Francisco, CA 94120-7456; 800-541-2233 ◆

The Dried Rose Bouquet is available as a kit including all the necessary materials. The cost is $19.95 plus $1.50 shipping and handling. To order the kit, send a check or money order for $21.45, or send your credit card number (we accept American Express, VISA, and Mastercard), the expiration date and an authorized signature to: Rose Kit, *Handcraft Illustrated,* P.O. Box 509, Brookline Village, MA 02147-0509.

Quick Projects

Using easy-to-find materials and a little imagination, you can transform ordinary metal or plastic switch plates into decorative accents. Any standard (2¾" x 4½") switch plate will work, or try your hand at decorating double, triple, or quadruple switch plates. Note: You may need to purchase longer screws to accommodate the applied materials.

Gold-leaf plastic — cut two 7" x 1½" (precut) lengths of gold Friendly Plastic down to 5" pieces. Put extra aside. Place strips in hot tap water for 3 to 4 minutes to soften. Make sure strips stay flat while they soak. Remove 1 strip at a time from the water, holding both ends with tongs. Center and press the strips onto the plate, folding the extra to the back. Press the warm plastic firmly to cover the plate. Poke holes for the screws with a pen or knitting needle and cut a hole for the light switch with an X-Acto knife before the plastic hardens. To make "ribbon" accents, cut remaining pieces of Friendly Plastic into ⅜" strips and heat. Shape plastic into bows and, while still warm, press firmly onto the plate taking care not to cover screw hole completely. If desired, hot-glue a gold leaf to ribbon as an accent.

Victorian filigree — spray-paint the switch plate gold using enamel paint. When dry, cut and hot-glue 2 identical embroidered appliqués to fit opposite 1 another on the plate front, leaving a space for the light switch. Cut holes for screws in appliqué using an X-Acto knife.

Continuous cord — measure and cut enough cord to cover entire surface of the plate (2 yards should cover a standard-size plate). To prevent the end of the cord from unraveling, wrap a piece of clear tape around the end and cut in the middle of the tape to leave a clean edge. Starting at one outside corner, hot-glue one end of cord in place. Run a line of hot glue and press on cord, following all around the contour of the plate and moving around to the inside switch hole until the plate is covered. When reattaching switch plate to wall, simply screw through the cord.

Starry night — spray-paint the switch plate royal blue. If using brass star findings designed for decorating fabric, be sure to snip off the small teeth on the back of the stars using pliers or junky scissors before gluing. When paint is dry, hot-glue brass stars on front of plate, taking care not to cover the light switch or screw holes.

Dutch still life — find attractive giftwrap with a central motif or overall floral design. Using the switch plate as a template, mark and cut the giftwrap ½" larger than the switch plate on all sides to allow for tucking under. Apply a thin coat of white glue on the plate front; center and press giftwrap image to plate front. Turn extra giftwrap to back and glue edges under. Cut hole for light switch using an X-Acto knife and poke holes for screw using a pen or knitting needle. ◆

Continuous cord

Starry night

Dutch still life

Gold-leaf plastic

Victorian filigree

Dried Rose Bouquet

Press rim of a terra-cotta flowerpot (4" in diameter and 4" high) onto a 5" cube of Styrofoam to create a pattern for cutting. Using a sharp knife, cut around indentation to form a cylinder. Pare away sides to create a tapered cylinder that fits inside pot. Push cylinder into pot for a snug fit. Trim foam so that it is even with rim of pot. Insert stem of one 8"-long dried pink rose into center of foam. Add 11 additional roses, keeping all flower heads at same height. Conceal foam with bits of moss (a 4" square will cover it). Tie a bow around stems with 1" wire-edged ribbon. To order this project in kit form, see page 32.

NUMBER THREE

SEPTEMBER/OCTOBER 1994

HANDCRAFT
~ILLUSTRATED~

BELLE EPOQUE FRAME

Transform Silk Flowers Into Sculptured Swags

Block-Print Grape Arbor

Use a Computer Mouse Pad to Print a Verdant Vine

Marbling Made Easy

5 Basic Steps Yield Hundreds of Patterns

Classic Teddy Bear

Sew This Early 1900s Replica In Under 5 Hours

HOW TO GILD ALMOST ANYTHING

QUICK WHEAT SHEAF CENTERPIECE

•

FAUX STONE FRUIT BASKET

SPECIAL INSERT:
FOLD YOUR OWN
DECORATIVE BOXES

$4.00 U.S./$4.95 CANADA

0 71486 02716 4

10

TABLE
OF CONTENTS

**CLASSIC STEIFF
TEDDY BEAR**
page 17

**FAUX STONE FRUIT
BASKET**
page 10

**GRAPE ARBOR
MURAL**
page 13

**APPLE HARVEST PIE
WITH DECORATIVE
CRUST**
page 22

**WHEAT SHEAF
CENTERPIECE**
page 9

**BELLE EPOQUE
FRAME**
page 26

HANDCRAFT
~ILLUSTRATED~

Editor
CAROL ENDLER STERBENZ

Executive Editor
BARBARA BOURASSA

Senior Editor
MICHIO RYAN

Managing Editor
MAURA LYONS

Directions Editors
CANDIE FRANKEL
SUSAN WILSON

Editorial Assistant
KIM RUSSELLO

Copy Editor
KURT TIDMORE

Art Director
MEG BIRNBAUM

Publisher and Founder
CHRISTOPHER KIMBALL

Editorial Consultant
RAYMOND WAITES

Marketing Director
ADRIENNE KIMBALL

Circulation Director
ELAINE VALENTINO

Circulation Assistant
JENNIFER L. KEENE

Production Director
JAMES McCORMACK

Publicity Director
CAROL ROSEN KAGAN

Treasurer
JANET CARLSON

Office Manager
JENNY THORNBURY

Customer Service
CONNIE FORBES

Handcraft Illustrated (ISSN 1072-0529) is published bimonthly by Natural Health Limited Partners, 17 Station Street, P.O. Box 509, Brookline, MA 02147-0509. Copyright 1994 Natural Health Limited Partners. Application to mail at second-class postage rates is pending at Boston, MA, and additional mailing offices. Editorial office: 17 Station Street, P.O. Box 509, Brookline, MA 02147-0509; (617) 232-1000, FAX (617) 232-1572. Editorial contributions should be sent to: Editor, *Handcraft Illustrated*, P.O. Box 509, Brookline, MA 02147-0509. We cannot assume responsibility for manuscripts submitted to us. Submissions will be returned only if accompanied by a large self-addressed stamped envelope. Subscription rates: $24.95 for one year; $45 for two years; $65 for three years. (Canada: add $3 per year; all other foreign add $12 per year.) Postmaster: Send all new orders, subscription inquiries, and change of address notices to *Handcraft Illustrated*, P.O. Box 51383, Boulder, CO 80322-1383. Single copies: $4 in U.S., $4.95 in Canada and foreign. Back issues available for $5 each. PRINTED IN THE U.S.A.

Rather than put ™ in every occurrence of trademarked names, we state that we are using the names only and in an editorial fashion and to the benefit of the trademark owner, with no intention of infringement of the trademark.

Note to Readers: Every effort has been made to present the information in this publication in a clear, complete, and accurate manner. It is important that all instructions are followed carefully, as failure to do so could result in injury. Natural Health Limited Partners, the editors, and the authors disclaim any and all liability resulting therefrom.

EDITORIAL

Autumn has always been a season of beginnings for me. In part, this is connected to the tradition of starting the school year. When I was young, each fall my sisters and I would get new shoes and hair ribbons and notebooks thick with smooth, lined paper. I am still made nostalgic by the scent of newly sharpened pencils and the rough texture of drawing paper.

Of course, I am not beginning school this September. But that sense of planning and expectancy is still in the air as my children prepare for school. They are of an age now where their September beginnings are more complex than those I think of. Genevieve and Rodney went off to college several years ago, and although it was a beginning for them, it felt like a kind of ending for me. Now Gabrielle, my youngest child, is about to leave for college.

As I sit on the stairs by the front door, I ponder the architecture of Gabrielle's seventeen years, now condensed into three suitcases, two duffel bags, and a trunk with several cardboard boxes on top. It is a profound beginning for Gabrielle, a woman now, no longer a child. But when did this transformation take place? She grew up before my eyes, and yet at times I hardly noticed.

Gabrielle is singing to herself as she brings another box into the foyer. I notice how tall she is. But whether just a toddler on eye level with me when I bent down to pick her up, or a girl staring through just-acquired glasses as she took her first driving lesson, I always saw a child who could draw joy from any day.

When Gabrielle was an infant, I measured my free time in baby naps and dryer loads. When I could, I would go to my workroom and try to get some work done on a project. I was quilting and seemed always to be in some stage of that, using her sleep time to cut out squares of fabric, letting the colors lead my scissors to the design, and thinking of the luxury of two old spinster sisters I'd heard who, after scrutinizing the quilting done at their "bee" one afternoon, closed their shutters and *re-quilted* an entire coverlet which failed to meet their standards. The demands of raising a family always seemed to shrink my dreamed-of queen-sized productions to considerably smaller proportions.

When Gabrielle was older she would stand in her playpen close to my worktable, singing and talking as I sewed. When she got impatient and wanted "o-u-t" and "n-o-w," I would lift her onto

CAROL ENDLER STERBENZ

my lap hoping I could sew another line before she shrieked for freedom. Sometimes I misjudged her patience and, encouraged by a sudden quiet, kept on sewing. Usually she had gotten hold of something. Careful as I was to keep the table free of small notions, once Gabrielle snatched a raspberry-shaped bead. She was about to put it into her mouth when I caught her. Disaster avoided, I dropped the bead into a button box and closed the lid.

There are other moments I recall now, and catch myself smiling. When she was five, Gabrielle appeared at breakfast every morning from autumn through winter wearing a gold lame bathing suit under her school clothes; no amount of coaxing convinced her to change. Sometimes in the evening, when she visited me in my workroom, she would be wearing the gold lame suit over her pajamas. She claimed she had better dreams, and I believed her.

When she was twelve, she joined me at the sewing machine, making doll clothes from fabric scraps. Soon we were making trips together to the fabric shop to stock up for our projects. It didn't matter if we had a project planned or not, we went anyway to load up with bolts of prints and solids, cottons and velvets, each ¼ yard an absolute necessity. We developed an unerring ability to find great fabrics and crafts supplies. And we never questioned our view that it was perfectly normal to purchase lengths of fabric so that we could cut them up in smaller pieces, only to sew them back together again!

Gabrielle is calling, waking me from my reverie. I follow her voice and find her in the foyer, where she is picking up some boxes that have toppled over, spilling little heaps of stuff across the carpet. I bend down and help her re-stack a pile of fabric squares into their box. As I replace one square after another into the box, I notice one in particular, gold lame with a small raspberry-shaped bead stitched to its center. The tears in my eyes surprise me. As many quilts as I have stitched, I will never come nearer to perfection than Gabrielle has in this one square. I tell her this, and she protests. I look down again at the small bead and realize that this beginning for Gabrielle is not necessarily an ending for me, but rather a great coming together of beginnings and endings in a never-ending circle. ◆

Carol Endler Sterbenz

NOTES FROM READERS

SUGARED ROSE PETALS

Can you tell me how to make sugared rose petals?

FIONA SELLEN
Houston, TX

Sugared rose petals make a beautiful decoration for cakes and pastries. Try this recipe: Take the petals of a rose apart and rinse each carefully under running water. Place the petals on a paper towel to dry. When the petals are dry, mix an egg white with a small amount of water and beat slightly. Dip each petal in this mixture, lift out with tweezers, then lay on granulated sugar. Press the petals gently into the sugar, then carefully turn the petal over and press the other side. Lay the sugared petal on wax paper to dry; when one side is thoroughly dry, flip the petal over to dry the other side. Seal the petals in a dark jar to preserve the color.

FLORIST FOAM VERSUS OASIS

What is the difference between florist foam and Oasis?

BARBARA SHOEMAKER
Lilleville, NY

In a word, nothing. Oasis is a brand name for floral foam. Both describe the fine-textured foam that is designed for use in fresh and dried flower arrangements; colors include bright green and dull green for use in fresh floral arrangements and brownish-green for use in dried floral arrangements. With a sharp knife, the foam can be cut easily into any shape or it can be cut to mimic the shape of a container. When using foam with fresh arrangements, be sure to soak it with water.

SUBSTITUTE FOR SPRAY ADHESIVE

Do you know of an environmentally safe substitute for spray adhesive?

LYNN EFFRACE
Chicago, IL

Daige Inc. of Albertson, New York, recently released the Rollataq 300 Adhesive System, a hand-held cartridge which dispenses a thin, even coat of permanent adhesive across a 2½" roller. The adhesive is odor free, and the roller includes a refillable squeeze bottle.

MAIL-ORDER REPRODUCTION WALLPAPER

I'm looking for a source of reproduction wallpapers for use on boxes and albums that I make myself and give as gifts. Can you help?

BETSY NOVAK
Tallahasee, FL

One company that exists solely to reproduce Victorian wallpaper is Bradbury and Bradbury, of Benicia, California. Sample packets of historic wallpapers (e.g., from the 1770s to 1920s) are available from Charles Rupert, of Victoria, Canada. Hardware Plus, of Garland, Texas, offers Lincrusta Anaglypta embossed wallcoverings.

TIPS ON GROWING HYDRANGEAS

I'm interested in growing my own hydrangeas for use in a fresh flower garland. What can you tell me about hydrangeas?

KARYN BETTER
Boston, MA

Long-living hydrangeas come in a variety of colors, including white, pink, blue, purple, and green. Their soil should be moderately rich and well drained, and they should be kept moist at all times. The more acidic the soil in which you plant them, the bluer the flowers; the more alkaline (or lime) the soil, the pinker the flowers. All hydrangeas, especially those growing in lime soils, which typically suffer from mineral deficiencies, will benefit from an additive composed of iron and aluminum. One of the heartiest kinds of hydrangea is the mopheaded Hortensia, which includes the Hamburg, General Vicomtesse de Vibraye, and Altona.

CATEGORIZING LEATHER

How is leather sold and categorized?

PAM COSTELLO
Burlington, VT

Leather is sold by the square foot and the ounce. Leather labeled 1-ounce weighs 1 ounce per square foot; 4-ounce leather, 4 ounces per square foot. A leather's weight is related to its thickness. The 1-ounce leather is ¹⁄₆₄" thick, while 4-ounce leather is ⁴⁄₆₄, or ¹⁄₁₆" thick. Depending on the nature of your project, you'll need to select the appropriate weight leather. Belts, for instance, call for 7- to 9-ounce leather; garments for 2- to 3-ounce leather; and upholstery for 1- to 4-ounce leather.

DRIED FOLIAGE FROM WEEDS

I've heard that some common weeds are actually ideal for use as dried foliage. Can you recommend some varieties?

DELLA BREESE
Montclair, NJ

Many common weeds make excellent dried foliage, and they're usually easy to find growing in the wild. Grasses like green foxtail, often found growing through cracks in the sidewalk, can be picked for drying when young and fresh. Abandoned lots may harbor mullein, teasel, cinquefoil, goldenrod, bittersweet vines, and/or purple loosestrife. Be sure to get permission before cutting plants from someone else's property. Lists of scarce or protected plants are available from your state's Department of Environmental Resources; check wildflower guide books for photos of poisonous plants.

DETERMINING PAINT QUANTITIES

Can you suggest an easy means of estimating how much paint I'll need to cover my living room?

MICHELLE KENNER
Derry, NH

To estimate the amount of paint needed to cover any space, you'll need two measurements: the square footage of the wall to be painted, and the number of square feet a gallon of the paint you're planning to use will cover. The label on the paint can usually specifies how many square feet a gallon will cover. To calculate the square footage of your walls, measure the perimeter of the room and multiply this figure by the room's height. Divide this number by the number of square feet a gallon of paint will cover and you'll end up with the number of gallons you'll need to complete the job.

TIPS FOR CLEANING IVORY

Can you suggest a way to clean ivory?
JOE BISHOP
Triangle, WY

When cleaning ivory, avoid large quantities of water. Ivory grows in layers, and excessive exposure to water may cause the layers to swell and separate. If the carving is very dirty, make a lukewarm solution of mild soap with as little water as possible and brush the surface of the ivory quickly with a soft toothbrush. Rinse under clean water and dry immediately. To polish, rub gently in circles with jeweler's rouge or a very fine abrasive powder; clean off any excess with a soft rag.

HOMEMADE FIRESTARTERS

Can you give me some simple designs for making firestarters?
LEANNE DYKSTRA
Bangor, ME

You can make quick and pretty firestarters using twigs, candle wax from saved candle stubs, and glitter. Collect a bundle of fifteen to twenty skinny, straight twigs, each measuring approximately 6" long. Bind the stems together at their midpoint using cotton string. Melt three to four used candle stubs in a double boiler placed over low heat. Lay the bundle in the wax and coat it liberally. Using kitchen tongs, lift the bundle out of the pot and quickly sprinkle gold, silver, or colored glitter onto the wax surface while it is still soft. Let the bundles dry on newspaper, then tie them with raffia or narrow ribbon.

HOW TO INLAY EGGSHELLS

I'm interested in learning the art of eggshell inlay. What can you tell me?
DUSTY BRECKER
Minneapolis, MN

Eggshell inlay, which results in a mosaic-like appearance, is actually quite simple. Remove and discard the contents of an egg; soak the eggshells in a solution of household bleach for at least two days to break down the membranes of the shell. Rinse them in vinegar and water. Apply white glue to a smooth or properly sealed object such as a frame or small box; press the eggshells into place until they crack and lay flat against the object. When all the spaces have been filled and the glue is dry, fill in the cracks with floor- or wall-tile grout. (For added contrast, use a colored grout.) Wipe

any excess grout off before it dries. When the grout is dry, rub the surface smooth and seal with varnish or shellac.

RECIPE FOR ROYAL ICING

I have been looking for a dependable recipe for royal icing, the icing used to make line decorations on cookies. Can you help?
MARY CONTURE
Elmira, NY

Try this recipe. Beat 2 large egg whites until fluffy. Add 1 pound confectioners' sugar, ½ cup at a time, until the icing is stiff. To test readiness, run the blade of a knife through the center of the icing. When the "walls" hold, the icing is ready. For variation, tint the basic white icing by spooning a small portion of the icing into a bowl and adding a drop of food color.

TIPS ON CLEANING VASES

How can I clean the bottom of my glass vases thoroughly and easily?
SUSAN CHILLER
St. Paul, MN

Dissolve 2 packets of denture cleaner in 2 cups of warm water. Pour the mixture in your vase and swoosh it around. Allow the mixture to stand 3 to 4 minutes and remove. If stains are particularly stubborn, repeat the process, or drop a rag in the bottom of the vase and use a wooden spoon to move the rag around. Rinse the vase thoroughly before use.

REMOVING DRIPPED-ON WAX

My candles dripped onto one of my best tablecloths. Can you suggest an easy way to remove the excess wax?
BETTY O'REGAN
Billings, MT

Try this simple technique. Scrape away as much wax as possible with a blunt knife, then place the waxy area between layers of paper towels and press with a warm iron. Repeat with clean paper towels as necessary. Sponge any leftover traces of wax with a household cleaning fluid.

ORIGIN OF MILK PAINT

What is the origin of milk paint?
KATY ANDOLINO
Wilmington, DE

Milk paint, popular in North America during the late eighteenth and nineteenth centuries, was made by mixing earth-colored pigments with buttermilk or skim milk and a

little bit of lime. Mostly associated with Colonial-style interiors, milk paint dries to a smooth, flat finish and mellows nicely with age. Nowadays, pre-mixed, lime-free milk paints are available from a number of manufacturers, including The Old Fashioned Milk Paint Company, of Groton, Massachusetts, and Stulb's Old Village Paint, of Fort Washington, Pennsylvania.

SELF-HEALING MATS

I've been using layers of newspaper to protect my work surface when using an X-Acto knife, but the paper invariably shreds, leaves printers ink on white paper, and doesn't protect against cuts in the table underneath. What can you recommend?
LOTTIE SHEETS
Denver, CO

Any time you use a cutting device with a sharp blade, you should protect your work surface with a self-healing mat. The principle behind such a mat is as follows: After a cut is made in the rubber, the flexible rubber closes up again. Such mats are available in a variety of sizes from 6" square to 72" x 36" and often come with a grid printed on them.

MAIL-ORDER STENCILS

Where can I order precut stencil designs?
LOUANN CHAMBERS
Thendara, NY

Stencil World, of Newport, Rhode Island, has over 200 precut stencil designs in a wide variety of styles, including borders, miniatures, verticals, and center motifs. Gail Grisi Stencils, of Haddonfield, New Jersey, offers a wide variety of precut stencil designs and paints. Another source, Stencil House of New Hampshire, in Hooksett, New Hampshire, carries over 180 hand-cut stencils traced from old New England, Victorian, and Early American designs.

ALL ABOUT MEDITERRANEAN SPONGES

What can you tell me about Mediterranean sponges?
COURTNEY LAUNCH
San Mateo, CA

The Mediterranean honeycomb sponge, also known as sea wool, is useful for painters and lithographers; it also makes a great bath sponge due to its large pores and durable nature. The Mediterranean silk sponge is another fine pore sponge, but it is less absorbent. It is excellent for use with ceramic or watercolors, or as a cosmetic sponge. ◆

Quick Tips

Mitering a Corner with Decorative Trim

Decorative trim applied around the edge of a box or picture frame looks neater and more professional if the corners are mitered. The mitering method shown here is best suited for paper, metallic, and tightly woven trims that will not ravel when cut. In addition to trim, you'll need sharp scissors and a hot-glue gun and glue sticks.

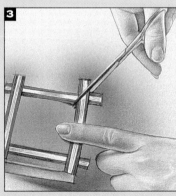

1. Cut two lengths of trim, each slightly longer than the edge of the box on which they'll be used. Position the strips on the surface of the box, allowing the ends to overlap at the corner.

2. Apply a small dot of glue under the center of each strip and tamp it down with your fingertips to secure. Let the glue set 1 to 2 minutes. Repeat steps 1 and 2 for other sides of the box.

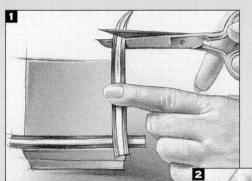

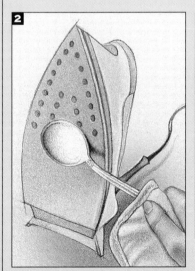

3. Lift the overlapped ends at one corner and slide the lower scissor blade under the ends. Cut diagonally through both strips of trim at once from the outside to the inside of the corner. Repeat the process at the three remaining corners.

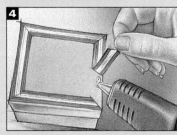

4. Apply a thin bead of glue under the loose sections of the trim and around the corner. Press the trim in place, aligning the cut edges for a perfect miter.

5. Repeat step 4 to miter the remaining corners.

Candle Decoupage

You can dress up a plain candle for a special occasion by affixing small printed pictures to the surface. For this simple decoupage technique, you'll need assorted small pictures (e.g., from giftwrap, glossy magazines, or brochures); a large, stocky candle; manicure scissors; a silver or silverplated soup spoon; an iron; and a pot holder.

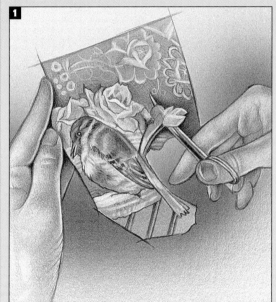

1. Cut out the picture using manicure scissors. Lay the candle on its side and hold the cutout against the surface to check the position.

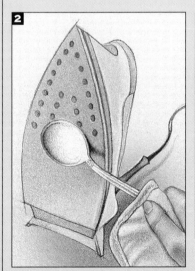

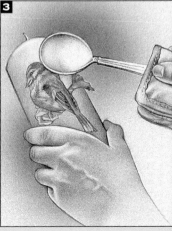

2. Turn on the iron to the linen setting. Grasp the handle of the soup spoon with a pot holder and press the bowl of the spoon against the hot iron for 30 seconds. Silver conducts heat rapidly, so be sure your fingers do not directly touch the spoon.

3. Position the cutout as desired on the candle and gently move the bowl of the hot spoon over the surface of the cutout, working from the center to the edges. The heat will soften the wax slightly, allowing the cutout to bond. Reheat the spoon and repeat as necessary. Continue adding cutout pictures as desired.

ILLUSTRATIONS BY HARRY DAVIS

Wiring Flowers in Bunches

Flowers in a fresh arrangement make a stronger color statement when similar blooms are grouped together instead of scattered. To wire several flowers together, you'll need florist scissors or pruning shears, an 18" length of 18-gauge florist stem wire, and a ruler.

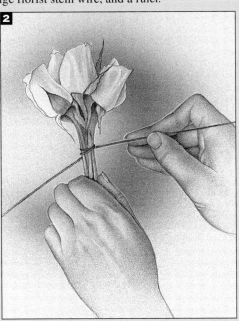

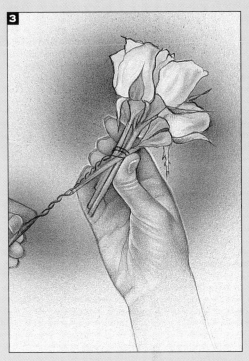

1. Trim the flower stems to 3½" using florist scissors or pruning shears. Strip away all the leaves except those surrounding the blossoms. Hold the stems together in one hand, and place the midpoint of the wire against the stems.

2. With your free hand, wrap the wire around the stems three times to secure.

3. Twist both wires together and bend downward to form a single false stem. Insert the wired flowers into the arrangement.

Wiring Individual Fruit

You'll find it easier to add apples, pears, oranges, lemons, and other fruits to still life arrangements if you wire them first. Since fruits are heavy, each piece must be wired individually using an 18" length of 18-gauge florist stem wire.

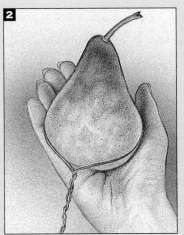

1. Push the wire straight through the lower third of the fruit, piercing the skin and exiting on the opposite side.

2. Adjust the wire so the ends are equal in length, then bend the wire around and under the fruit. Twist the wire together to form a false stem. Insert the wired fruit into the arrangement.

Easy Nail Removal

Knowing how to remove a protruding or skewed nail without damaging the wood surface is a skill you'll welcome during furniture refinishing or simple construction projects. To remove a nail, you'll need a curved claw hammer and scraps of wood 2" to 3" square or larger in assorted thickness.

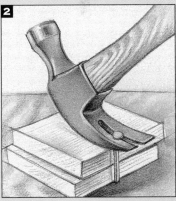

1. Examine the protruding nail. Select a scrap of wood that rests ⅛" to ¼" below the nail head when laid alongside it. Rest the hammer claw on the wood scrap, and maneuver into position to grip the nail head.

2. Gently pull the handle of the hammer back slightly to pull the nail straight out in small increments. Continue raising the nail. To avoid widening the entry hole, place a second scrap of wood under the hammer claw and complete the nail removal.

How to Gild Almost Any Surface

The secrets of gilding everything from plaster to paper.

BY MICHIO RYAN

Gilding, or applying gold leaf, is both simple and forgiving, and even beginners can produce professional-looking results. The key, as I discovered, lies in choosing an appropriate item for gilding and properly preparing that item's surface.

Gilding can be broken down into four major steps: preparing the surface, applying size (another word for glue) and letting it dry until tacky, arranging gold leaf on the sticky size, and burnishing (and sometimes sealing) the gilded surface.

All of my testing involved composition gold leaf, an alloy of copper and tin which is readily available by mail order and in art supply and craft stores. Only professionals opt for real gold leaf, mostly because of its price: real gold costs $35 and up per book, versus $4 to $8 per book for composition gold leaf. The latter is also thicker and tougher, making it easier to work with and mistakes less expensive and easier to fix.

Composition gold leaf comes in bound 5½"-square books. The thin metal leaf is sandwiched between pages of tissue. One book contains 25 sheets and will cover about 4 square feet. Instead of ordinary glue, gilding uses synthetic oil size, which is basically a special varnish. Unlike other varnishes, it dries in two stages. After application, it quickly dries to a sticky glaze and remains tacky for up to 3 hours before finally drying to a hard coating. It is during this "tacky" window of opportunity that the leaf is applied. After the size dries, the item is buffed to a final shiny finish and, if necessary, sealer is applied.

A few other notes about gilding: Be sure to work in a well-ventilated area free of dust and wind (metal leaf is easily blown away). Even the smallest particles of dirt will be visible under the leaf, as will pet hair or other foreign materials. Be sure to work atop several layers of newspaper to protect surfaces.

Size an area no larger than what you can reasonably expect to cover with leaf within half an hour, say 1 square foot at most. Size is thinner in consistency than ordinary paint or varnish. It is important to apply a thin, even coat so the whole area reaches the same stage of stickiness at once. Use a 1"-wide disposable brush for small items, a 2"-wide brush for larger surfaces, or a fine-grain foam brush for flat surfaces. (I recommend foam brushes for sizing flat surfaces because they give a smooth coat without brush marks. Natural bristle brushes are preferable for sizing shapes with curves or high relief.)

Depending on temperature and humidity, the sized surface will be ready for gilding in 1 to 3 hours. If it feels sticky like Scotch tape, it's ready. If it has dried too much and has no tack, allow it to dry thoroughly for several more hours, then start again, recoating and waiting until the desired tack is reached.

Size is easily cleaned from brushes and surfaces with turpentine or mineral spirits.

Where to Start

The first question to ask when considering gilding is an aesthetic one. Quite simply, the material you choose should be aesthetically suited to gilding. Of course, this is highly subjective; I've seen gold leafed rocks which were beautiful. Since gold leaf highlights the finest details of surface texture, the result should complement rather than detract from the object's form. A terra cotta pot with molded details that have been cleverly picked out in gold can be beautiful, but a brick that has been gilded will merely look like a gold brick, even though both are made of rough, unglazed clay.

In my search for ideal items for gilding, I tested a variety of materials. My top nine materials for gilding (discussed in detail below, with results highlighted in the chart on page 7) include plain or cast metal, unglazed or glazed ceramic, plastic, plaster, wood, and paper.

As a general rule, anything that can be painted or varnished successfully can also be gilded. But there are some exceptions. Certain plastics, including styrene and urethane, are sensitive to the solvents in the size, and will crackle or blister when it is applied. Styrene is most commonly found in clear plastic cups; urethane is used in pliable plastic grapes. If in doubt, do a patch test (*see* Plastic, page 8).

Most fabrics are also not suitable, because there is not enough surface area for the size and leaf to stick to. Even though the surface of plastic-like fabrics such as vinyl is smooth, the flexibility of the fabric makes it unsuitable.

Older veneer that has lifted away from the underlying substrate, causing ripples or bubbles, is not a good choice for leafing because the bubbles and ripples will show. You could reattach the veneer, but it's a fairly complicated process best left to professionals. I suggest choosing another object. Papier-mâché, unfortunately, is too lumpy to serve as a good base without extensive preparation, so I don't recommend it.

If you're considering an object other than those discussed in this article, ask yourself if the surface is hard, smooth, and nonporous. If the answer is yes to all three questions, your object can probably be gilded.

Preparation of the Material

One key to successful gilding is proper preparation of the item's surface. Follow these guidelines before moving to the directions on page 8.

Metal

Metal is the easiest material to leaf because it's hard, nonabsorbent, and smooth. However, both plain and cast metal should be primed before sizing. To promote adhesion, apply a coat of canned spray enamel primer before sizing.

If your metal object is older, check the surface carefully for defects such as corrosion or rust spots. Although you can't do much about scratches or dents, rust should be removed using 180-grit sandpaper. Plated metal, such as brass-plated lamp parts, often has small bumps erupting through the brass from the base metal. Since you'll want to preserve the polished surface of the brass, use a fine emery paper (220-grit) lubricated with water and a circular motion to remove these.

Wood

In general, wood is an excellent material for gilding, but as with any material, it needs proper preparation.

If the wood is raw but reasonably smooth, sand it with a coarser sandpaper (120-grit), then proceed to 180-grit paper, and finish with 200-grit. Seal with two coats of wood sealer, such as those made by Minwax, sand with 220-grit emery paper, and proceed to size.

If the wood is raw and the grain is rough, fill the grain with water putty. (I recommend Durock, because it mixes easily, sets quickly, and sands to a smooth finish.) Apply it with a putty knife, let dry following the manufacturer's instructions, and then sand following the steps discussed above for a smooth surface. Seal the object with two coats of sealer before leafing. If your wood has already been sanded and sealed, lightly roughen the finish with very fine (grade 000) steel wool before sizing.

The Best Materials for Gilding

MATERIAL	PREPARATION	SPECIAL NOTES	END RESULT
Plain metal (e.g., lamp part)	Prime with spray enamel. Sand rust spots or pits with appropriate sandpaper; wash with steel wool or stiff wire brush and water, then cover with rust-inhibiting primer such as Rustoleum.	If object will be exposed to humidity, seal with Varathane Diamond Finish Transparent IPN Coating. It appears milky and cloudy when first applied, but dries clear and can be handled in a few minutes.	PLAIN METAL
Cast metal (e.g., curtain tieback)	Prime with spray enamel. Sand rust spots or pits with appropriate sandpaper, then cover with rust-inhibiting primer such as Rustoleum.	Select objects with minimal molding seams or grinding marks. If leafing cast metal objects, examine them carefully for rough surfaces.	CAST METAL
Wood (e.g., carved frame)	For raw but smooth wood, sand and apply two coats wood sealer. For raw but rough wood, seal grain with water putty, then sand and apply two coats wood sealer. Remove any damaged finishes with paint thinner before sanding and sealing.	Avoid objects where veneer has loosened from underlying material. If you like the look of leafed wood grain, select an object made from ash or oak, as the grain will be very apparent.	WOOD
Glazed ceramic (e.g., vase)	Most glazed ceramic needs no preparation. In general, look for simple shapes with clean lines. Some molded ceramic with relief designs should be avoided, as mold seams and glaze drips will show through the leafing.	Do not gild items intended for serving food. Avoid gilding items with prominent mold seams or visible drips of glaze. Do not gild areas that will be exposed to water, such as the inside of a vase.	GLAZED CERAMIC
Unglazed ceramic (e.g., terra cotta)	Mature porcelain and stoneware need no preparation. Seal absorbent materials such as earthenware and terra cotta with one coat of wood sealer.	Over time, leaf that is exposed to water (e.g., if the pot is used to house a plant) may turn partially green. If this is not desirable, avoid this use of gilded terra cotta.	UNGLAZED CERAMIC
Plastic (e.g., cherub)	Do a patch test to determine if your plastic will react to the solvents in size. Several types of plastic will react to the solvents and cannot be gilded.	Avoid gilding objects made from styrene or urethane. With other clear plastics, note that the amber color of size may show through.	PLASTIC
Plaster (e.g., wall bracket)	Seal with two coats of wood sealer. Plaster also nicks and chips rather easily, and should be examined carefully before leafing. As with other surfaces, barely detectable minor defects become glaringly apparent when leafed.	If size seeps beyond sealed area, remove amber stain by scraping with the tip of an X-Acto knife, or cover the stain with a thin coating of white gesso thinned with water. Avoid gilding papier-mâché.	PLASTER
Porous Paper (e.g., book cover)	Seal with a single coat of wood sealer and allow to dry thoroughly before applying size. Heavy papers, such as two-ply Bristol, are better than thin papers.	Since paper is inherently fragile, gilded paper is not as durable as other gilded materials. Best uses include wrapping paper or cards, or as an accent on paper projects, such as the book at right.	POROUS PAPER
Glossy paper (e.g., giftwrap)	Glossy or coated card stock and magazine stock papers do not need sealing.	Since paper is inherently fragile, gilded paper is not as durable as other gilded materials. Gilded glossy paper works well as giftwrap.	GLOSSY PAPER

If your wood's finish is chipping or flaking, remove the finish with paint stripper such as 3M's Safest Stripper. If the wood's finish is in good condition, lightly sand the surface with 400-grit emery paper and seal with wood sealer. Newly veneered items typically don't need any special preparation.

Glazed Ceramic

Like metals, most glazed ceramic is a good choice for leafing, as the surface is hard, non-absorbent, and smooth. One important exception should be noted, however. Items used for food serving should not be leafed, as the leaf will not survive the wear of use or the heat of washing.

Consider sealing your finished project with Varathane Diamond Finish Transparent IPN Coating by Flecto, a very thin, transparent, water-based finish, which will protect the gilded surface from scratches and tears. One note: Sealer takes some of the luster away from gold leaf, so eliminate this step if you want particularly bright gold color and if you can properly protect your ceramic item.

If you're leafing a vase that will ultimately hold water, be sure to stop the process at least an inch or two away from any area that will be touching water.

Unglazed Ceramic

Gilding the rougher surface of unglazed ceramic results in a markedly matte leafed surface. Unglazed but mature porcelain and stoneware are virtually nonabsorbent, and can be sized directly without the benefit of a sealer. Earthenware and terra cotta should be sealed with a coat of wood sealer before sizing.

Aesthetic considerations raised in the previous section apply here as well. Consider leafing the rim band of an otherwise plain terra cotta flowerpot, for instance, and leaving the rest bare. With water and time, the pot body will become salty and the gilding partially green with verdigris. Another option is to choose a pot with garlands or other decoration and seal

some areas once and others twice to give a mixture of matte and glossy leaf.

Plastic

Many plastics are very good for leafing, as they are smooth and hard. But some will react to the solvents in size. If you're not sure what type of plastic you're dealing with, I recommend doing a test. Take a ¼" dab of size, apply it to an inconspicuous place, and allow it to dry completely. If cracks, bubbles, or ripples appear, the item is not appropriate for leafing.

Plaster

Plaster, an extremely absorbent material, must be sealed with two coats of wood sealer before sizing. Bright white plaster can be beautiful when partially gilded, but care must be taken when applying the size. Don't let it seep beyond the sealed surface, as it will bleed into the plaster and leave a pronounced amber stain. If this happens, you can remove the stain by scraping the affected area with the tip of an X-Acto knife, or cover the stain with a thin coating of white gesso thinned with water.

Paper

Paper is fragile and leaf doesn't wear well on the surface, but for items that are only used for a short time, such as gift wrapping or cards, leafing adds a beautiful touch well worth the effort. Most papers (with the exception of glossy paper) are inherently absorbent, so they must be sealed before sizing. Use a single coat of wood sealer and allow to dry thoroughly.

GILD ANY SURFACE

1 object for gilding with properly prepared surface
1 book composition gold leaf
1 4-ounce can quick-dry synthetic gold size varnish

You'll also need: Two 1"- or 2"-wide flat paintbrushes or fine-grain foam brushes; soft

cloth or flannel rag; table knife; several sheets clean paper; small metal container; newspaper; tack cloth; and mineral spirits for cleanup.

Other items, if necessary: Varathane Diamond Finish Transparent IPN Coating by Flecto; 1"-wide brush for sealing; and 1"-wide brush for removing loose flakes from carved surfaces.

1. Cover work space with newspaper. Remove dust from object with tack cloth.

2. Pour small amount of size into clean, metal container. Apply thin, even coat of size to object's surface using appropriate brush.

3. When object is fully coated, remove with a swipe of the brush any drips of size from bottom edges or any buildup in crevices. Even out coat of size by going over heavy areas with clean brush. Clean brushes with mineral spirits.

4. Let dry for 1 to 3 hours. Test surface by touching with clean finger.

5. Open book of composition gold leaf and lay flat. Using clean hands, remove protective tissue paper to expose sheet of leaf. Touch edge of leaf with table knife moistened with breath and trail onto flat, clean piece of paper. To release leaf from knife, hold down opposite corners of leaf with finger and roll knife blade off. Break gold leaf into random pieces using perfectly dry fingertips.

6. Use fingertip to lift and position gold leaf. Tap lightly into place, and remove any air bubbles using fingertip. To close gap between pieces, apply leaf that is larger than size of gap and tap into place. (Any excess will drop off.)

7. When entire object is gilded, remove sheet of tissue from book and lay over gilded surface. Gently rub finger over tissue to further adhere gold leaf. For a carved surface, use light, wispy strokes of clean 1"-wide brush to remove loose flakes. Let dry overnight, or until hard to the touch.

8. Burnish surface using a wad of natural cotton or soft cloth with a gentle circular motion. If necessary, apply thin coat of sealer using 1"-wide brush. ◆

Four Steps to Guilding

1. Apply a thin, even coat of size to the item's surface using the appropriate brush.

2. Touch the edge of the leaf with a table knife moistened with your breath and trail it onto a flat, clean piece of paper. Break the gold leaf into random pieces using perfectly dry fingertips.

3. Use your fingertip to lift and position the gold leaf, then tap lightly into place and smooth out any air bubbles.

4. Burnish the surface using a gentle circular motion with a soft cloth or flannel rag.

PHOTOGRAPHS BY RICHARD FELBER

Wheat Sheaf Centerpiece

An ordinary soup can serves as the base for this traditional autumn bouquet.

You can make this traditional autumn centerpiece in under thirty minutes.

The wheat sheaf, a traditional fall talisman, makes a tasteful autumn centerpiece. In the past, creating such a piece might have required six or eight bouquets each of wheat and rye, but you can make this piece with half that many materials. The key is an everyday soup can, which serves as a base for the sheaf and creates the illusion of bulk. Using a hot-glue gun and three packages each of wheat and rye, you can bring a fall harvest indoors in less than thirty minutes.

Wheat Sheaf Centerpiece

3 4-ounce packages natural triticum wheat
   (about forty 22" stems per package)
3 4-ounce packages rye grain (about forty
   22" stems per package)
1 unopened 4-ounce can of soup, any type
1 jumbo braided hair elastic
½ yard waxed string (*see* "How to
   Make Waxed String," right)
1 yard natural-fiber, 24-strand raffia

You'll also need: scissors or pruning shears; hot-glue gun and glue sticks; ruler or yardstick; pencil; and masking tape. ◆

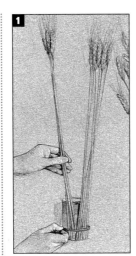

1. Remove the wrapping from the wheat stems. Cut a 19" length of masking tape and stick it down on the work surface. Lay a single wheat stem along the tape so the tip of the grain head is even with the end of the tape. Using scissors or pruning shears, trim the lower stem until it is even with the other end of the tape. Repeat this process with 2 or 3 stems at a time until all the stems are cut to 19". (Discard any shorter stems.) Slip the hair elastic around the soup can about 1½" from the bottom of the can. Slip a group of 5 wheat stems under the elastic and distribute them so the snipped ends line up with the bottom of the can and lay close to one another. Continue adding stems around the can in groups of 5 until the entire can is covered.

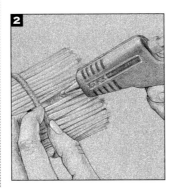

2. Lay the can on its side and part the adjacent stems below the hair elastic. Apply a small dot of hot glue near the base of the can. Shift the stems back into position over the glue and press in place. Repeat this process until all the stems are glued to the can. Stand the can upright. Do not remove the hair elastic. Let the glue set about 5 minutes.

3. Cut the ½-yard length of waxed string in half. Draw one 9" length around the stems 4" to 5" below the grain heads and tie in a half-knot to secure the core of the bouquet. Adjust the tension so the gathered core is narrower than the can diameter, then finish tying the knot and snip off the extra string.

4. Remove the plastic wrapping from the rye stems. Draw a line on the masking tape 15½" from one end and trim the rye stems to 15½" lengths using the method outlined in step 1. After cutting 1 stem, hold it against the wheat bouquet. The rye grain heads should fall just below the wheat heads. Adjust the length marked on the tape if necessary. Turn the can on its side and repeat the appropriate parts of steps 1 and 2 with the rye. When all the rye stems are glued in place, gather the stems with the remaining 9" length of waxed string (about 1" below the rye heads) and tie off. Trim the ends of the string. Stand the bouquet upright. Twist 12 strands of raffia into a rope and tie around the bouquet to conceal the waxed string. Trim the ends even. Using the remaining 12 strands, twist a second rope and tie over the hair elastic at the bottom of the bouquet. Knot at the back and trim the strands.

HOW TO MAKE WAXED STRING

To make your own waxed string, you'll need a ball of butcher twine or similar all-purpose cotton string, 2 cakes of paraffin wax or quilter's beeswax, and scissors.

1. Cut string to desired length. Stack 2 wax blocks in one hand and slip free end of string between them so tip emerges slightly.

2. Grab tip of string with free hand. Pressing wax blocks together, draw string through them until desired length is coated.

Faux Stone Fruit Basket

Bring the look of weathered stone indoors with this papier-mâché sculpture.

BY MICHIO RYAN

Weathered stone fixtures or sculptures work well in a garden or on a patio or doorstep, but most are too large and heavy to use on delicate indoor furniture or mantels. Using a basket, papier-mâché, and plastic fruit, however, you can create a faux stone sculpture with a fraction of the weight.

The faux stone finish on this sculpture is created using a combination of paint, sand texture paint additive, and rottenstone. I used the following brands, but you're free to substitute. For the medium-gray, water-based acrylic paint: Rustoleum Acrylic Water Base Coating, Navy gray #5786. For the light and dark gray craft paints, respectively: Folk Art dove gray #708 and charcoal gray #613. For sand additive and rottenstone, respectively: Permalite San-Finish and Rainbow Colors rottenstone.

This project makes a half-relief sculpture suitable for narrow shelves and flat backdrops, but you can make a pair of matching fixtures by doubling the fruit and papier-mâché and purchasing two additional foam bricks. (One basket will yield two halves for the pair, and there will be enough of the other materials and supplies for both.) By varying the arrangement and type of fruit in each basket, you can create a customized pair of sculptures that clearly make up a set, but are distinct from each other.

To further customize your basket(s), consider making additional fruit from instant papier-mâché. (*See* "Making Other Fruit Using Papier-Mâché," page 12.) You'll find directions on how to make pomegranates and miniature melons, but you can also make nuts, berries, or fruit of any kind.

You can make this single faux stone basket, or make a pair of matching fixtures by doubling the amount of fruit and papier-mâché and purchasing two additional foam bricks.

FAUX STONE FRUIT BASKET

1 flared oval basket: 13" across top, 11" across bottom, and 7" high, with thick, pronounced, open-weave canes
2 4½" x 9" x 3" florist foam bricks
1 4-ounce box methyl cellulose wallpaper adhesive
1 sheet double-weight chipboard or ⅛"-thick oaktag
½ pint matte finish, medium gray, water based acrylic paint
1 2-ounce bottle light gray acrylic craft paint
1 2-ounce bottle dark gray acrylic craft paint
1 pint gesso
1 6-ounce package sand texture paint additive
1 8-ounce package rottenstone
1 16-ounce package instant papier-mâché Assorted stiff plastic fruit: 3 apples; 3 pears; 3 plums; 2 peaches; 2 lemons; 2 oranges; 6–8 cherries or other pieces small fruit

You'll also need: 1¼" round stencil brush; two 1"-wide disposable paint brushes; coarse sea sponge; 3 pairs latex gloves; 2 disposable plastic plates; newspaper, self-healing mat, or scraps of cardboard; hot-glue gun and glue sticks; 1½"-wide masking tape; pruning shears; X-Acto knife or utility knife; felt-tip pen; ruler; 9"-square (or larger) disposable aluminum pan; long-blade serrated kitchen knife; drop cloth; paint stirring stick; tablespoon; 12" x 18" cutting board; aluminum foil; wax paper; plastic wrap; butter knife; chopstick; high-tack white craft glue; and Teflon scouring pad (if using flocked fruit).

Preparing the Basket

1. Turn basket upside down. Stick masking tape in one continuous strip down side, across bottom, and up other side, with tape running across basket's longer width. (The tape serves as guide for cutting basket in two.)

2. Using pruning shears, cut straight down center of tape on sides and across bottom to cut basket in two. Reinforce cut edges with additional tape to prevent canes from unraveling.

3. Place cut edge of one half against chipboard or oaktag. Using felt-tip pen, trace

around outside of basket sides and bottom. Remove basket.

4. Using ruler, draw a line on chipboard straight across top of basket to connect the sides. Measure in 1" from both sides on horizontal line. Free-hand draw an upside-down, U-shaped arc. Uppermost point of arc should be 5" to 6" above horizontal line.

5. Lay down 15 to 20 sheets of newspaper, several pieces of scrap cardboard, or self-healing mat. Using utility or X-Acto knife, cut through chipboard or oaktag along all lines except the one connecting the sides.

6. Position half of basket on cut-out backing; secure outside edges temporarily with tape. Apply hot glue generously to inside joint where basket meets backing, injecting glue between canes to secure them to each other as well as to backing. Let glue cool, then remove outside tape and check joint for adhesion. Apply hot glue from outside to secure any loose canes, holding them in position until glue hardens. Once glue is hard, remove any remaining tape and remove excess glue from outside with X-Acto knife.

7. Pull on latex gloves. In disposable aluminum pan, mix 1 ounce (¼ package) cellulose wallpaper adhesive in 1 pint water following manufacturer's directions. Let stand 10 minutes to thicken.

8. Tear (don't cut) 24 sheets of newspaper into strips measuring about 2" x 5".

9. Skim newspaper strip across surface of wallpaper paste to coat one side. Place strip, paste side down, on basket lengthwise along woven grain. Working from center of strip out, gently nudge moist paper into basket crevices using dry 1"-wide paintbrush, making paper conform to basket surface. Work carefully to avoid tears. If the paper is too dry and doesn't mold easily, brush surface with wallpaper paste and further nudge into crevices. Tear additional strips of newspaper as needed.

10. Continue applying strips, overlapping edges ½", until entire front and bottom of basket are covered. Stick strips from bottom and sides onto chipboard backing, overlapping at least 2" onto backing. Brush lightly with paste to help secure bond. Be sure to coat top 2" of basket with paste and paper, as well as inside of basket bottom. Let dry overnight. Clean up using warm water.

11. When first layer of newspaper is thoroughly dry, repeat steps 7 to 10 to apply second coat. Be sure to press out all wrinkles and folds and tap any tears or gaps into place with brush or fingertips. Let dry overnight.

Preparing and Arranging the Fruit

1. In medium-sized mixing bowl, combine 12 ounces (¾ package) instant papier-mâché with water following manufacturer's directions. Knead with fingertips into a wet powder, then cover bowl with aluminum foil and let

Preparing the Basket

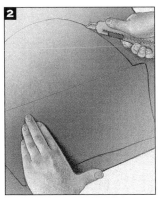

1. Turn the basket upside down and place the masking tape across the basket bottom and up the sides. Using pruning shears, cut straight down the center of the tape on the sides and across the bottom to cut the basket in two.

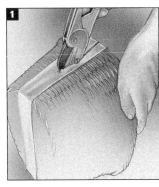

2. Place one half of the basket against the chipboard and trace around the sides and bottom. Free-hand draw an upside-down U-shaped arc. Using a utility or X-Acto knife, cut through the chipboard along the outside lines.

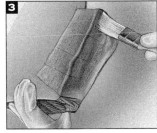

3. Cover the entire front and bottom of the basket with strips of newspaper skimmed in wallpaper adhesive. Gently nudge the moist paper into the basket crevices using a dry 1"-wide paintbrush. Paste the strips of paper from the bottom and the sides of the basket onto the chipboard backing, overlapping the paper at least 2" onto backing.

Preparing and Arranging the Fruit

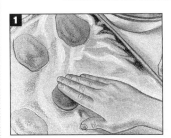

1. To make the leaves, cover the cutting board with foil. Pull off golf ball-sized lumps of papier-mâché, roll them into balls, and flatten into oval-shaped pancakes measuring 4" x 2" x ⅜".

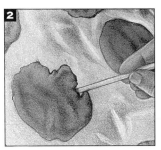

2. To serrate the leaves, press in sharply along the edges of the pancakes with the pointed end of a chopstick. Start at the top and work down toward the stem.

3. After serrating the edges, dip a butter knife in water and run the flat blade firmly across the surface to smooth out bumps and holes.

4. To scribe the veins, use the blade of the butter knife, then widen the veins using the tip of a chopstick.

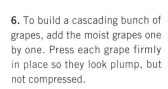

5. With the basket standing upright, center a foam brick in it vertically and up against the chipboard. Cut the second block in half and wedge the halves into place beside the first brick.

6. To build a cascading bunch of grapes, add the moist grapes one by one. Press each grape firmly in place so they look plump, but not compressed.

7. Arrange the leaves one by one, positioning them so they curl realistically over the fruit and the rim of the basket. Glue in place with white tacky glue.

stand 10 minutes, or until clay is evenly moist and semisolid.

2. To make grapes, take a grape-sized lump of papier-mâché and roll it into ball between palms. If papier-mâché sticks to your hands, dampen them. Dip palms in warm water before completing last few rolls to fuse any cracks and smooth grape's surface. Make about 15 grapes, varying sizes slightly. Lay on sheet of wax paper and cover with plastic wrap until ready to use.

3. To make leaves, cover the cutting board surface with aluminum foil. Pull off golf ball–sized lump of papier-mâché, roll into a ball, then flatten into an oval-shaped pancake measuring 4" x 2" x ³⁄₈". Lay pancake on cutting board and smooth edges with fingertips. Make 6 pancakes.

4. To make serrated leaves from pancakes, press in sharply along pancake edges with pointed end of chopstick, starting at one end and working down to the other. Mend tears and cracks by smoothing area with dampened fingertip. After serrating edges, dip butter knife in water and run flat blade firmly across surface to smooth out bumps and holes. Scribe veins on leaves using blade of butter knife, then widen veins slightly using tip of chopstick.

5. To make smaller round leaves, pull off walnut-sized lump of clay and repeat step 3 to make 4 smaller pancakes measuring 2½" x 2" x ³⁄₈". Lay on cutting board, smooth edges, and scribe veins with knife. Cover all leaves with plastic wrap and set aside.

6. Using X-Acto knife, scrape mold marks from plastic fruit. If using flocked fruit, such as peaches, soak fruit in warm water for 15 minutes, then scrub with Teflon scouring pad to remove flocking and adhesive.

7. Using 1"-wide paintbrush, cover all plastic fruit with a light, even layer of gesso; set aside on wax paper and let dry 2 hours.

8. Lay basket flat on back. Coat bottom of basket with a light, even layer of gesso; then coat front of basket and chipboard. Stand basket upright on wax paper and coat back of chipboard and any missed edges. Leave upright on wax paper until thoroughly dry, about 2 hours.

9. When basket is dry, center a foam brick vertically inside, pushed up against chipboard. Cut second brick in half using serrated kitchen knife, and wedge each piece into place at sides of first foam brick, shaving off foam as necessary for a tight fit.

10. Arrange 5 or 6 large pieces of gesso-coated fruit along back and rim of basket. Hot-glue fruits to each other, to basket rim, to backing, and to foam.

11. Using illustration 6 on page 11 as guide, build a cascading bunch of grapes by adding the moist grapes one by one. Press each grape firmly in place so they look plump but compressed and affix using white tacky glue. (Hot glue will not adhere to moist papier-mâché.)

12. Peel moist leaves off foil and arrange one by one using illustration 7 on page 11 as reference. Position leaves so they curl realistically over fruit and rim of basket. (If clay does not bend easily or develops cracks, dampen slightly with fingertip to restore pliability.) Glue in place with white tacky glue.

13. Fill in any gaps with remaining plastic fruit; hot glue in place. Secure any loose pieces of fruit with hot glue. (Loose grapes or leaves should be affixed using white tacky glue.) Let dry overnight.

14. Apply second coat of gesso to entire piece, starting with basket front and bottom and moving up to fruit and leaves. Stand basket upright on wax paper and apply coat of gesso to back. Brush gesso into any missed spots or crevices. Cover any exposed hot glue or small cracks in papering of basket, to make sculpture waterproof and smooth. Stand upright on wax paper and let dry overnight.

Painting the Arrangement

1. Put on latex gloves and spread drop cloth over work surface. Add 1 generous tablespoon sand texture additive to ½ pint matte finish, medium-gray paint; stir well with paint stick.

2. Lay sculpture on drop cloth. Using 1"- wide brush, paint entire surface with sandy paint mixture. Work paint into all crevices, encouraging grit to accumulate in crevices to simulate natural wear. (The ¼" round brush will be particularly useful in reaching crevices between fruit and leaves.) Stand sculpture upright on wax paper, and examine fruit carefully. Paint over any missed areas. Coat back of sculpture last. Let dry 1 hour, or as recommended by paint manufacturer. Apply second coat and let dry 4 hours. Clean up paint materials and brushes using warm water.

3. Squeeze approximately 1 tablespoon light gray paint onto plastic plate, add a few drops of water, and stir until creamy using ¼" round brush. Clean brush in warm water. Repeat process with dark-gray paint.

4. Put on latex gloves. Dip moistened sea sponge into light-gray paint, squeeze out excess, and lightly dab surface of sculpture. (Avoid dabbing large amounts of light gray paint into crevices, as those will be covered with dark gray paint to simulate aging.) Let dry ½ hour. Wash sea sponge in warm water.

5. Using ¼" round brush, dab crevices with dark gray paint, then immediately dab area with clean, damp sea sponge to remove excess paint and blend. Proceed one area at a time with dark-gray paint, alternating brushwork and sponging, to bring sculpture into relief. Pay special attention to textures such as basket weave and leaves. Apply additional paint as desired. Let dry completely. To finish, shake a light dusting of rottenstone over entire surface with clean, dry 1"- wide brush. Blow off any excess rottenstone out-of-doors. ◆

Grape Arbor Mural

Block-print a lifelike grapevine in an afternoon's time.

BY STU AND VI CUTBILL

You don't need a paintbrush to create this beautiful grape arbor in your home. This vine was created using block printing, a time-honored technique that is amazingly forgiving even for beginners. The concept is easy: Transfer an image onto a printing pad, cut out the shape of the image, paint the pad with glaze, and block print directly onto your wall.

You can purchase precut block printing pads, or cut your own from a computer mouse pad, a potato, or a sheet of synthetic rubber using the patterns below. All three materials have a smooth, even texture and can be cut and scored to produce detailed templates. Pads cut from the mouse pad or synthetic rubber can also be washed and reused. Although there is some variation in the prints from each material, results are fairly comparable (*see* the samples on page 15). The vine shown here was created using a computer mouse pad. For specific directions on cutting your own pads, *see* "How to Cut Your Own Printing Pads," page 15.

Whichever material you use, practice on a plain, painted surface or scrap paper before working on the wall. You'll notice that

THE PATTERN PIECES

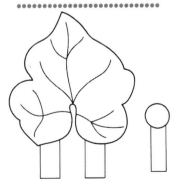

Enlarge the templates above until the grape leaf measures about 3⅛" wide and the grape measures ⅝" wide.

the pad can be used several times before it must be reloaded with glaze. The pressed image will go from a heavy, saturated look to a light, wispy one as the amount of glaze on the pad diminishes. This effect is very useful in creating three-dimensionality, as darker print images suggest objects in the foreground, while the lighter prints suggest objects in the background.

Over the years, we've discovered that glaze is far better for use in block printing than paint. Paint consists of a powder pigment dissolved and suspended in a binder (e.g., linseed oil) and thinned with a diluent (e.g., turpentine). Glaze is essentially paint with different proportions of binder and diluent, making it translucent rather than opaque. When glaze is applied to a wall, a hint of the wall color will still show through. In addition, when glaze dries, the extra binder gives it a bit of a sheen.

For this project, we used premixed latex glazes. You can also mix your own glazes very easily using oil- or water-based paints; *see* "Making Your Own Glaze," on page 15, and the color palette, below. To create a grape arbor with a spring, summer, or autumn color palette, *see* "Seasonal Grape Arbors," page 15.

Start by determining the location for your block print effect and, if necessary, removing any grime or dust with liquid detergent and a sponge or rag. Your project needn't be limited to painted walls, however—block printing also works well on wallpaper or glass or anything paintable, including furniture, lampshades, curtains, placemats, or even metal or ceramic containers.

GRAPE ARBOR MURAL

2-ounce jars glaze, one each in the following colors:

You can block print this arbor design using a printing pad cut from one of three materials: a computer mouse pad, a sheet of rubber, or a potato.

vivid violet, forest green, deep forest green, clear, and umber brown, *or* homemade glazes

You'll also need: grape and leaf blocking pads, precut or handmade; two ½"-wide, flat paintbrushes; ¼" round tapered paintbrush; ¼"-wide masking tape; heavy-duty paper or plastic plates; zip-close plastic bags for storing pads; turpentine; soap; access to a copy machine; and scrap paper for experimenting with block prints.◆

Stu and **Vi Cutbill** are one of Canada's leading faux artist teams and inventors of The Cutbill System of Block Printing.

Color Palette

Shown here are the colors used to create the grape arbor above. If mixing your own glazes, use these colors as a guide.

deep forest green **forest green** **umber brown** **vivid violet**

Block-Printing the Grape Arbor

1. To mark the vines, start near the floor and work upward. Apply ¼" masking tape continuously from the roll in a random, squiggly line to represent a vine. Adjust placement as needed. Repeat process to mark a second, intertwining vine.

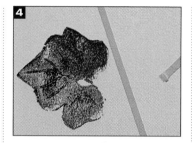

2. Hold the grape leaf pad in one hand, scored veins facing up, with your thumb and forefinger holding one or both tabs to prevent shifting. Brush deep forest green glaze onto one half of the pad, taking care to keep the glaze off the tab area, then cover the other half with forest green glaze. Brush glaze out to edges and let it seep into the vein cuts.

3. Position the pad face down on the wall near the lower end of the tape so the leaf appears to be growing out of the vine. Press your fingertips across the pad to ensure all the glazed areas touch the surface.

4. Lift the pad off the wall to reveal the first leaf block print. If the first press seems too saturated, press off onto a piece of paper, then continue on the wall with the second press.

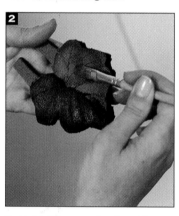

5. Without reapplying the glaze to the pad, and rotating pad slightly to alter the angle of each leaf, print three more leaves in the same vicinity to create a cluster. To suggest overlapping foliage, make a partial print by pressing down on one half of the pad. Make some leaves imperfect so the overall coloration is natural.

6. Recoat the pad with green glazes and print the second cluster of leaves about 12" up the vine. Continue adding clusters of full and partial leaves along the entire taped line, recoating the pad, occasionally switching colors on either side, and mixing additional glaze as necessary. Rotate the pad in different directions for a varied, spontaneous look. Step back occasionally to view your work. Fill out any clusters that seem sparse.

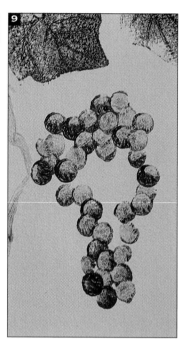

7. Apply dime-sized blobs of deep forest green, umber brown, and clear glazes on a paper plate. If mixing your own glaze, substitute thinned linseed oil for clear glaze when painting with oils, or thinned acrylic medium for clear glaze when painting with water-based acrylics. Thin a dime-sized puddle of linseed oil with a few drops of turpentine and mix well; thin the same amount of acrylic medium with a few drops of water. Dip the bristles of the ¼" round brush into all three glazes without mixing the colors on the brush. Starting at one end, peel up the first tape, while at the same time gently trailing the wet brush along its path, making a ¼"- to ½"-wide vine. Twist and turn the brush as you trail it along to merge the green and brown glaze at random. Reload the brush as necessary. Paint right over the intersection of the first and second tape, or break off and repeat the process following the path of the second tape vine. Add the tendrils as desired.

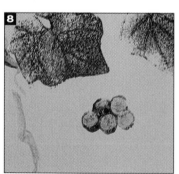

8. To block print grapes, apply a thin layer of vivid violet glaze to the clean pie plate or work from the jar. Press the pad into the glaze to coat it or apply glaze with a brush. Keep the tab free of paint. Select an opening in the leaf mural and press the pad against the wall surface four or five times in succession to make a small cluster.

9. Reload the grape pad and continue printing, expanding the cluster until it resembles the coastline of Africa or South America.

10. Fill in the outline with additional pressings, overlapping some to create an illusion of depth. Continue printing the grape clusters as desired over both the vines. Clean acrylic glazes from the brushes and pads with soap and cool water. Clean oil-based glazes with an odorless turpentine followed by soap and water. Be sure to clean the residue from the scored vein lines of the pads. Wipe the pads dry and store in a zip-close plastic bag.

PHOTOGRAPHS BY THOMAS M. HORBETT

How to Cut Your Own Printing Pads

Y ou can make the grape leaf printing pad from a ¼"-thick computer mouse pad, a sheet of synthetic rubber, *or* an extra large potato. (You'll also need an average size potato for the grape pad.)

The results are comparable, but will vary a small amount from one material to another. For all three materials you'll need tracing paper and a pencil. If making the pad from rubber or a mouse pad, you'll

also need an X-Acto knife, dressmaker's transfer paper, a ballpoint pen, and a cutting board. For the potato version, you'll also need a large knife, an X-Acto knife, paper towels, and scissors.

Mouse pad

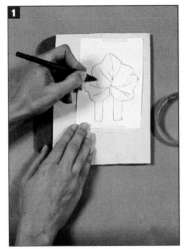

Synthetic rubber

Potato

1. Enlarge the leaf and grape patterns on page 13, then trace them using tracing paper and a pencil. (For variation, draw your own designs, or trace found images. Be sure to leave a small tab on one edge for holding the pad.)

3. *For the potato,* use a large knife to slice the potato in half to reveal the broadest surface possible. Cut out the traced image using scissors and press it onto the flat, cut surface of the potato. (The moisture from the potato will hold it in place.) Using an X-Acto knife, cut ⅜" deep into the potato along the traced lines.

2. *For the computer mouse pad or synthetic rubber,* lay the mouse pad (fabric side up) or rubber on a flat work surface. Lay a sheet of dressmaker's transfer paper face down on the mouse pad or rubber. Lay traced patterns on top of the transfer material. Pressing firmly with a ballpoint pen, trace over the pattern outlines and veins to transfer the images to the mouse pad or rubber. Remove the papers. Set the mouse pad or rubber on a cutting board. Using an X-Acto knife, cut through the entire thickness of the pad following the marked outlines. As shape emerges, pull on the pad slightly to facilitate cutting through the top fabric layer. Cut the veins about halfway through the pad thickness.

4. Remove the tracing. Using an X-Acto knife, cut into the potato from the sides, parallel to and ¼" below the flat surface, until you reach the outline cuts. Carefully pick out any loose potato flesh so the design stands in relief. Blot any juice with a paper towel before applying the glaze.

SEASONAL GRAPE ARBORS

U sing the sample prints provided here, you can create a grape arbor with springlike or summerlike foliage, or one with the colors of autumn. For the spring palette, mix a spring green with bright gold. For a summery look, combine teal-green glaze and deep forest green. For the autumn colors, mix bright moss green with warm brown.

Spring

Summer

Autumn

MAKING YOUR OWN GLAZE

2-ounce tubes oil or acrylic artist's paint, one each in the following colors: forest green, deep forest green, umber brown, and vivid violet to match color palette on page 13

Glaze medium or linseed oil (if using oil paints) *or* acrylic gel medium (if using acrylic paints)

You'll also need: heavy-duty paper or plastic pie plates and palette knife.

Other items, if necessary: odorless turpentine (if using oil paints).

1. *To mix oil-based glaze,* place a 1"-long squeeze of paint on pie plate. Add half to one time as much of glaze medium or linseed oil and mix

well with palette knife. Thin with a few drops of turpentine if necessary to achieve a syrupy, but not runny, consistency.

2. *To mix acrylic glaze,* place a 1"-long squeeze of acrylic paint on pie plate. Using palette knife, add one to three times as much acrylic gel medium and mix well. Thin with water to achieve a syrupy consistency.

Fold Your Own Decorative Boxes

Use the original box designs bound into this issue to make exquisite gift packaging.

These beautiful boxes, designed using turn-of-the-century lithographs, can be folded and ready for use in less than fifteen minutes. Consider filling the pillow-shaped box with several small scented soaps or a scarf. The triangular box can hold a pen and pencil set or a pair of candles. Cut and fold each box for immediate use, or accent them following the suggestions below.

You can fold the boxes found on the following pages, or create multiple boxes by making color copies of the designs provided on heavyweight paper. For best results when folding, start all folds in the middle of the crease and work outwards.

DECORATIVE BOXES

Box prints (*see* special insert, following pages)

You'll also need: damp sponge; scissors; straightedge; butter knife; Scotch tape; high-tack craft glue; 2–3 rubber bands; heavy book; and felt-tip pen.

1. Cut out each box along outlines.

2. Lay box, printed side up, on flat surface. Using straightedge as guide, make creases along fold lines or between fold marks with dull side of butter knife. Turn box over, blank side facing up, and score same lines, following indentations made from front side.

3. Fold crease lines by placing crease along table edge, printed side facing up, and press on crease with fingers. Fold long side creases first, followed by tabs. Fold curved creases by hand. Address triangular box with felt-tip pen.

4. Run a ¹⁄₁₆"-wide bead of glue along tab marked "tab to glue" and fold box closed. Wipe off any excess glue with damp sponge. Hold glued portion together until set, then set aside to dry for 15 minutes. Clamp pillow-shaped box in place with heavy book and hold triangular box sides closed with rubber bands.

5. To close triangular box, tuck tab A under tab B; then tuck tab B under tab C. Glue tab C under tab A with small drop of glue. Insert gift and repeat process at other end of box, but tape shut instead of gluing.

6. To close the pillow-shaped box, tuck one oval-shaped tab under the other and glue in place with small beads of glue. Insert gift and close opposite end using tape. ◆

To make multiple versions of these beautiful gift boxes, copy the designs found on the next page onto heavyweight paper stock using a color copier.

Dressing Up Your Boxes

Following are a few suggestions for dressing up the boxes.

For the Triangular Box

➤ Tie a length of ½"-wide ivory-colored satin ribbon into a bow and add a cluster of three or four lavender, pink, and rose satin roses by running the wire stems through the knot. Affix to one end of the box using a hot-glue gun.

➤ Before folding the box, use a fine-point Pilot gold marker and a straightedge to create pinstripes along the top and bottom bands. Add gold highlights to the basket weave and on the leafy garlands.

➤ Cover the medallion with a foiled chocolate coin; affix it using white tacky glue.

➤ Using fabric paint from a fine-nibbed squeeze bottle, add pearlescent gold dots atop the berries in the laurel leaves.

For the Pillow Box

➤ Before folding the box, use a finepoint Pilot gold marker and a straightedge to create pinstripes along the top and bottom bands. Create wide stripes by making closely adjacent lines with a fine-point gold pen; add narrow pinstripes with one pass of the pen.

➤ Using fabric paint from a fine-nibbed squeeze bottle, add ivory pearlescent dots atop the berry clusters in the frieze band. Use orange fabric paint to build up the oranges in the topiary. Highlight the centers of the square medallions.

➤ Tie a 1"-wide, wire-edged, metallic gold mesh ribbon around the "waist" of the box (atop the topiary) and finish with a bow. Hot-glue it in place. Tuck several bay leaves, a sprig of boxwood, a berry cluster, or other decorative foliage (fresh or dried) under the bow and hot-glue it in place.

See instructions,
page 16.

Fold along curve and
glue under adjacent tab

Tab to glue

Fold along curve and
glue under adjacent tab

See instructions, page 16.

Classic Steiff Teddy Bear

Sew this replica 1900s bear in less than a day's time.

BY PAT CASTKA

This classic bear, modeled after the earliest designs from the German teddy bear maker Steiff, can be assembled in under a day. While the finished result looks quite professional, making the bear simply requires learning about fur, a minimal amount of sewing, and a quick lesson in attaching jointed limbs. Once the bear is assembled and stuffed, adding the finishing touches to his face to give him personality and character involves a small amount of handsewing.

Like the teddy bears made by Steiff prior to World War I, this bear features jointed, elongated limbs; large paws and stitched-on claws; small, black eyes; widely spaced, unstuffed ears; a tapered muzzle; and a slightly humped back. The bear can be sewn using mohair, a fur commonly used on teddy bears in the early 1900s, or made from more commonly found (and less expensive) synthetic plush fur.

Prior to the early 1900s, dolls and trains topped the list of best-selling toys. An incident in 1902, however, involving then-President Teddy Roosevelt, propelled the bear to the front of the toy industry. In November of that year, the President attended a bear hunt in Mississippi. He found no game except for a bear cub, which he refused to shoot. The incident was illustrated in *The Washington Post* by political cartoonist Clifford Berryman, and through this cartoon the teddy bear came to symbolize the President.

Within a year, the bear had been transformed into a toy for children. Steiff, which had launched a mail-order stuffed animal business in the 1880s, was one of the first firms to manufacture teddy bears in large quantities. Between 1903 and 1908, Steiff expanded its

This bear was sewn with mohair, but synthetic fur, soft brown velvet, or cream-colored wool will work equally well.

teddy bear factory three times to keep up with the growing demand. Over that period, known as the *Barenjahre* (Bear Years), the number of teddy bears produced annually rose from 12,000 to about 975,000.

Since that time, two classes of teddy bears have emerged: classic collectibles, like the one pictured here, and those designed for children. As a collectible, it should be noted that this bear does not feature child-proof eyes, nor

are its jointed limbs or hand-stitched features sturdy enough for a child's heavy handling. In addition, if you sew the bear from mohair, it will not be machine-washable, a desirable feature of bears designed specifically for children.

If you have never worked with fur, keep the following points in mind. Like fabrics such as velvet and corduroy, fur has a nap. The nap is, quite simply, the direction of fur growth, much like on a dog. If you run your hand with the nap (or pet a dog along the direction of fur growth), the fur is smooth and silky. If you run your hand against the nap, the fur is roughed up. (*See* "Working with Fur," below.) Determining the direction of nap is as simple as brushing your hand over the fur to find the direction in which it is smooth and silky.

The pattern diagram on page 18 is designed to serve two purposes. It includes the bear pattern pieces for enlarging, and it serves as a placement diagram for cutting out the pattern pieces. When enlarging pattern pieces, enlarge a total of eight pieces. Omit the shaded pieces.

After the pattern pieces have been enlarged, lay out the fur wrong side (backing side) up and nap toward you. Arrange the pattern pieces as shown in the diagram, with the arrows on the pattern pieces running in the direction of the nap. (When pinning the pattern pieces onto the

WORKING WITH FUR

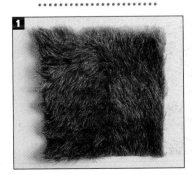

1. Fur on the left side runs against the nap; fur on the right, with the nap.

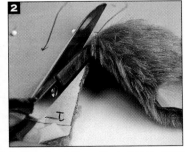

2. To cut out the pattern pieces, open the scissors and slide the sharp edge of the lower blade along the underside of the fur to part the hairs. Take care to cut only through the backing.

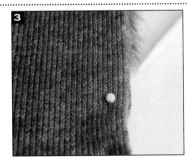

3. Before sewing any bear pieces together (right or furry sides together), tuck in any stray hairs using the tip of a knitting needle and pin through both layers to prevent shifting.

4. Turn pieces right side out, then use the tip of a knitting needle to pick out hairs caught in the seams.

Pattern Pieces to Cut from Fur

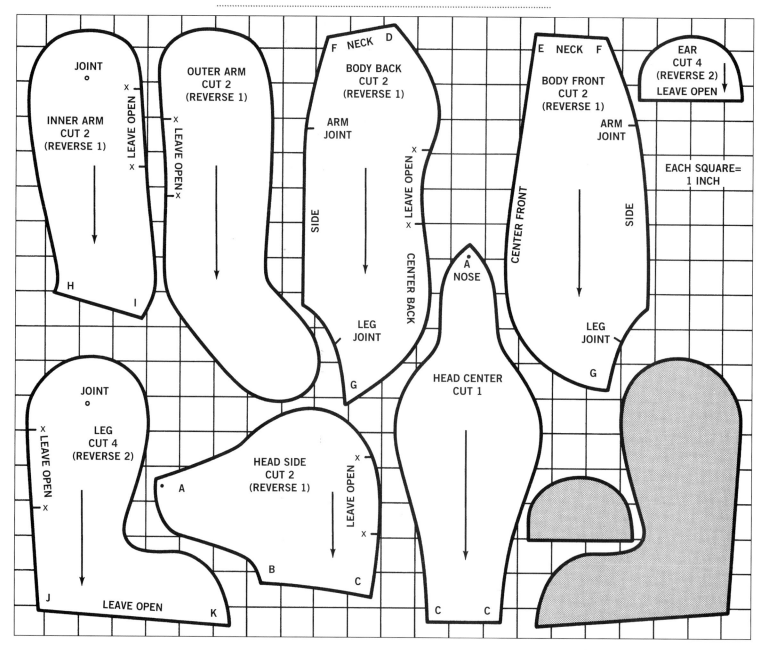

JOINT
○

**INNER ARM
CUT 2
(REVERSE 1)**

x
x
LEAVE OPEN
x

x
X LEAVE OPEN
x

H
I

**OUTER ARM
CUT 2
(REVERSE 1)**

F **NECK** D

**BODY BACK
CUT 2
(REVERSE 1)**

**ARM
JOINT**

SIDE

X **LEAVE OPEN**
x

CENTER BACK

**LEG
JOINT**

G

E **NECK** F

**BODY FRONT
CUT 2
(REVERSE 1)**

**ARM
JOINT**

CENTER FRONT

SIDE

**LEG
JOINT**

G

**EAR
CUT 4
(REVERSE 2)
LEAVE OPEN**
↓

**EACH SQUARE=
1 INCH**

A
NOSE

**HEAD CENTER
CUT 1**

JOINT
○

**LEG
CUT 4
(REVERSE 2)**

x
LEAVE OPEN
x

J

LEAVE OPEN

K

•A

**HEAD SIDE
CUT 2
(REVERSE 1)**

B

C

x
LEAVE OPEN
x

C C

This diagram serves two purposes: it includes the pattern pieces for enlarging, and serves as a placement diagram for cutting out the pieces. When enlarging, omit the shaded pieces for a total of eight enlarged pieces. To cut out the pieces from the fur, arrange them as shown in the diagram, with the arrows on the pattern running in the direction of the fur nap.

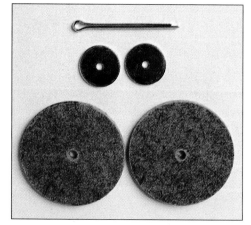

The joint set consists of three kinds of pieces: the cotter pin (top), the metal washers (middle), and the hardboard joints (bottom).

fur backing, take care to pin only through the fur backing. Pins should not show on the right (furry) side of the fabric.)

You must cut two each of the following pieces in mirror image—the inner and outer arm, the body front and back, and the head sides. To cut a mirror image pair, lay out the pattern pieces following the cutting diagram, and cut out and mark each piece. Then remove the pattern pieces from the fur, turn over each piece, and lay them out again, following the cutting diagram, on the remaining fur backing. (If you are sewing this bear from a fabric with-

out a thick napped pile, such as wool, you can fold the fabric in half, lay out the pattern pieces as shown, and cut out two of each piece at once. Because of the pile, however, this approach will not work with fur. Instead, you must cut out each piece individually.)

You will also need to cut two mirror images of the legs and ears, for a total of four legs and four ears. (The placement for the extra leg and ear are indicated by the shaded pattern piece on the diagram.) You'll cut only one head center.

When you are ready to cut out the pattern pieces, open your scissors and slide the sharp

PATTERN BY ROBERTA FRAUWIRTH, PHOTOGRAPH BY RICHARD FELBER

edge of the lower blade along the underside of the fur in order to part the hairs. Cut only through the backing, taking care to leave the long hairs intact.

When sewing fur, care must be taken not to stitch the hair into the seam, or to remove the hair from the seam once sewn. Before sewing, and after right (furry) sides have been placed together, tuck any stray hairs inside using the tip of a knitting needle, then pin through both layers to prevent shifting. After sewing and turning the pieces right side out, use the tip of a knitting needle to pick out and separate any hairs caught in the seams.

When stuffing the bear's body, you can use a variety of fillers, depending on the desired look and feel. I used polyfill; you can stuff it as loosely or as densely as you like. Fabric scraps will add weight and give the bear a lumpy, older look, but it will not be easily shaped. Pellets will make the bear very poseable and heavy, somewhat like a bean bag. The head is best stuffed with polyfill.

COLLECTIBLE TEDDY BEAR

1 ½ yard 45" or 60" brown fur or natural mohair, ⅜" to ½" pile
1 8" x 11" piece brown wool fabric or felt
1 9" x 13" piece white cotton broadcloth
1 spool brown sewing thread
1 spool white sewing thread
1 spool brown heavy-duty button, craft, or carpet thread
5 2" hardboard doll joint sets
1 12-ounce package polyfill (or filling of choice)
1 pair 8mm black glass eyes
1 skein size 3 black or dark brown perle cotton
1 ½ yard 1"-wide burgundy ribbon

You'll also need: Access to copy machine; scissors; quilter's 1¾" ball-head pins; felt-tip permanent marker; knitting needle; sewing machine; hand sewing needle; iron; ruler; safey pin; needle-nose pliers; and 5" dollmaking needle.

Enlarging and Cutting Pattern Pieces

1. Make a copy of entire pattern diagram on page 18 and pattern above. Cut out each piece. Enlarge each piece individually until grid squares measure 1" square. Trim any excess paper off pattern pieces.

2. Determine fur nap. Lay fur wrong side (backing side) up. Following diagram on page 18, arrange appropriate pattern pieces on fur backing so nap arrow on pieces matches nap of fur. Pin pieces in position, slipping each pin through fur backing only.

3. Cut out pattern pieces, taking care to only cut through backing. Turn up outside edges of pieces slightly, and transfer any markings from

PAW PAD AND COLLAR PATTERNS

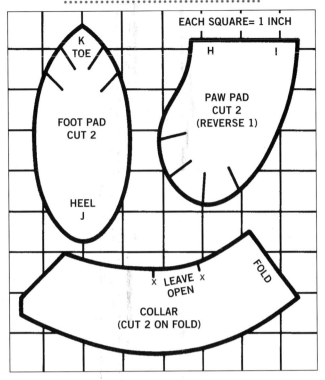

Enlarge the pattern pieces for the paw pads and collar and cut them from felt and broadcloth, respectively.

piece to fur backing using marker. If necessary, remove pins, reposition or reverse piece, and re-cut duplicate or quadruplicate pieces; transfer any markings to fur backing. When finished, you should have 2 head sides, 1 head center, 4 ears, 2 body fronts, 2 body backs, 2 outer arms, 2 inner arms, and 4 legs.

4. Pin paw pad and foot pad pattern pieces in place on brown wool or felt and cut out. Transfer any markings to cut pieces. Position and pin collar pattern piece on folded cotton broadcloth and cut out two pieces; transfer any pattern markings to cut collar.

Sewing the Bear

Sew together bear pieces as directed below. For all pieces, place fabric right sides (furry sides) together, tuck any stray hairs in using tip of knitting needle, and pin through both layers to prevent shifting. Sew ¼" from edges using brown sewing thread. Be sure to leave areas between "x's" open. After turning pieces right side out, use blunt tip of knitting needle to pick out and separate hairs caught in seams.

Sewing the Bear's Head

1. Sew head sides together from A to B to form chin.

2. Sew head center to each head side from C to A, matching dots and pivoting at A to form nose. Leave area open between "x's" on one head side piece only. Turn head right side out.

3. Sew ears together in pairs along curved

edges; leave straight edges open. Turn right side out.

Sewing the Bear's Body

1. Sew body backs together from points D to G.

2. Sew body fronts together from points E to G.

3. Matching seams and joint marks, sew body front to body back at sides from F to G. Turn right side out.

Sewing the Bear's Arms

1. For each arm, sew paw pad to inner arm along straight edge between points H and I.

2. Sew each outer arm to inner arm. Turn right side out.

Sewing the Bear's Legs

1. Sew legs together in pairs along curved edges from points J to K. Leave straight edges (between points J and K) open.

2. Machine baste around edge of each foot pad. Pull thread ends slightly to take up ease. Sew each pad to leg, matching points J and K. Turn right side out. Remove basting if desired.

Assembling the Bear

1. Arrange bear's body, head, arms, and legs on flat surface. Using brown heavy-duty thread, hand-sew a running stitch around neck openings of head and body. Pull thread ends to gather each neck opening closed into a tight circle. Tie off ends.

2. Separate hardboard doll joint into following pieces: washers, disks, and cotter pin. (*See* photograph, page 18.) Slip washer and then disk onto cotter pin. Insert cotter pin into side opening of head and out through neck opening of head so disk lodges firmly inside neck.

3. Insert cotter pin into neck opening of body.

4. Turn body inside out so it surrounds head. Place second hardboard disk then washer on cotter pin.

5. Use illustrations 5A through 5C on page 20 as guide for next few procedures.

A) Slide all disks and washers down cotter pin, compressing fur in between as tightly as you can. Hold this "sandwich" with one hand.

B) With free hand, use needle-nose pliers to separate and flare cotter pin prongs into a narrow "V" shape. Bend tip (about ⅛") of each prong in toward center at right angle.

C) Bend each prong backwards (away from center) in a sharp upside-down "U," so flattened tips rest on washer surface. If cotter pin is bent correctly, joint should be snug with

Assembling the Bear

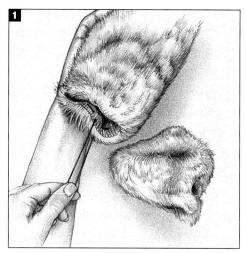

1. Using brown heavy-duty thread, hand-sew a running stitch around the neck openings of the head and body. Pull the thread ends to gather each neck opening closed and tie off the ends.

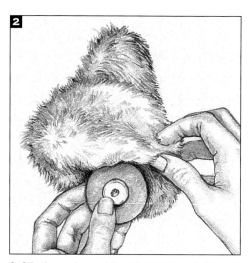

2. Slip the washer and then the hardboard disk onto the cotter pin. Insert the cotter pin into the side opening of the head and back out through the neck opening so the disk lodges firmly inside the neck.

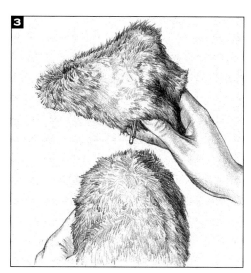

3. Insert the cotter pin into the neck opening of the body.

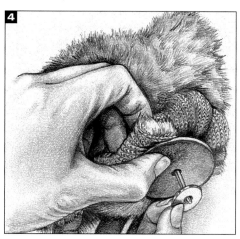

4. Turn the body inside out so it surrounds the head. Place the second hardboard disk and then the washer on the cotter pin.

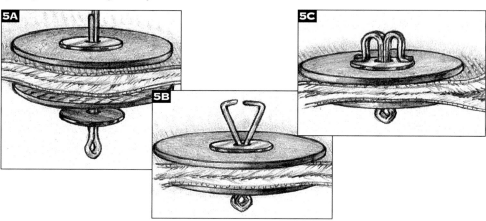

5. (A) Slide all of the disks and washers down the cotter pin, compressing the fur as tightly as you can. (B) With your free hand, use a needle-nose pliers to separate and flare the cotter pin prongs into a narrow "V" shape. Bend the tip (about ⅛") of each prong in toward the center at a right angle. (C) Bend each prong backwards (away from the center) in a sharp upside-down "U," so the flattened tips rest on the washer surface.

Stuffing the Bear

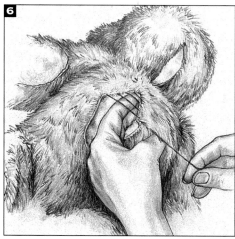

6. Hand-sew all openings closed with brown thread.

Sewing the Claws

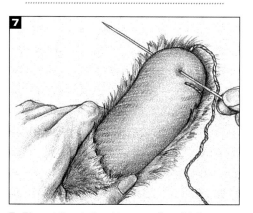

7. Thread the dollmaking needle with brown or black perle cotton and sew four or five straight stitches about ½" in each paw and foot pad. Pull the thread snug after each stitch.

Attaching the Ears

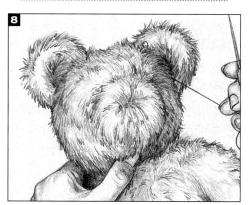

8. Position the bear's ears so each straddles a side seam. Cup each ear slightly toward the bear's face, secure with pins, and sew in place using small, firm stitches.

ILLUSTRATIONS BY JUDITH LOVE, PHOTOGRAPH BY STEVEN MAYS

a "stiff" swivel.

6. To join arms and legs to body, start by turning an upper arm partially inside out, enough to reveal joint mark on inner arm. Slip washer and then disk on cotter pin, and push cotter pin through joint mark and out fur side. Turn right side out, concealing disk inside arm. Locate corresponding joint mark on bear body (paws should face inside and forward). Push cotter pin through fur to inside, slip disk and then washer onto pin, and bend cotter pin into position as noted in step 5 and illustrations 5A through 5C on page 20. Attach remaining limbs the same way, making sure feet face forward.

Stuffing the Bear and Sewing Pad Claws

1. Insert stuffing into arms and legs and push down firmly into paws and toes. Pad stuffing around disks at upper arms and thighs to mask hard edges. When limbs are fully stuffed, stuff body and head.

2. Hand-sew all openings closed with brown thread. Use blunt tip of knitting needle to free hairs caught in stitches.

3. Thread 5" dollmaking needle with 36" length of brown or black perle cotton and knot end. Insert needle into seam, give sharp tug to lodge knot in batting, and make four or five straight stitches about ½" in each paw and foot pad. Pull thread snug after each stitch to indent surface and simulate claws.

Creating the Bear's Face

The most expressive feature of any bear is, of course, the face. The expression depends on the tilt of the ears, the position of the eyes, and the stitching used for the nose. Don't be concerned if your bear is slightly different from the one pictured here—the variations will give your bear a personality of its own.

1. To attach ears, turn raw edges of each ear ¼" to inside and whipstitch opening closed. Position ears on head so each one straddles a side seam at its highest point. Cup each ear slightly towards the face, and secure with pins. Sew in place with brown thread, using small, firm stitches.

NOSE AND MOUTH OPTIONS

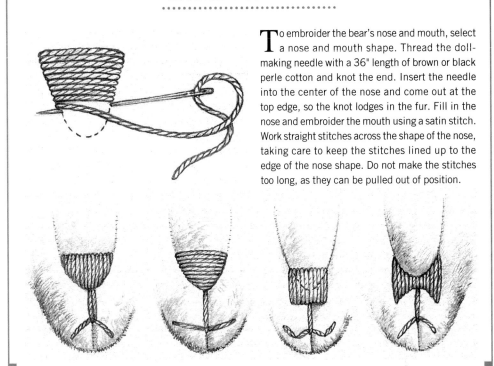

To embroider the bear's nose and mouth, select a nose and mouth shape. Thread the doll-making needle with a 36" length of brown or black perle cotton and knot the end. Insert the needle into the center of the nose and come out at the top edge, so the knot lodges in the fur. Fill in the nose and embroider the mouth using a satin stitch. Work straight stitches across the shape of the nose, taking care to keep the stitches lined up to the edge of the nose shape. Do not make the stitches too long, as they can be pulled out of position.

2. To attach glass eyes, hold eyes on or near face side seams to test position and pin in place. Eyes may appear closer together after sewing, so allow more space between them than may look natural.

3. Thread dollmaking needle with 36" length of brown heavy-duty thread, double over thread, and knot end. Following diagram at right, insert needle into bear head at 2 and draw it out at 1, lodging knot in fur. Slip on eye shank. Reinsert needle at 1 and draw out at 2 to secure first eye. Sew second eye at 2 in same manner. Carry needle back and forth several times between 1 and 2, catching eye shanks on each pass; end at 2. Slip needle through shank, reinsert at 2, and come out at 3, just below ear. Reinsert needle at 3 and come out at 2, pulling thread snug to indent eye. Reinsert at 2 and come out at 4. Repeat stitching sequence to indent eye on right side. Check eyes to make sure they are even, and make additional stitches if necessary. End stitching at 4 and knot thread.

4. To embroider the bear's nose and mouth, select a nose and mouth shape from illustrations above.

5. Thread dollmaking needle with 36" length of brown or black perle cotton and knot end. Insert needle into center of nose and come out at top edge, so knot lodges in fur. Fill in nose and embroider mouth using satin stitch. Work straight stitches across shape of nose, taking care to keep stitches lined up to edge of nose shape. Do not make stitches too long, as they can be pulled out of position.

Attaching the Eyes

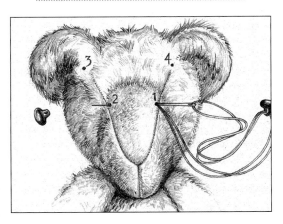

To attach the bear's right eye, insert a threaded needle at 2 and draw it out 1; slip on the eye shank and re-insert the needle at 1.

Adding the Collar

1. Place collar pieces right sides together and sew around shape with white thread, leaving area between "x's" open for turning collar inside out. Clip corners and curves; turn right side out. Pick out corners with pin, stitch opening closed with white thread, and press.

2. Fit collar around bear. Sew top corners together under chin with white thread. Tie ribbon into bow and attach to collar front with small safety pin. ◆

Pat Castka, a professional seamstress, specializes in teddy bear designs.

Apple Harvest Pie with Decorative Crust

Use ordinary cookie cutters to create apple and leaf shapes for quick pie decorations.

Whether you're an experienced baker or a beginning cook, your apple pies needn't look ordinary. Using this simple design and two aluminum cookie cutters, you can create a sumptuous, edible pie top that resembles a work of art. Apply the crust to an apple pie made with the *Cook's Illustrated* recipe provided on page 23, or decorate a pie made with your own favorite recipe.

The pastry recipe included with this project yields enough dough for an 8" or 9" double-crust pie, as well as the decorations for the top. If you only need pastry for the decorations, use a third of the recipe. Because this recipe uses only a small amount of water, the dough is delicate and may tear when handled. If this happens, simply patch it using a small dab of water. Once the pie is cooked, the patches won't show.

Although most of the leaves will be applied directly to the pie before cooking, five or six leaves will be cooked separately on a tube of foil. Once both these leaves and the pie are cooked, make a small opening with a knife, then insert the leaves into the pie top to give height and three-dimensionality.

APPLE HARVEST PIE TOP

1 uncooked 9" double-crust apple pie and extra pastry dough (*see* "The Best Apple Pie" and "Perfect Pie Pastry," page 23)
2 tablespoons white flour
1 egg
½ cup heavy cream

You'll also need: pastry brush; two 2½" round cookie cutters; aluminum foil; waxed paper; paring knife or sharp wooden skewer; rolling pin; spatula; fork or whisk; and 2 cookie sheets.

1. Adjust oven rack to lowest position and pre-

You can create this decorative pie top using a pair of ordinary cookie cutters. Bend one into the shape of a leaf; use the second as is to stamp out apples.

heat oven to 350 degrees.

2. Sprinkle 2 tablespoons white flower on flat, clean counter surface or cutting board. With rolling pin, roll out extra pastry dough to thickness of ⅛".

3. Cut out 2 circles using round cookie cutter. To form apples, indent top and bottom slightly with thumb and first finger. Transfer to cookie sheet using spatula, cover with waxed paper, and refrigerate until ready for use.

4. To bend second cookie cutter into leaf shape, pinch on two opposite sides using thumb and first finger. Hold against leaf template at

left to further refine shape. As the cookie cutter is slightly larger than the resulting leaf, you may end up with "leftover" cookie cutter. Bend this unused portion to side of oval leaf shape. Cut out 35 leaves, gathering up pastry scraps and re-rolling dough as necessary.

5. Using template as guide, scribe veins on leaves using tip of paring knife or point of a wooden skewer.

6. To make glaze, beat egg until foamy using fork or whisk. When foamy, mix in cream using fork or whisk.

7. Roll a large piece of foil into a 5" to 6"

LEAF TEMPLATE BY ROBERTA FRAUWIRTH, PHOTOGRAPH BY STEVEN MAYS

Perfect Pie Pastry

BY CHRISTOPHER KIMBALL

This recipe and a full discussion of pie pastry can be found in the September/October 1994 issue of *Cook's Illustrated*.

3½ cups all-purpose flour
1½ teaspoons salt
3 tablespoons sugar
16 tablespoons (2 sticks) chilled unsalted butter cut into ¼" pieces
11 tablespoons chilled all-vegetable shortening
6–9 tablespoons ice water
Food processor

1. Mix flour, salt, and sugar in food processor fitted with steel blade. Scatter butter pieces over flour mixture, tossing to coat butter with a little flour. Cut butter into flour with five 1-second pulses. Add shortening and continue cutting in until flour is pale yellow and resembles coarse cornmeal with butter bits no larger than small peas (about four more 1-second pulses). Turn mixture into medium bowl.

2. Sprinkle 5 tablespoons of ice water over mixture. With blade of rubber spatula, use folding motion to mix. Press down on dough with broad side of spatula until dough sticks together, adding 1 to 4 tablespoons more water if dough will not come together. Divide dough into three parts, one slightly larger than others. Shape into balls with your hands, then flatten into 4"-wide discs. Dust lightly with flour, wrap in plastic, and refrigerate for 30 minutes before rolling to thickness of about ⅛".

long tube, about 1" wide, and place on second cookie sheet. Lay 5 or 6 leaves over tube to make them curve. Brush with glaze using pastry brush, and put cookie sheet into oven for 15 minutes, or until leaves are brown. When done, set aside to cool until ready to put on cooked pie. Turn up oven to 400 degrees.

8. Add lifelike folds and shape to remaining 29 or 30 leaves by pinching tips with index finger and thumb. Transfer each leaf to cookie sheet, cover with waxed paper, and refrigerate until ready for placement.

9. Cut 2 strips of dough measuring ¼" wide by 2" long to be used as stems. Transfer to cookie sheet, cover with waxed paper, and refrigerate until ready for use.

10. Using pastry brush, glaze top of pie. Working along outside perimeter, arrange 12 to 14 leaves in a ring. Add a second ring of 12 to 14 leaves, positioning them between and overlapping the leaves already in place. Further shape each leaf as desired.

11. When second ring of leaves is in place, position 2 dough apples in center of pie. Using photograph on page 22 as guide, add stems and remaining leaves. Lightly brush entire pie with glaze. Cut 4 to 6 slits in pie top to allow steam to escape.

12. Cover top of pie with sheet of foil and bake 15 minutes; remove foil and bake another 10 minutes. Reduce oven temperature to 350 degrees, and continue baking until crust is rich golden brown and apples can be pierced easily with knife, about 50 minutes. Transfer pie to wire rack and cool for at least 1 hour before serving. Position leaves cooked on foil tube on top of pie by making a small opening with knife and inserting stem portion into pie. ◆

The Best Apple Pie

BY STEVEN SCHMIDT

For this pie, the apples are macerated in sugar so they shrink slightly before rather than during baking. This pie is best when consumed within a few hours of baking, but can be stored at room temperature, covered by an inverted bowl, for a day or two. This recipe also appears in the September/October 1994 issue of *Cook's Illustrated*.

2½ pounds (5 to 6) Granny Smith apples, peeled, quartered, cored, and cut into ⅜" slices (5 to 6 cups)
¾ cup sugar
2 tablespoons all-purpose flour
½ teaspoon ground cinnamon
Pinch of salt
Perfect Pie Pastry, left
2 tablespoons unsalted butter, cut into small pieces

1. Toss first 5 ingredients in large bowl; let stand until apples soften and shrink a bit, 10 to 15 minutes.

2. Roll larger dough disc on a lightly floured surface into a 12" circle, about ⅛" thick. Transfer dough to 9" Pyrex pie pan, leaving dough that overhangs lip of pan in place. Turn apple mixture, including juices, into shell; scatter butter over apples.

3. Roll smaller dough disc on lightly floured surface into 10" circle. Lay over top of pie. Trim top and bottom dough edges to ¼" beyond pan lip. Tuck this rim of dough underneath so that folded edge is flush with pan lip. Flute dough in your own fashion, or press with fork tines to seal.

MAKING THE PIE'S DECORATIVE ELEMENTS

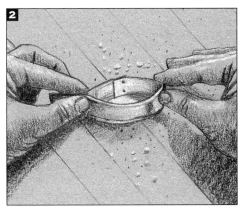

1. Shape the circles of dough into apples by indenting the top and bottom.

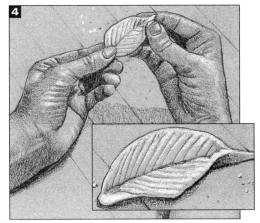

2. Pinch opposite sides of the second round cookie cutter into an oval shape; refine as necessary by holding up to the leaf template on page 22.

3. Scribe the leaf veins using the tip of a paring knife or sharp wooden skewer.

4. To add realistic folds, hold the leaf in one hand and gently shape it with your other hand.

Three Simple Napkin Folds

Folded napkins dress up a table and hold small favors, place cards, or flowers.

BY GENEVIEVE A. STERBENZ

Each of these folded napkin designs was created with several objectives in mind. In addition to dressing up a formal table, each also holds a small favor or gift, a place card, or a miniature bouquet of dried or fresh flowers. I chose napkin folds which appear difficult, but which are, in reality, quite simple and straightforward.

The Tulip Fold, below, holds a small wrapped gift or favor, while the Deco Fold, on page 25, holds a place card or personal note. The Fanfare Fold, also on page 25, can be decorated with a small cluster of dried flowers; I chose roses and boxwood.

For best results, first practice each fold with paper to avoid creasing or wrinkling your napkin. Then starch your napkins with an iron at the hottest possible setting until they are perfectly flat and square at the corners. I used 15" polyester napkins for these designs. In general, cotton or linen napkins are easier to fold; polyester and polyester blends may require extra starch in order to hold their folds, but the result is worth the added effort.

Tulip Fold

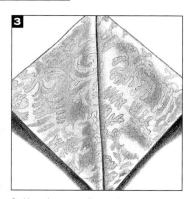

3. Keeping your finger in place at the center, fold the left point down and in to meet the bottom point.

4. Bring the top point down to within 1" of the bottom point.

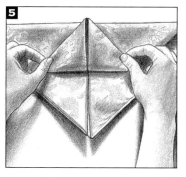

5. Fold the same point up to the center point of the top straight edge.

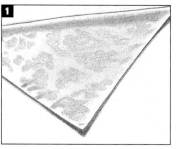

6. Turn the napkin over so that the folded point from step 5 faces the work surface. Hold the right corner in your right hand and the left corner in your left hand. Bring the corners together at the center, then tuck the left corner inside the right fold. If necessary, hold the tucked corners in place with a paperclip.

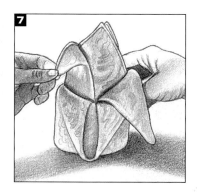

7. Hold the napkin at the tuck, stand it upright on the table, and shape so the base is rounded. Pull down the right folded edge to form the first petal. Repeat with the left folded edge. Insert your fingers between the top points and push the back rear layer to form the gift pouch.

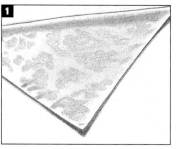

1. Lay the napkin flat and position it as a diamond shape. (If using a napkin with right and wrong sides, position it with the wrong side up.) Bring the top point down, folding the napkin in half to form a triangle.

2. Place your finger at the top center. Fold the right point down and in to meet the bottom point.

ILLUSTRATIONS BY WENDY WRAY, PHOTOGRAPHS BY STEVEN MAYS

Deco Fold

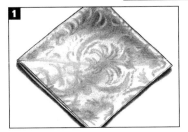

1. Fold the napkin in half to form a rectangle, then fold in half again to form a square. (If using a napkin with right and wrong sides, begin with the wrong side up.) Position as a diamond shape with the open points at the bottom.

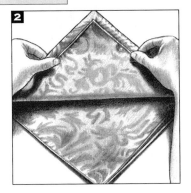

2. Fold up the first bottom point to within ¾" of the top point.

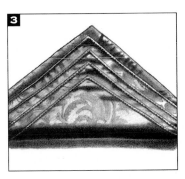

3. Fold up the second point to within ¾" of the first point; repeat with the third and fourth points.

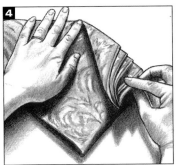

4. Turn the napkin over so the points are face down on the table and pointing toward you. Place your finger at the center of the top edge and fold it down to the middle of the right edge.

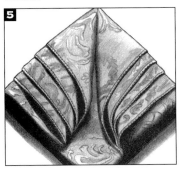

5. With your finger still in the center, fold over the left point to match the right.

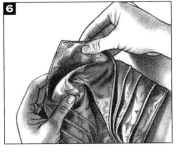

6. To form the pocket for the place card, hold the bottom of the napkin in your left hand. With your right hand, pull up on one layer of the material from the back of the napkin.

7. Rotate the napkin so the pocket is facing toward you; fold the top portion to finish the pocket. Arrange the place card as shown.

Fanfare Fold

1. Position the napkin as a square. (If using a napkin with right and wrong sides, position it with the wrong side up.) Fold it in half, right side over left.

2. Fold up 1" of the bottom edge and smooth the fold with your fingers. Holding 1" fold at each side, form accordion pleats to within 3½" of the top edge.

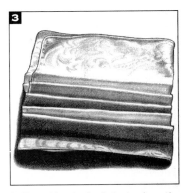

3. Press the stack of pleats along the folds using your fingertips.

4. Stack the pleats face down on the table, with an extra 3½" of the napkin on top of the stack. Hold the pleats in the middle and bring the right side over the left.

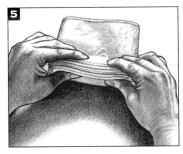

5. Hold the folded stack in both of your hands and squeeze it tightly to further crease the folds.

6. Rotate the creased napkin so the folds stand vertically. Place your finger at the top edge of the pleats and fold the top right corner of the extra 3½" of material down to form a triangle. Run your fingers along the fold to crease. Repeat this with the opposite side. (These two folds will support the fan when the napkin is standing up. If necessary, hold the two folds together with a paper clip.) Using the color photograph as reference, stand the folded napkin upright on the table and slowly release the pleats, one side at a time, allowing them to fan outwards. Arrange the dried roses and boxwood as shown.

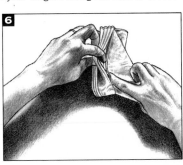

Belle Epoque Frame

Transform an ordinary frame into a nineteenth century masterpiece using beading and silk flowers.

The silk flowers on this frame are stiffened with a setting agent, arranged in a draped swag, and finished with gold paint and rottenstone.

Elaborately hand-carved or molded gold frames were a common sight in late nineteenth century homes. These belle epoque frames combined the neoclassical geometry of a rectangular frame with the softening effects of draped floral bouquets, garlands, or exuberant scrollwork.

Recreating the look and feel of such opulence is deceptively simple. This gold-finish frame was assembled using an ordinary frame and mat, silk flowers, beading, and gold paint. To stiffen the flowers, use Petal Porcelain setting agent, which transforms everyday artificial flowers into hard, plastic-like facsimiles. Once the flowers are stiffened and arranged, finishing the frame is as simple as applying gold paint and various aging agents.

Artificial or silk-look flowers come in many shapes, sizes, colors, and brands. For specific examples of the flowers used in this project, *see* "Buying the Flowers," at right. Almost any artificial flower may be used, but avoid blooms with frayed or crumpled edges, and steer clear of flocked flowers, as they will absorb too much setting agent.

Choose a mat with a textured finish as this will be aesthetically pleasing and help hide stray glue marks.

BELLE EPOQUE FRAME

1 16" x 20" wood or plastic frame, any color
1 16" x 20" mat with oval opening measuring 10½" x 13½"
2 yards bead strand, ⅛" or 3mm diameter, any color
1 8-ounce jar Petal Porcelain setting agent
   Various silk flowers with leaves (*see* "Buying the Flowers," below, for details)
1 12-ounce can spray-on primer
1 12-ounce can gold spray paint
1 1-pound box rottenstone
½ fluid ounce Rub n' Buff, gold color

You'll also need: cotton flannel or other soft cloth rags; Q-tips; clean sponges; 4 same size pieces scrap wood at least 1" high; scissors; newspaper; fine-point marker; ruler; latex gloves; ⅜"-diameter round brush with stiff bristles or ⅜"-wide stiff strip of cardboard; stiff ¾" brush; 1" soft round paintbrush; high-tack craft glue; mineral spirits or turpentine; and 2 wide, shallow bowls.

Other items, if necessary: tweezers (for inserting leaves); 4 cans soup or canned vegetables (for frames without clips to hold mat in place while glue dries); 1 sheet 220 grit sandpaper (for removing dirt, rust, or debris from frame).

Preparing the Frame

1. Cover work space with newspapers. Lay frame face down. Remove clips or staples holding cardboard and glass. Remove cardboard and glass from frame; set aside glass in safe place. If necessary, clean any dirt, rust, or loose paint from frame using sandpaper or cloth dampened with mineral spirits. If using plastic frame, lightly rough up surface with sandpaper. Wipe frame with dry cloth or rag to remove dust or mineral spirits.

2. Squeeze a ⅛"-wide line of glue along inside ledge of frame (where glass sits) on all four sides. Spread glue evenly along ledge using ⅜" round brush or strip of stiff cardboard. Place mat, textured side or face down, into frame; run a finger along edge of mat to ensure adhesion. If frame uses clips to hold glass in place, reinsert clips while glue is drying. If frame

does not use clips, place a soup or vegetable can at each corner of mat**.** Let dry ½ hour.

3. Remove cans or clips and flip frame over. Remove drips of glue from front of mat or frame with damp sponge. (Do not use too wet a sponge or too vigorous a scrubbing motion to remove drips, as either may damage mat.) Place frame face down until dry (½ hour).

4. Turn frame face up. Cut two 20" and two 16" lengths of bead strand to fit each side of frame. Check fit carefully, and if necessary trim until each strand fits perfectly. Holding glue bottle at 45-degree angle, squeeze a ⅛"-wide line of glue along one inside edge of frame where it meets mat. Push beaded strand into glue with finger until whole strand is embedded in glue. Holding one end of strand with fingertip, drag damp sponge along beaded strand to remove excess glue. Repeat process for each side of frame. Let frame dry at least 1 hour, or until glue is completely clear.

5. Always wear latex gloves and work in a well ventilated area when using spray paint. To

BUYING THE FLOWERS

For this project you will need the following artificial flowers (including their leaves), or their equivalents (clockwise starting at bottom left and ending with the center): One 1½"-diameter large single rose and 2 medium of same type rose (not shown); 22 small "dried look" roses (3 stems); 12 bellflowers (1 or 2 stems); 1 bunch paper rosebuds, 12 buds per bunch; 3 small roses (1 stem); one 1¾"-diameter large single rose; and one 2"-diameter large single rose.

To decorate swags, position roses first, followed by bellflowers.

The corner cluster is made up of a medium-sized rose, a small rose, and a bellflower.

prevent frame from sticking to paper after painting, prop frame, face up, on top of scrap wood pieces, one at each corner. Spray front of frame with primer. For best results, hold spray can nearly upright, 8" to 10" away from frame, and move evenly across surface. Let dry thoroughly, following paint manufacturer's recommended drying times.

6. When frame is dry, locate garland swag by marking midpoint on top inside edge of frame (it will be about 7¾" from sides). Using illustration 2 as guide, draw smooth, symmetrical arcs from midpoint mark to each side.

Preparing and Positioning the Flowers

1. For the following steps, work in an area where the frame can be left undisturbed overnight. Lay frame face up on several sheets of newsprint. Undo bundle of paper rose buds. Separate stems and set aside. For remaining flowers, pull flower heads off stems or use scissors to clip stems approximately ¼" from head. Clip or pull off rose leaf sets (3 leaves per set), leaving a ¼" to 1½" stem. Clip bellflowers off about ¼" from head.

2. Organize flowers and leaves into following groups. For center crown cluster use 3 large roses, 1 small rose, 2 paper rosebuds, and 2 large rose leaf sets. For each swag use 10 small "dried look" roses, 5 bellflowers, 5 paper rosebuds, and 5 medium rose leaf sets. For each lower right and left cluster use 1 medium rose, 1 small "dried-look" rose, 1 small rose, 1 bellflower, and 1 small rose leaf set.

3. Pour 1½" setting agent into wide shallow bowl. Replenish as necessary to maintain depth. Fill second bowl with water for washing fingers. Starting with flowers for corner clusters, dip flower heads into setting agent, holding flower head by stem stub. Squeeze out excess setting agent with fingertips by rolling flower between fingers. Using close-up of frame as guide, position medium rose at outside edge, followed by smaller rose and single bellflower. Adjust petals and position as desired. Tap each flower lightly into place.

4. Repeat process with leaves. To remove excess setting agent on leaves, drag between two fingers. Position leaves using fingers or

tweezers, tucking each leaf under floral cluster so points peek out. Repeat process with other corner cluster. If setting agent drips onto frame or mat, remove with wet Q-tips or damp sponge. Remove fingerprints with damp sponge.

5. To place flowers on swag, repeat steps 3 and 4, starting with top left side. After dipping flowers in setting agent and squeezing, place largest roses at lowest point of arcs, followed by roses of varying sizes on remaining portion of swag. Insert bellflowers between roses. Place small paper rose at outer end of swag. Position 1 leaf set under paper rose so it extends beyond edge of frame. Hold 3 paper rosebuds by wire stems at different heights and twist together. Dip in setting agent, squeeze excess setting agent from flowers, and place below rose at endpoint.

6. To create central floral cluster, dip, squeeze, and place 2 medium roses directly above frame's edge at top center point. Position largest rose between other two, followed by small rose at bottom of cluster. Tuck in several leaves. Wire together two paper rosebuds at different lengths and place under center of cluster, hanging slightly below top of oval opening of mat.

7. After all flowers have been placed, remove pools or drops of setting agent from mat and frame using wet Q-tips or damp sponge. Clean up brushes, bowls, and surfaces with soap and water. Let frame dry. When setting agent is dry, individual petals will be stiff and solidly in place. If any flowers come loose from frame, glue in place using high-tack glue, and let dry at least ½ day longer.

Finishing the Frame

1. To cover flowers with primer, repeat appropriate portions of step 5 from "Preparing the Frame," page 26. To reach crevices and areas between flowers, use short spurts of spray, depressing and releasing nozzle quickly. Shake can between spurts. When flowers are covered with primer, set aside to dry at least ½ hour.

2. Apply two coats of gold spray paint, allowing at least 10 minutes between each coat. After final coat, let dry at least 4 hours.

1. Holding the glue at a 45-degree angle, squeeze a narrow line of glue along one inside edge. Push a beaded strand into the glue with your finger until the whole strand is embedded in the glue.

2. When the frame is dry, locate the garland swag by marking the midpoint on the top inside edge of the frame (it will be about 7¾" from the sides). Then mark a point on each side of the frame even with the top of the oval opening. Using the illustration as a guide, draw smooth, symmetrical arcs from the midpoint mark to the marks on each side.

3. Position the leaves using your fingers or tweezers, tucking each leaf under the floral cluster so the points peek out.

3. To add brighter gold highlights, apply Rub n' Buff to frame with fingertip; apply to flowers with stiff ¾" brush. Buff to a high shine using a soft cloth. Burnish flowers with clean, stiff brush or Q-tips. Clean up using mineral spirits or turpentine.

4. Work in a well-ventilated area, protected from wind. Load 1" soft brush with rottenstone and dust entire surface generously, working it into crevices. Remove excess rottenstone from face of mat and high relief areas with cotton flannel or soft cloth rag. Replace glass behind mat if framing a print or a photograph. Leave glass out if framing a painting. ◆

How to Make Marbled Paper

Decorate paper with a stone pattern by floating acrylic paint on water.

BY LAURA SIMS

This article will teach you how to create a stone pattern, the most basic of all marbling patterns. It's possible to create hundreds of variations from the stone pattern by varying the type of paint, the colors, the order in which the colors are applied, the color paper used, or how the paint is manipulated. Marbling is like the ocean—you can enjoy the surface, or take it to any depth.

No one formula will ever produce the exact same print, but therein lies one of the great appeals of marbling. As a marbler and teacher for eight years, I have found marbling to be a nonthreatening means of introducing people to the creative process. I encourage you to experiment with color, sequence, and movement before marbling the "keeper" sheet of paper, the one you finally use. Once you've marbled that keeper sheet, use it to embellish anything from a book cover to desk accessories to a lampshade, a small box, or a picture mat.

The techniques for marbling paper, in various forms, have existed for hundreds of years. In principle, the process involves floating paint on a liquid surface and transferring the design to paper. I've broken down that process into four basic parts: preparing a marbling bath, floating paint on the bath, preparing and laying paper into the bath, and drying the paper.

Every marbling project starts with the bath, in this case a mix of carrageenan (a pre-cooked, powdered seaweed) and tap water. The carrageenan thickens the marbling bath to control the movement of the paint. Once the bath is prepared, specks of paint are dropped onto the surface using a marbling whisk, and the paint immediately spreads and forms translucent "stones" of color on the surface of the bath. (The last color applied generally becomes the most dominant color, as the first colors are pushed into veins.)

Before floating the paper on the surface of the bath, coat it with alum to improve paint adhesion. Alum, short for aluminum sulfate, is available in craft and dye supply stores and some pharmacies. When dry, it is safe to touch. However, I recommend wearing latex gloves when using alum, as it can be absorbed into the skin. Because it is used in septic systems, it can be disposed of down the drain.

For this project I've used jars, versus tubes of Liquitex paints, because I found the liquid paints easier and quicker to mix. If you use tube paints, they are more concentrated, and may

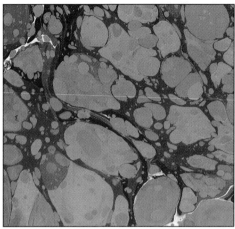

To create this stone pattern, paint was dropped onto the water's surface using a whisk.

need more mixing to avoid clumping. (You may also substitute such paints as Ceramacoat or Folkart, but all paints mix and spread differently, so you may need to experiment.) Virtually all marbling requires pre-mixing of paints, as pigment straight from the jar is usually too harsh. Take a look at the color sample above, and notice that most of the colors are diluted. All of these tones can be created by mixing in varying amounts of white or black. (The mixing recipes for the stone pattern pictured are found below.)

For best results, keep the paints and the marbling bath at room temperature, no less than 60 degrees and no more than 80 degrees. This helps ensure that the paints form smooth stones on the surface of the bath.

Paint may be applied using a marbling whisk, which can be purchased at any marbling supply store, or assembled from a few strands of an old broom (*see* "Making a Marbling Whisk," page 29). You can vary the basic stone pattern by dragging a hairpick or stylus through the paint. (*See* "Creating a Zigzag Pattern," page 29).

MARBLED PAPER

- 2-ounce jars Liquitex acrylic paints, one each in the following colors: raw umber, metallic copper, ultramarine blue, phthalocyanine green, ivory black, and titanium white
- Ivory-colored paper cut or torn into sheets measuring 14" x 9½"

1–4   marbling whisks (commercial or handmade, *see* "Making a Marbling Whisk," page 29))
Aluminum sulfate (also called alum)
Carrageenan

You'll also need: 10 small (4-ounce or larger) containers for diluting and mixing paint (e.g., empty yogurt containers or baby-food jars); aluminum roasting pan (15¾" x 11" x 2½"); paper towels; measuring spoons; 3 smooth, flat boards, at least 1" larger than paper; newspaper; sponge; latex gloves; clothesline and clothespins; blender; pencil; 6–8 Popsicle sticks or plastic spoons; sink; cup or empty plastic container; artist's apron or work clothes; soap and water for clean up; and several heavy books.

Other items, if needed: dishwashing liquid (for stabilizing paint).

Preparing the Bath and Paper

1. Mix 2 tablespoons carrageenan to 1 gallon of water as follows: Add 1 tablespoon carrageenan into blender filled with 1 quart agitating warm water. Blend 30 to 60 seconds, then place contents in roasting pan. Repeat for second quart; add to pan. Then add 2 additional quarts fresh water to pan. Let bath sit covered with newspaper for 24 hours.

2. Dissolve 2 tablespoons aluminum sulfate in 1 pint water. Make a small mark with a pencil in the corner of each piece of paper. This mark will indicate which side of your paper has not been coated. (Paint will only adhere to paper coated with alum.) Put on latex gloves. Dip sponge in alum solution and lightly coat the unmarked side of paper, taking care to cover the entire surface. Sandwich up to 12 sheets of paper, alum side down, between 2 boards for 1 hour, weighting boards with books. For best results, marble with sheets of paper slightly damp, keeping them between boards until it is time to print. (This prevents the edges of paper from curling.) If marbling with dry paper, flatten between boards weighted with books overnight, then stack sheets of paper, alum side down.

Preparing and Applying the Paint

1. Set paint jars or containers on work surface. Use a jar to dilute each color by mixing equal parts (any measurement, e.g., 8 teaspoons) paint and water. Using diluted paint

and clean jars or containers, mix up marbling paints using following recipes: **Dark umber:** 6 teaspoons raw umber plus 2 teaspoons metallic copper plus 3 teaspoons ivory black. **Dark blue:** 7 teaspoons ultramarine blue plus 2 teaspoons ivory black. **Dark green:** 6 teaspoons phthalocyanine green plus 5½ teaspoons ultramarine blue plus 4 teaspoons ivory black. **Light green:** 6 teaspoons dark green mix plus 4½ teaspoons titanium white.

2. Work in an area where flecks of paint will not get on walls, furniture, or rugs. Cover work space with newspapers, and wear artist's apron or work clothes. Using illustration 3 as guide, position board in sink at 45-degree angle for rinsing. If necessary, prepare whisks following "Making a Marbling Whisk," below. Place roasting pan filled with carrageenan solution in middle of work space.

3. Rip a 3"-wide strip of newspaper and drag it over surface of bath to remove any film or excess paint; discard newspaper. Repeat process.

4. Dip whisk into jar of dark umber paint; hold over marbling bath and gently tap whisk across wrist of other hand as you move it above the surface of the pan. Apply other colors in the following order: dark blue, dark green, and light green. Use a different whisk for each color, or rinse the whisk between paint applications and pat dry with paper towels. If at any time the paint stops spreading, there may be too much paint on the surface of the bath. If this happens, next time add a few drops of diluted dishwashing liquid to the paint (3 drops dishwashing liquid per ½ cup of paint).

5. When the surface is covered, the design is ready to transfer to paper. Hold paper by diagonally opposite corners, alum side down. Starting with corner closest to you, gently roll paper onto surface of bath in one continuous motion. Work quickly to prevent air from getting trapped between paper and bath surface. (Any air bubbles will show up as unprinted spots on the paper.)

6. Leave paper in bath for a few seconds, then grasp the two uppermost corners, pull paper out of bath, and place it face up on the rinse board in the sink. Fill cup or plastic container with water and pour it over marbled paper to wash off carrageenan.

7. Hang paper to dry on clothesline (about 1 hour). To flatten, lay between the two boards and weight with heavy books.

8. Before repeating marbling process, skim paint off bath with strips of newspaper. (If paint goes under surface of bath, that's okay.) Repeat steps 4 to 7 for additional prints.

9. When finished, store diluted paints in sealed container, or dispose of by pouring on newspaper and throwing away when dry. Liquitex cleans up with soap and water. ◆

Laura Sims operates the Indigo Stone Marbling Studio in Asheville, North Carolina.

Five Steps of Marbling Paper

1. Sponge the entire surface of your paper with the aluminum sulfate and water solution and press between boards. Skim the surface of the bath with a 3"-wide scrap of newspaper to remove any film. For random distribution of paint, tap the whisk lightly on your wrist above the surface. When the surface of the bath is covered with stones, the design is ready for transferring to paper.

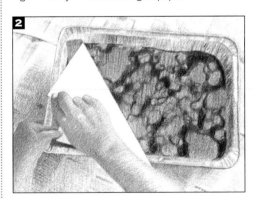

2. Roll the paper onto the bath in one smooth, continuous motion. After a few seconds, lift the paper out of the bath by the two top corners.

3. Rinse the paper on a board set at a 45 degree angle in the sink.

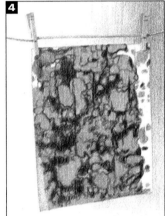

4. Hang the paper on a clothesline to dry.

5. When the paper is completely dry, flatten it between two boards.

MAKING A MARBLING WHISK

To make your own marbling whisk, you'll need an old broom, scissors, and two rubber bands.

1. Hold broom flat and cut off 30 to 40 bristles above stitching on broom head. Pull broom bristles out and gather into a bunch, with the unfrayed ends even.

2. Wrap two rubber bands, 1" to 2" apart, around bunch about 6" from unfrayed end. Trim back frayed end to within ½" of rubber band to create handle. Trim unfrayed end so bristles are even.

CREATING A ZIGZAG PATTERN

Adding zigzags to your marbled pattern is as simple as dragging a ballpoint pen (or any object with a single point, such as a knitting needle or skewer) back and forth across the marbling bath before the design is transferred to paper.

Experiment by creating zigzags after applying three or four colors, then use the whisk to apply flecks of color over the surface.

Field Guide to Beeswax Candles

Candles create instant atmosphere, and beeswax candles, which release a slight honey fragrance, bring a special warmth to any room. Although beeswax candles can take a variety of forms, each is made from beehive wax that has been separated from the honey. The wax sheets are either melted down for molded or dipped candles (such as the tree-shaped candle, center) or hand-rolled around a wick and cut to various sizes and shapes.

As a beeswax candle burns down, it creates an outside "wall" around the wick. Trim this wall to about 1" above the candle's center to prevent the flame from going out from lack of air. If the flame is too low, pour out any melted wax that has collected around the wick; if the flame is too high, trim the wick to ¼". Remember, never leave burning candles unattended and keep them out of drafts and away from flammable materials. ◆

MEASUREMENT AND SOURCE

1. 9" high, 3" in diameter; Perin-Mowen
2. 4½" high, 3¾" in diameter; Pottery Barn
3. 2½" high, 2½" in diameter; Pottery Barn
4. 4" high, 3" in diameter; Pottery Barn
5. 5" high, ⅞" in diameter; Perin-Mowen
6. 9" high, 5" in diameter; Perin-Mowen
7. 8" beehive; 4¾" base; Perin-Mowen
8. 6" high, 2" in diameter; Zona
9. 12" high, 5" wide; Perin-Mowen
10. 16" high, 1¼" in diameter; Wolfman-Gold
11. 18" branch; Wolfman-Gold
12. 9" high, 3¾" in diameter; Perin-Mowen
13. 8" beehive, 4¾" base; Perin-Mowen
14. 12" tapers; Pottery Barn
15. 12" high, 3¾" in diameter; Perin-Mowen

PHOTOGRAPH BY STEVEN MAYS

SOURCES
AND RESOURCES

Most of the materials needed for the projects in this issue are available at your local craft supply, hardware, paint store, florist, fabric shop, or bead and jewelry supply. Following are specific mail-order sources for particular items, arranged by project. Suggested retail prices listed below are current at press time. Contact suppliers directly to confirm up-to-date prices and availability.

Notes from Readers; pages 2–3
Sugared Rose Petals: Roses for $35 per half dozen from Village Flowers. Weck Canning Jars for $13 per set of 4 from Williams-Sonoma. *Florist Foam versus Oasis:* 8" x 4" x 3" florist foam for 87¢ from Craft King. 3" x 7" x 3" Oasis block for $2.50 from Village Flowers. *Substitute for Spray Adhesive:* Rollataq 300 Adhesive Roller for $22.95 and 16-ounce adhesive refills for $7.95 from Daige. *Mail-order Reproduction Wallpaper:* Victorian wallpaper from $39 to $59 per roll from Bradbury and Bradbury. Sample packets of historic wallpapers for $5 from Charles Rupert. Lincrusta Anaglypta embossed wallcoverings from $20 to $50 for double roll from Hardware Plus. *Tips on Growing Hydrangeas:* Climbing hydrangea, pot- grown plants for $19.95 from White Flower Farm. *Categorizing Leather:* Leather scraps in various weights, colors, and finishes for $4 per pound from Earth Guild. *Homemade Firestarters:* Paraffin wax for $1.90 per pound from Earth Guild. Glitter for $2.50 for 15gm and natural raffia for $3.45 for 8 ounces from Craft King. Natural twig bundles for $4.95 for 1 bundle from Mills Floral. Wide variety of ribbons from $1.35 for 5 yards from Newark Dressmaker Supply. *How to Inlay Eggshells:* Bond's Victory Glue for $1.59 for 1¾ ounces, tile grout for $7.28 for 1 quart, and shellac for $7.80 for 1 quart, all from Pearl Paint. *Removing Dripped-on Wax:* Irons from $12 from Service Merchandise. *Origin of Milk Paint:* Milk paint for $8.50 for 1 pint from The Old Fashioned Milk Paint Company. Buttermilk paints for $8.25 for 1 pint from Stulb's Old Village Paint. *Self-healing Mats:* 18" x 24" Olfa Self-healing Cutting Mat for $18.75 from Newark Dressmaker Supply. *Mail-order Stencils:* Large selection of pre-cut stencils starting at $3 from Stencil World (catalog $3.50), Gail Grisi Stencils (catalog $2.50), and Stencil House of New Hampshire. *All About Mediterranean Sponges:* Mediterranean Honeycomb Sponge for $7.40 and Mediterranean Silk Sponge for $1.85 from Earth Guild. Also available at Jerry's Artarama for $3.79 and $1.49.

Quick Tips; pages 4–5
Mitering a Corner with decorative Trim: Metallic trims from $1.10 for 5 yards, large selection of fabrics from $4 per yard, scissors from $10.75, Low Temp Glue Gun for $12.95, and Low Temp Glue Sticks for $3 for 8, all from Newark Dressmaker Supply. *Candle Decoupage:* 7" square potholder for $2.05 and 4½" embroidery scissors for $6.06 from Craft King. Wide variety of candles from $3 from Pourette Candle Making Supplies. Irons from $12 from Service Merchandise. Wide selection of gift wrap for $2.95 per 4 sheets from Dover Publications. *Wiring Flowers in Bunches:* Fiskars Craft Snip for $11 and C-Thru Plastic Ruler for $3.75 from Newark Dressmaker Supply. 18 gauge 18" stem wire for 69¢ for 25 pieces from Sunshine Discount Crafts. Large selection of flowers from $4.95 a stem from White Flower Farm. *Wiring Individual Fruit:* 16 gauge 18" stem wire for 69¢ for 16 pieces from Sunshine Discount Crafts. *Easy Nail Removal:* Estwing Claw Hammer for $27.70 from Frog Tool Company.

How to Gild Almost Any Surface; pages 6–8
5½" Composition Leaf for $5.65 for book of 25 sheets, variety of metallic leafing materials from $5.65, Odorless Mineral Spirits for $4.50 for 1 pint, Daniel Smith Series 33-33 Flat Bristle Brush for $12.42 for 1"-wide brush and $23.44 for 2½"- wide brush, and small clamp-on tin palette cups starting at $2.50, all from Daniel Smith. Cheesecloth for $1.10 for 1 yard and Super-Dri Flannel for $11 per yard from Newark Dressmaker Supply. Rolco gold varnish (size) for $2.90, spray-on primer for $3.95 for 10 ounces, Rustoleum for $6.05 for spray and $11.58 per quart, Minwax for $12.19 per quart, water putty for $1.66 per pound, Five Star paint thinner for $2.20 per quart, white gesso for $5 per ½ pint, sandpaper for 29¢ per sheet, safest stripper for $9.44 per quart, steel wool for 69¢, and Varathane Diamond Finish Transparent IPN Coating for $8.64 for 8 ounces, all from Pearl Paint. 1"-wide foam brush for 45¢ and Surgrip Utility Knife, $4.99 for plastic retractable and $6.59 for metal retractable, from Co-op Artists' Materials. Steel wire brushes from $1.70 from Torrington Brushes.

Wheat Sheaf Centerpiece; page 9
Triticum wheat for $4.95 per 8-ounce bunch, Rye for $2.95 per 6-ounce bunch, and Raffia Hank for $5.20 for 12 ounces (approx. 100 strands), all from Mills Floral. Waxed linen for $1.99 for 75-foot spool and metallic elastic for $3.99 for 50-yard spool from Enterprise Art. Non-slip ruler for $6.99, ½" masking tape for $1.45, Magic Melt Low Temp Glue Gun for $7.99, and glue sticks for $5.99, all from Jerry's Artarama. Laser Scissors from $7.41 from Craft King. Paraffin wax for $1.90 per pound, cotton blend netting twine for $3.80 per ½-pound ball, and beeswax for $8 per pound, all from Earth Guild.

Faux Stone Fruit Basket; pages 10–12
16" flair large princess oval basket (includes hard liner with 9" opening, 7" height and 15" handle) for $5.49 from The Elizabeth Company. 8" x 4" x 3" florist foam for 87¢, rubber gloves for $1.23 per 5 pairs, Claycrete Instant Papier Mâché for $3.88 per 1 pound bag, Mini Magic Melt Lo-Temp Glue Gun for $6.15, mini low-temp glue sticks for $2.75, and stencil brushes for 95¢ for size 2, all from Craft King. Drop cloth for 69¢ for 9" x 12" plastic cloth, rottenstone for $2 per 1 pound box, 32" x 40" x ⅛" chipboard for $3.72, coarse sea sponge for $6.40, cellulose wallpaper adhesive for $9.99 per 1 pound box, all from Pearl Paint. Surgrip Utility Knife, $4.99 for plastic retractable and $6.59 for metal retractable, Winsor & Newton Artists' Acrylics in Neutral Gray (light) and Paynes Gray (dark) for $2.49 each per 2-ounce tube, Liquitex Acrylic Gesso from $8.11 for 16 ounces, Matte Medium for $5.99 for 8 ounces, 1½" masking tape for $3.10 for 60 yards, 18" non-slip ruler for $6.99, Scenic Sand Art for $4.89 per 5 pound bag, Sobo Glue for $1.70 for 4 ounces, 1"-wide (size 12) Color Magnet Bristle paintbrush for $6.99, 12" x 18" Cutting Board for $12.59, and Tech-liner tipped pen for $2.29, all from Jerry's Artarama. Cane cutters for $9.75 from Frank's Cane & Rush Supply. Set of 14" Bamboo Cooking Chopsticks for $1, F. Dick Cutlery serrated slicer for $25.20, and heavy-duty cleaver for $32, all from A Cook's Wares. Soft plastic fruits for $2.40 includes 3½" peach, 3" lemon, 4" pear, 3½" tomato, and 8" banana; 10" green grapes for $4.90 for 90; and 8" wine grapes for $3.90 for 48, all from May Silk. Natural Dried Fruit apples, oranges, and grapefruit for $5.95 per bag (10 pieces) from Newark Dressmaker Supply. 20mm cherries for 99¢ a dozen from Creative Craft House. 18" x 24" Olfa Self-healing Cutting Mat for $18.75 from Newark Dressmaker Supply.

Grape Arbor Mural; pages 13–15
2-ounce jars of glaze in purple (BG 20), moss green (BG 03), hunter green (BG 05), clear (BG24), brown (BG 22), and various other colors, for $5.99 each, block printing pads starting at $10.99, ¼" masking tape for $2.95, and 3" x 5" sheet of uncut synthetic rubber material for $14.95, all from Stenciler's Emporium. Grumbacher Red Sable round paintbrushes from $5.10 and Black Bristle ½"-wide easel brush for $3.66, Purified Linseed Oil for $4 per 8 ounces, Odorless Turpenoid for $4.95 for 8½ ounces, Liquitex Gel Medium for $8.05

for 8 ounces, Canson tracing paper for $3.99 per 50-sheet pad, Surgrip Utility Retractable Knife, $4.99 for plastic and $6.59 for metal, 5½" x 12" plastic palette for $6.99, and Bob Ross Palette Knife for $8.25, all from Co-op Artists' Materials. Dressmaker's transfer paper for $1.55 for 6 sheets and scissors from $10.75 from Newark Dressmaker Supply. Cutting boards from $7.50 from A Cook's Wares.

Fold Your Own Decorative Boxes; page 16
Jumbo rubber bands for 56¢ per dozen, Plaid's Tacky Glue for 89¢ per 4 ounces, variety of fabric paints from 99¢, 8-ounce squeeze bottle for 71¢, craft cord for $2.08 for 27 yards, 4mm pearl beads for 36¢ for 8gm package, assortment of brass filigree for 95¢ each, and extra fine-tip gold pen for $2.54, all from Craft King. Tech-liner black ink tipped pen for $2.29, 18" non-slip ruler for $6.99, natural sponges from $1.49, Magic Melt Low Temp Glue Gun for $7.99, and glue sticks for $5.99, all from Jerry's Artarama. Scissors from $10.75, ⅜" ivory ribbon for $1.35 for 5 yards, 1½" metalique ribbon for $1.60 for 5 yards, and satin rose buds for $1.35 for bundle of 12, all from Newark Dressmaker Supply. 3mm Berries for 55¢ for package of 48 from Kirchen Brother Crafts. Boxwood for $6.90 for 1 bunch, and variety of other dried foliages from Mills Floral. ½" double-coated tape for $5.90 from Co-op Artists Materials.

Classic Steiff Teddy Bear; pages 17–21
⅜" Nap Standard Mohair for $50 for ½ yard, 8mm black glass eyes for 80¢ pair, 55mm plastic joint set for $3 or 2" hardboard joint set for $3.50, Heavy #3 Black perle cotton skein for $1, all from Bear Clawset. Stuff & Fluff fibre fill for $2.20 per 12-ounce bag, 5½" doll needles for 50¢ for 2, brown and white sewing thread for $1.65 each per 300 yard spool, 1¾" quilter's pins for $3.95 for 200, Sharps hand sewing needle for 70¢ for package of 20, brass safety pins from $2.70, scissors from $10.75, extra heavy-duty brown thread for $2.25 for 250 yard spool, 1"-wide ribbon in a variety of colors for $1.75 for 5 yards, 45" wide 100 percent cotton white broadcloth for $4.25 per yard, and C-Thru Plastic Ruler for $3.75, all from Newark Dressmaker Supply. 9" x 12" brown felt for 22¢ and Pigma Micron permanent marker for $1.99 from Sunshine Discount Crafts. 4½" long-nose pliers for $7.99 from Enterprise Art. Selection of irons from $12 and sewing machines from $140 from Service Merchandise. Knitting needles from $3.09 from The American Needlewoman.

Apple Harvest Pie with Decorative Crust; pages 22–23
Pastry Cloth (20" x 24") and 20" x 2" Bakery Rolling Pin for $9, 1½" to 3½" circle cookie cutter set for $4 for set of 5, 9½" soft spat-

SOURCES
AND RESOURCES

ula for $2, 3" Victorinox Paring Knife for $5.80, pastry brush for $5.60, Village Baker cookie sheet for $10, all from A Cook's Wares. 9" Pyrex pie plate for $4.25 from Corning Revere.

Three Simple Napkin Folds; pages 24–25
Hotel Cocktail Napkins for $12 for set of 12 and Hotel Dinner Napkins for $18 for set of 12 from Williams-Sonoma. Boxwood for $6.30 for 1 bunch and miniature rose heads for $4.50 for 1 ounce from Mills Floral. Irons from $12 from Service Merchandise.

Belle Epoque Frame; pages 26–27
16" x 20" Americana oak wood frame including unbreakable acrylic glass, backing board, and beveled pre-cut mat up to size 18" x 24" for $29, Sobo glue for $2.39 per 4 ounces, large selection of round brushes from $1.59, all from Jerry's Artarama. Permanent fine-point marker for $1.09, 24" ruler for $5.80, stainless steel scissors for $15.30 from Co-op Artists' Materials. Spray-on primer for $3.95 for 10 ounces, gold spray paint for $3.95 for 10 ounces, Rub n' Buff gold leaf color tube for $2.40 for ½ fluid ounce, rottenstone for $2 per 1 pound box, and turpentine for $4.25 for 1 quart, all from Pearl Paint. Petal porcelain setting agent for $3.25 for 8 ounces, Pearls By the Yard for $2.50 for 5 yards, Precision Tweezers for $4.75, Miniature Rose Buds on a 2½" stem for $1 per 6 buds, single rose for $1.25, C-Thru Plastic Ruler for $3.75, and cheesecloth for $1.10 yard, all from Newark Dressmaker Supply. Rose Spray for $1.19 per stem (3 flowers) from Sunshine Discount Crafts. Bellflower Spray for $2.90 for 20" stem from May Silk. 1½" blossom rose bud for 66¢ and 1" blossom ribbon roses for 89¢ per dozen from Creative Craft House. Rubber gloves for $1.23 for 5 pairs from Craft King. Sandpaper pads for 69¢ and natural sponges from $1.49 from Jerry's Artarama.

How to Make Marbled Paper; pages 28–29
Alum (aluminum sulfate) for $4.50 for 1 pound, carragheenan for $12.75 for ½ pound, 1-ounce eyedroppers for 50¢ each or 35¢ each for 6 or more, Davey Board for pressing alummed papers for $2.50 for full sheet (minimum of 10 half-sheets for $12.50 for mail order), applicator bottle for color for $1.10 each for 4 ounces, paper washing tray for $25, and broom corn (to make marbling wisk) for $4 per ½ pound, all from Colophon Book Arts Supply. 19" x 25" Canson Mi-Teintes paper in a variety of colors for $1.50. Neatness jars for $1.69, Liquitex Jar Colors in raw umber, ultramarine blue, phytalocyanine green, ivory black and titanium white, 2-ounce size for $2.69, and Elephant Ear Sponge for $2.75, all from Co-op Artists' Materials. Rubber gloves for $1.23 for 5 pairs, clothespins for $2.58

for 40 pieces, ⅜" x 4½" wood craft sticks for $3.55 per 1,000 pieces, and jumbo rubber bands for 56¢ per dozen, all from Craft King. Heavy Duty Measuring Spoon Set for $2.50 from A Cook's Wares. Scissors from $10.75 from Newark Dressmaker Supply.

Field Guide to Beeswax Candles; page 30
Beeswax for $8 for 1 pound, candle wicks from 12¢ for 1 yard, and wick bases for 20¢ per dozen, all from Earth Guild. Candle Pillars for $12 for a set of 3 and Candle Tapers for $12 for a set of 3 from Pottery Barn. 6" high, 2" diameter beeswax candle for $14 from Zona. Assortment of beeswax candles from $10 from Perin-Mowen and Wolfman-Gold.

Quick Projects; page 33
3¾" candle ball for $4.20 from Pourette Candle Making Supplies. *Beaded Garland and Ribbon:* ½" double-coated tape for $5.90 from Co-op Artists' Materials, Super Strength Needle-Steel pins for $2.40 for box of 300, and ribbon from $1.35, all from Newark Dressmaker Supply. Pearl Bead Garland for 69¢ for 5 feet from Craft King. *Copper Leaf:* Wide variety of ribbons from $1.35 for 5 yards from Newark Dressmaker Supply. Copper Leaf for $7.50 for book of 25 sheets from Daniel Smith. *Tuxedo Stripe:* Crayola Crayons for 84¢ for 8 and ½"-wide masking tape for $4.89 from Co-op Artists' Materials. Assortment of brass filigree for 95¢ each and candle wax for $1.59 for 1 pound from Craft King. Super Strength Needle-Steel pins for $2.40 for box of 300 from Newark Dressmaker Supply. *Gold and Copper Silk Leaves:* Rolco gold varnish (size) for $2.90 from Pearl Paint. Large selection of silk flowers from $2 from May Silk. Copper Leaf for $7.50 for book of 25 sheets, and gold colored Composition Leaf for $5.65 for book of 25 sheets from Daniel Smith. Super Strength Needle-Steel pins for $2.40 for box of 300 from Newark Dressmaker Supply. *Star Studs:* 9mm Star Brass Studs for 79¢ for 24 from Sunshine Discount Crafts. *Rose Garland Decoupage:* Wide selection of giftwrap for $2.95 for 4 sheets from Dover Publications. Irons from $12 from Service Merchandise. Scissors from $10.75, miniature rose buds for $1 for 6 buds, and 1"-wide satin ribbon for $1.75 for 5 yards, all from Newark Dressmaker Supply. 7" square potholder for $2.05 from Craft King. *Fern Sprigs:* Irons from $12 from Service Merchandise. Low Temp Glue Gun for $12.95, Low Temp Glue Sticks for $3 for 8, miniature dried rose buds for $1 per 6 buds, and scissors from $10.75, all from Newark Dressmaker Supply. Candle wax for $1.59 for 1 pound and 7" square potholder for $2.05 from Craft King. Dried Bracken Fern for $3.95 for 10 piece bunch from Mills Floral. *Twisted Cord and Autumn Leaves:* Bright Jewels Metallic Green Cord for $2.26 for 27

yards from Craft King. Super Strength Needle-Steel pins for $2.40 for box of 300 from Newark Dressmaker Supply. Variety of silk leaves from $2 from May Silk. 3mm Red Holly Berries for 55¢ for package of 48 or Mini Leaves and Berries for 79¢ for 2 branches from Kirchen Brothers Crafts.

Della Robbia Centerpiece; back cover
Yellow roses for $50 per dozen and standard Oasis block (3" x 7" x 3") for $2.50 from Village Flowers. Pedestal Table Vase for $65 or Iron Pedestal Floor Vase for $85 from Pottery Barn. Florist wire for $1.15 for 10-yard spool and scissors from $10.75 from Newark Dressmaker Supply. Large selection of produce from Frieda's.

....

The following companies are mentioned in the listings above. Contact each individually for a price list or catalog.

A Cook's Wares, 211 37th Street, Beaver Falls, PA 15101; 412-846-9490

The American Needlewoman, P.O. Box 6472, Fort Worth, TX 76115; 800-433-2231

Bear Clawset, 27 Palermo Walk., Long Beach, CA 90803; 310-434-8077

Bradbury and Bradbury, P.O. Box 155, Benicia, CA 94510; 707-746-1900

Charles Rupert, 2004 Oak Bay Avenue, Victoria, B.C., Canada V8R 1E4; 604-592-4916

Co-op Artists' Materials, P.O. Box 53097, Atlanta, GA 30355; 800-877-3242

Colophon Book Arts Supply, 3046 Hogum Bay Road NE, Olympia, WA 98516; 206-459-2940

Corning Revere, P.O. Box 1994, Waynesboro, VA 22980; 800-999-3436

Craft King Discount Craft Supply, P.O. Box 90637, Lakeland, FL 33804; 800-769-9494

Creative Craft House, P.O. Box 2567, Bullhead City, AZ 86430

Daige Inc., 1 Albertson Avenue, Albertson, NY 11507; 800-645-3323 or 516-621-2100

Daniel Smith, P.O. Box 84268, Seattle, WA 98124-5568; 800-426-6740

Dover Publications, 31 East 2nd Street, Mineola, NY 11501 (telephone orders not accepted)

Earth Guild, 33 Haywood Street, Asheville, NC 28801; 800-327-8448

The Elizabeth Company, 21 Ellisville Green, Plymouth, MA 02360; 800-229-7538

Enterprise Art, P.O. Box 2918, Largo, FL 34649; 800-366-2218

Frieda's, P.O. Box 58488, Los Angeles, CA 90058; 213-627-2981

Frank's Cane & Rush Supply, 7252 Heil Avenue, Huntington Beach, CA 92647; 714-847-0707

Frog Tool Company, P.O. Box 8325, Chicago, IL 60661; 800-648-1270

Gail Grisi Stencils, P.O. Box 1263, Haddonfield, NJ 08033; 609-354-1757

Hardware Plus, 701 E. Kingsley Road, Garland, TX 75041; 800-522-7336

Jerry's Artarama, P.O. Box 1105, New Hyde Park, NY 11040; 800-U-Artist

Kirchen Brothers Crafts, P.O. Box 1016, Skokie, IL 60076; 708-647-6747

May Silk, 13262 Moore Street, Cerritos, CA 90703; 800-282-7455

Mills Floral, 4550 Peachtree Lakes Drive, Duluth, GA 30136; 800-762-7939

Newark Dressmaker Supply, 6473 Ruch Road, P.O. Box 20730, Lehigh Valley, PA 18002; 800-736-6783

The Old Fashioned Milk Paint Company, P.O. Box 222, 436 Main Street, Groton, MA 01450; 508-448-6336.

Pearl Paint, 308 Canal Street, New York, NY 10013; 800-221-6845

Perin-Mowen, 270 Lafayette Street, 9th Floor, New York, NY 10012; 212-219-3937

Pottery Barn, 100 N. Point Street, San Francisco, CA 94133; 800-922-9934

Pourette Candle Making Supplies, P.O. Box 15220, Seattle, WA 98115; 206-525-4488

Service Merchandise, P.O. Box 25130, Nashville, TN 37202; 800-251-1212

Stencil House of New Hampshire, P.O. Box 109, Hooksett, NH 03106; 800-622-9416

Stencil World, P.O. Box 1112, Newport, RI 02840; 800-274-7997

The Stenciler's Emporium, 800-229-1760

Stulbs Old Village Paint, P.O. Box 1030, Fort Washington, PA 19034; 215-654-1770

Sunshine Discount Crafts, P.O. Box 301, Largo, FL 34649; 813-581-1153

Torrington Brushes, P.O. Box 56, Torrington, CT 06790; 800-262-7874 or 800-525-1416

Village Flowers, 297 Main Street, Huntington, NY 11743; 516-427-0996

White Flower Farm, P.O. Box 50, Litchfield, CT 06759; 203-496-9600

Williams-Sonoma, P.O. Box 7456, San Francisco, CA 94120-7456; 800-541-2233

Wolfman-Gold, 116 Green Street, New York, NY 10012; 212-431-1888

Zona, 97 Greene Street, New York, NY 10012; 212-925-6750 ◆

Quick Projects

Beaded Garland and Ribbon

Copper Leaf

Tuxedo Stripe

Gold and Copper Silk Leaves

Star Studs

Rose Garland Decoupage

Fern Sprigs

Twisted Cord and Autumn Leaves

With a little creativity and some paint, ribbon, preserved foliage, or copper leaf, you can dress up a 3"-high, 3"-diameter white candle to match any decorating scheme. Use these ideas as presented, or as a starting point for developing your own designs.

Beaded Garland and Ribbon—Insert 8 straight pins at even intervals around top third of candle. Loop beaded garland as shown, and secure ends with short piece of double-sided tape. Wrap length of ribbon around bottom of candle, and secure end with short straight pins. Wrap length of beaded garland around base and secure with small piece of double-sided tape.

Copper Leaf—Break 2 to 3 squares copper composition leaf into pieces using perfectly dry fingertips. Apply irregularly shaped pieces, one at a time, to candle surface, smoothing each piece in place with fingers to create a broken pattern. Tie 1"-wide copper-colored ribbon around base of candle.

Tuxedo Stripe—Melt 3 blue crayons and two 3" white candle stubs in top of double boiler using low heat. Meanwhile, cut or pull off eight ¼"-wide strips of high-tack masking tape. Position tape strips vertically with even spaces between them to create striped pattern. Hold candle at ends and quickly roll in melted crayon until evenly coated. Remove candle and continue turning in air (to prevent drips) until wax hardens. Slowly peel off tape. Mount gold embroidered medallion to side of candle with short straight pins.

Gold and Copper Silk Leaves—Remove 8 to 10 leaves of any size from stem of silk flowers. Paint leaves with gold size and allow to dry for 15 minutes or until sticky to touch. Meanwhile, break sheets of gold and copper composition leaf into pieces. When size is tacky, press bits of gold and copper composition leaf on silk leaves. When dry, pin leaves around base of candle in overlapping pattern using short straight pins.

Star Studs—To plan overall design, press star studs onto candlewax using light, even pressure. When satisfied with arrangement, push stars into wax.

Rose Garland Decoupage—Cut out rose garland image from gift wrap and arrange flowers in "U" shape on lower third of candle. Adhere the image to the candle following the directions in Quick Tips, "Candle Decoupage," page 4. Loop ½ yard 1"-wide ribbon under candles as shown, and accent with dried rose bud.

Fern Sprigs—Melt half of a block of paraffin in top of double boiler using low heat. Meanwhile, cut 8 to 10 artificial, silk, or live fern tips and attach to base of candle following the directions in Quick Tips, "Candle Decoupage," page 4. Dip candle base into melted paraffin to secure ferns. Hot-glue small red flowers between fern sprigs.

Twisted Cord and Autumn Leaves—Attach one end of ½ yard twisted green cord to candle base using straight pin. Wrap cord around candle and pin other end in place. Accent with silk leaves and berries. ◆

Della Robbia Centerpiece

Cut a 2½" x 3" x 3" block of green Oasis and soak with water. Place block in center of pedestal dish. Heap grapes on top of Oasis, interspersing 2 or 3 large bunches dark purple grapes with 1 or 2 bunches light green grapes. To hang grapes, wind florist wire around main stem and anchor end into Oasis. Nest one yellow pear on top of grapes; slice another pear in half, and then in quarters. Dip pear pieces in lemon juice to prevent browning and arrange as shown. Cut stems of 6 to 8 yellow roses to 5". Trim remaining stem portions (those with leaves attached) to 5" and insert into foam, then insert yellow roses at same points.

NUMBER FOUR

NOVEMBER/DECEMBER 1994

HANDCRAFT
~ ILLUSTRATED ~

Victorian Christmas Cornucopias

30-Minute Ornaments from Our Vintage Design

SPECIAL INSERT

Turn-of-the-Century Place Cards

Dress Up Any Table With Cut-and-Fold Place Cards

Gingerbread Birdhouses

Bake and Decorate Miniature Houses in Minutes

Low-Sew Tree Skirt

PRINT YOUR OWN GREETING CARDS

•

SECRETS OF ANTIQUING FABRIC

•

QUICK TRASH BAG GARLAND

•

EASY-TUFT FOOTSTOOL

$4.00 U.S./$4.95 CANADA

0 71486 02716 4   1 2

RE-CREATE AN AUTHENTIC VICTORIAN CHRISTMAS WITH THIS VINTAGE CORNUCOPIA ORNAMENT

HANDCRAFT
~ILLUSTRATED~

Editor
CAROL ENDLER STERBENZ

Executive Editor
BARBARA BOURASSA

Senior Editor
MICHIO RYAN

Managing Editor
MAURA LYONS

Directions Editors
CANDIE FRANKEL
SUSAN WILSON

Editorial Assistant
KIM N. RUSSELLO

Copy Editor
KURT TIDMORE

Art Director
MEG BIRNBAUM

Photo Stylist
SYLVIA LACHTER

Publisher and Founder
CHRISTOPHER KIMBALL

Editorial Consultant
RAYMOND WAITES

Marketing Director
ADRIENNE KIMBALL

Circulation Director
ELAINE REPUCCI

Circulation Assistant
JENNIFER L. KEENE

Production Director
JAMES MCCORMACK

Publicity Director
CAROL ROSEN KAGAN

Treasurer
JANET CARLSON

Office Manager
JENNY THORNBURY

Customer Service
CONNIE FORBES

Handcraft Illustrated (ISSN 1072-0529) is published bimonthly by Natural Health Limited Partners, 17 Station Street, P.O. Box 509, Brookline, MA 02147-0509. Copyright 1994 Natural Health Limited Partners. Application to mail at second-class postage rates is pending at Boston, MA, and additional mailing offices. Editorial office: 17 Station Street, P.O. Box 509, Brookline, MA 02147-0509; (617) 232-1000, FAX (617) 232-1572. Editorial contributions should be sent to: Editor, *Handcraft Illustrated*, P.O. Box 509, Brookline, MA 02147-0509. We cannot assume responsibility for manuscripts submitted to us. Submissions will be returned only if accompanied by a large self-addressed stamped envelope. Subscription rates: $24.95 for one year; $45 for two years; $65 for three years. (Canada: add $3 per year; all other foreign add $12 per year.) Postmaster: Send all new orders, subscription inquiries, and change of address notices to *Handcraft Illustrated*, P.O. Box 51383, Boulder, CO 80322-1383. Single copies: $4 in U.S., $4.95 in Canada and foreign. Back issues available for $5 each. PRINTED IN THE U.S.A.

Rather than put ™ in every occurrence of trademarked names, we state that we are using the names only and in an editorial fashion and to the benefit of the trademark owner, with no intention of infringement of the trademark.

Note to Readers: Every effort has been made to present the information in this publication in a clear, complete, and accurate manner. It is important that all instructions are followed carefully, as failure to do so could result in injury. Natural Health Limited Partners, the editors, and the authors disclaim any and all liability resulting therefrom.

EDITORIAL

CAROL ENDLER STERBENZ

I remember last Christmas; it had been snowing all afternoon. I was standing at my kitchen counter mixing dough for gingerbread. Genevieve and Rodney had gone to pick up my mother, who was coming to visit. This was the first time in a long while that we had all been together as a family. It was two days before Christmas, and the kitchen was filled with the mingled scents of cinnamon and cloves, carried by the warm air of an afternoon fire. Christmas is my favorite time of year; at no other time is our family more filled with the spirit of being together and making things.

I had kept up my tradition of decorating the house in the weeks and days before Christmas, and every room was touched by some humble object made years ago. Little bears that had been tucked away all year were unwrapped one by one and arranged knee-deep in fresh evergreen, which twinkled with tiny lights on the mantel. Woven, paper hearts hung from every window; my mother taught me to cut and weave these hearts from shiny colored paper when I was a child. By Christmas morning they would be filled with candies, nuts, and chocolate.

There are several activities that we do together during the holidays, traditions we have upheld despite the changes that time and circumstance have brought. We always make gingerbread houses, and we always go out to pick a Christmas tree. I remember the gingerbread sections cooling on the kitchen stove. Later on we joined them together and decorated them, then together we hung the houses on the tree.

Our gingerbread house design has gone through several versions since we started this tradition fifteen years ago. The earliest model was styled like a Danish farmhouse, a reminder of the farmhouse where my father spent his summers as a boy; we even molded a little marzipan gnome who, legend told us, would eat the bowl of porridge we left out each Christmas Eve.

As the children got older, the art of their gingerbread decoration began to reflect their age, their developing skills, and their divergent tastes. Each of them was given an entire side of the gingerbread house to decorate. At nine, Genevieve decorated her side with orderly rows of white squiggles, curls, and flowers, methodically and symmetrically beautifying the windows, the base, and the door. But when you turned the corner on this house, you found a tableau worthy of Jackson Pollack, created by Gabrielle, aged three. Around another corner was seven-year-old Rodney's work, which he created by squeezing a thick layer of icing around the gingerbread foundation. He then "crashed" his Matchbox car against the side of the house, using a liberal sprinkling of pepper for skid marks. Art imitates life indeed.

Inevitably, the tradition of decorating a gingerbread house each Christmas required another change, since the gargantuan structure took a lot of time to make. As the children got older, some of that time went to other activities, but they were adamant about maintaining the gingerbread house tradition. Last year, they came up with a solution to make smaller, separate dwellings. (I made a silent protest, but went along with the change, preparing enough sections of gingerbread to allow them to make any style house they fancied.)

Just as I finished, I heard the car door slam. A rush of fresh air announced the arrival of my mother and the children. Everyone was talking at once, and in only a minute, it seemed, five gingerbread houses were standing on the counter, constructed and decorated, one for each of the children, one for my mother, and one for John and me. When dinner was finished, we put on our coats and headed for the neighborhood garden nursery.

It didn't take long for us to find the perfect tree, barter for a good price, and tie the tree to the top of the car. When we got home, John and Rodney brought the tree inside, and we spent the rest of the evening hanging the lights and ornaments, and arranging the gingerbread houses among the other ornaments.

P.S. Late that Christmas Eve, I stood in the living room, which was dark except for the glow of the lights on the tree, and looked at the decorations, remembering years gone by. Then my gaze rested on a row of five little houses—four condos, and a Victorian house with an ornate roof—all hanging on the same branch. Yes, art imitates life, and I'm glad. May the spirit of the season fill your days as it does mine. ◆

Carol Endler Sterbenz

NOTES FROM READERS

PAINT CHOICES FOR STENCILING

I've done some experimenting with stenciling, and can't seem to find a paint that works well consistently. What do you recommend?

LAURA ROGERS
Marlboro, MA

Paint is one of your most important stenciling purchases, since its performance under daily use can make the difference between success and failure. A stenciled floor, for instance, will need paint that stands up under wear. These considerations are different for a clock case, which is not handled very often.

Acrylic paints (which are water-based) and Japan paints (which are special, quick-drying, oil-based paints) are best for stenciling. Both types of paint are generally widely available and come in a variety of colors. In general, Japan paints wear better than acrylic.

Because acrylic paints are water-based, clean-up is a simple matter of washing everything with soap and water. Acrylics are also quick-drying, which means that the time when the brush is dry enough to stencil but moist enough to use is relatively short. It can be difficult to keep the paint from hardening on the brush, although this problem can be alleviated by mixing retarder into the paint to lengthen the drying time. Acrylic paint also has the potential to become chalky-looking, and cause the stenciling to appear slightly raised—an effect you may or may not want.

Clean-up is messier with Japan paints, as your tools must be washed with turpentine or mineral spirits. Japan paint also dries quickly, but in general you have more control over it than acrylic, since the oil in the paint helps to keep the brush damp, pliable, and evenly distributed with color.

FAST FIX FOR ROLL-UP SHADES

Can you suggest a fast and easy way I can jazz up my plain white roll-up shades?

SUZANNE LECHTER
Cincinnati, OH

There are plenty of terrific ways to add character to your shades. If your shades have pull rings, consider replacing them with other objects, such as tassels, vintage beads, chande-

lier crystals, or ball knots made from silk or rayon cord. You can also replace the pull rings with those made from burnished metal, colored Lucite, Bakelite, textured wood, or ceramic. Most of these objects or rings can easily be applied with a hot-glue gun or white tacky glue.

You could also create interest along the bottom edge of the shade by gluing on a thin strip of ribbon or lace or any of the colorful trimmings available by the yard at fabric shops, including moss fringe, tasseled fringe, and tiny silk-covered pom-poms. You could also block print or stencil on a design, or apply cut-out images using decoupage.

IDEAL HEIGHT FOR HANGING PICTURES

Is there an ideal height at which to hang a picture on a wall?

STUART JACOBSON
Ann Arbor, MI

We took your question to Peter Sullivan, art preparator and registrar at Hirschl & Adler Modern gallery in New York. Sullivan says that if the picture is three feet tall or less, it should be hung so that its center is fifty-eight to sixty inches above the floor. If the picture is greater than three feet tall, its center should be fifty-five to fifty-seven inches above the floor. This assumes that the picture is being hung on an eight-foot wall with no physical obstructions. Different ceiling heights and the presence of architectural elements such as moulding will affect this rule of thumb.

THE DEFINITION OF NONTOXIC

I always buy my children art materials that are labeled "nontoxic," but a friend recently told me that just because a product was labeled "nontoxic" didn't mean it was 100 percent safe. Is she right?

TARA REEVES
San Francisco, CA

According to the Health Hazards Manual for Artists (published by the now defunct Foundation for the Community of Artists, or FCA), the term "nontoxic" can be somewhat misleading. Many children's art materials "have not been tested for long-term toxicity," nor do

"most art material manufacturers have toxicologists or other personnel competent to evaluate the materials they are testing." The FCA suggests that you buy products that have been endorsed by the Art and Craft Materials Institute (ACMI). Such products display the Institute's Certified Product (CP) or Approved Product (AP) seal of approval, which means they have been "certified by an authority on toxicology."

USING EDIBLE FLOWERS IN ICE CUBES

I tried making ice cubes with edible flowers for a holiday cocktail party—with terrible results. The flowers sank to the bottom of the tray and the water was cloudy. What did I do wrong?

THERESA BRUCE
Albany, NY

Try this method. Fill an ice-cube tray about one-third full with water that you have first brought to a rolling boil, then cooled to room temperature and put in the refrigerator. (Boiling the water makes the ice more transparent.) Freeze the trays until ice crystals begin to form, about fifteen minutes, then remove the trays from the freezer and arrange an edible flower (or other edible garnish) on top of each partly frozen ice cube. Add more of the cold, boiled water until each compartment is three-quarters full, then put the trays back in the freezer until the cubes are frozen solid.

TIPS ON CARING FOR AN AMARYLLIS

I just received a beautiful salmon-colored amaryllis from a coworker, and I feel obliged to keep it in the window of my office. The room gets plenty of sun, but the problem is, I have no idea how to care for it once the flowers die.

SANDRA JENKINS
Bridgeport, CT

After the flowers die, simply cut the stalk down to the base of the plant with a very sharp knife, being careful not to injure the leaves. Place the plant in or near the window. Water it when the soil is dry to the touch, and fertilize it with a standard houseplant fertilizer every two weeks (Peter's Professional Plant Food is a good choice). In mid-September, cut the leaves off and store the plant in a cool, dark place (a sixty- to sixty-five-degree basement is ideal). Some people put their amaryllises in boxes to ensure that the dormant plants are not exposed to light.

In the beginning of December, remove the bulb from the pot, shake off the loose soil, and replant it in fresh potting medium. Place it near a sunny window and water sparingly to keep the bulb from becoming waterlogged. As the bulb begins to sprout, you can give it more water. Your plant should be in bloom for the holiday season, but don't despair if it doesn't bloom the first year, as an amaryllis doesn't always flower every year.

PROTECTING A NEWLY REFINISHED TABLE

I just had my dining room table refinished. Can you give me any pointers on protecting it?
JENNY SUMMERS
Houston, TX

Apply several thin coats of a high-quality furniture wax. Liquid or paste wax works equally well, although paste wax is preferable if your table receives heavy use. Let the wax dry before buffing it with a soft cloth; if you don't, you'll just be pushing the wax around.

Don't use a silicone product, because should you ever decide to refinish the table again silicone could prevent a new finish from adhering. Lemon oil is not a good choice either, as it can injure the finish.

TYPES OF WATERCOLOR PAPER

What are the differences between hot press, cold press, and rough watercolor paper? Is one type better than another?
ABIGAIL DWYER
Nashville, TN

These terms refer to the finish of the paper. Cold press paper has a medium to coarse finish, rough paper has a high-relief texture, and hot press paper has a smooth finish. Cold press paper is a good choice for novices, as it is ideal for practicing traditional techniques. The more pronounced texture of rough paper makes it more difficult to work with, so it is a better choice for the more experienced watercolorist. The fine tooth of the hot press paper makes it a better choice for pen and ink or charcoal, as water tends to pool up on its surface, making it difficult to use for traditional watercoloring.

Finding a paper that suits your needs is not so cut-and-dry, however. Manufacturers often use different methods of finishing their papers. One brand of hot press paper may be smooth to the touch, while another brand may resemble the texture of cold press paper. Rough papers can vary in texture as well.

You can alter a paper's absorbency by adjusting the amount of size it contains. Size, a gelatin mixture, is often incorporated into the paper by the manufacturer. It can be adjusted by applying a commercial product known as "prepared size." The more prepared size you apply, the less absorbent the paper's surface becomes. To decrease the size (and thereby increase absorbency), place the paper in a water bath for several hours.

REJUVENATING OLDER FURNITURE

I recently inherited an old mahogany dresser. I cleaned it with my usual furniture spray, but it still looks dingy. Is there anything I can do?
BARBARA TEMPERTON
Portland, ME

Try cleaning the dresser with mineral spirits and a soft cloth. This will remove the film, but it will also strip the wood of its natural oils. To return the wood to good condition, wipe on a mixture of lemon extract and mineral oil (two to three drops of lemon extract per cup of mineral oil), then use a thin coat of high-quality paste wax to protect the surface.

TIPS ON SANDING INTRICATE ITEMS

Do you have any suggestions for sanding turned table legs and chair rungs? I have a project in mind, but the woodworking is so intricate I'm afraid I wouldn't be able to do an even job.
RANDY DIXON
Seattle, WA

You have a variety of options available, including curved sanding blocks or abrasive string. You can also purchase sanding sponges, which are available in two types—either with a fine grit on one side and a medium grit on the other, or a medium grit on one side and a coarse grit on the other. These flexible sponges can be cut smaller if necessary, which makes it easier to sand hard-to-reach places with them.

You can also back any sandpaper with duct tape (which is tough and will minimize tearing), then cut the paper into whatever width strips you need.

DETERMINING PAPER GRAIN

I recently tried gluing paper to a mat board to make my own postcards, but the results were pretty warped. What did I do wrong?
ROSALYN HENRY
Cambridge, MA

Most likely the grains of the two papers weren't going in the same direction when you glued them together. Paper, like the wood from which it is made, has a grain. If you're bonding two pieces of paper together, make sure the grain of each is going in the same direction. If you don't, the papers will curl away from each other and warp as they dry.

Use this simple test to find the direction of the grain: Bend the sheet (or board) in half. If it bends easily, you're folding with the grain. If it is resistant, you're folding across the grain. Mark the direction of the grain on each piece of paper to avoid confusion.

HOW TO MAKE A GREETING CARD PUZZLE

Can you tell me how to make a greeting card puzzle?
PATTY JOHNSON
Princeton, NJ

A greeting card puzzle is fun and easy to make. All you need are a sheet of bonded paper; a thin mat board; a stiff, flat brush; a mat knife or X-Acto knife; a felt-tip, permanent marker; liquid glue (like Sobo or Elmer's); and a 1"-diameter wooden dowel. Optional items include a lead pencil and stencils for tracing shapes.

First, using the instructions outlined in the item "Determining Paper Grain," above, find the grain of the mat and the paper. Then, starting at the center and working toward the edges, brush the glue evenly over the mat board. Working from one end to the other, glue the paper to the board, making sure the grain of the paper and the grain of the board are going in the same direction. Smooth out any wrinkles or bubbles as you go by rolling a 1"-diameter dowel over the surface. Let glue dry completely.

To cut your puzzle in a specific shape, you can trace around a stencil, or draw the shape freehand. Use the lead pencil to lightly trace the shape onto the back of the mat, cut out the shape, then write your message on the paper side of the mat using the marker.

After you've written your message, cut the card into several large puzzle pieces with the mat knife or X-Acto knife on the papered side of the puzzle. When mailing your puzzle, be sure to use extra postage, as the card will be heavier than a normal letter.

ORIGINS OF RAFFIA

What is raffia and where does it come from?
EILEEN O'CONNOR
Nashua, NH

Raffia is the fiber found in the large leaves of the raffia palm of Madagascar. It is often used to make baskets or mats, and to tie plants. Raffia is currently enjoying great popularity as a component of dried-flower arrangements and as an alternative to gift-wrapping ribbon. ◆

Quick Tips

Making a Starched Fabric Bow

To make a fabric bow that holds its shape for use on indoor and outdoor wreaths or garlands, you'll need a strip of muslin 2½" x 32"; liquid decoupage glue (such as Plaid Royal Coat); latex gloves; a shallow, washable container about 8" across; a nonporous, washable work surface; and soap for cleanup. The directions that follow are for a 5" bow with 7½" streamers.

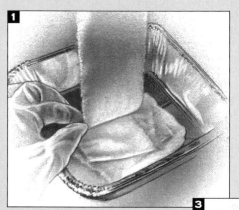

1. Slip on the latex gloves and pour a thin layer of decoupage glue in the bottom of the washable container. Lower the muslin strip accordion-style into the glue, and press it down to moisten it.

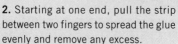

2. Starting at one end, pull the strip between two fingers to spread the glue evenly and remove any excess.

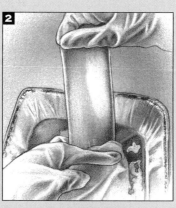

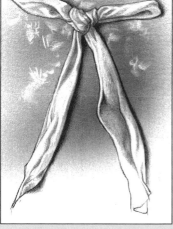

3. Tie the wet strip into a bow, concentrating on size, not shape, and lay it flat on a nonporous, work surface, such as plastic.

4. Shape the bow and streamers with your fingers, coaxing the edges of the muslin under. Let it dry overnight. Clean up with soap and water.

Building a Beaded Tassel

This tassel is easy to make using prestrung 8mm (¼") beads sold as a tree garland, one 20mm (¾") bead, and some 24-gauge brass beading wire. Make several for use as tree ornaments, or use them to decorate gift packages. You'll also need scissors or wire cutters.

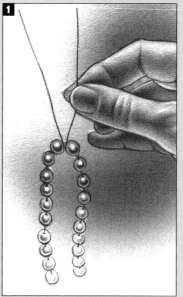

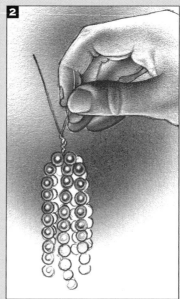

1. Cut four 20-bead lengths of prestrung 8mm beads from the tree garland, then cut a 6" length of brass wire. Bend the wire in half to form a V. Center a length of beads over the V so 10 beads fall to each side.

2. Repeat with the remaining lengths of beads. Twist together the wire directly above the beads to secure them.

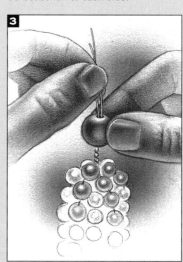

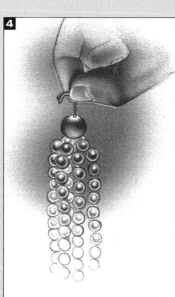

3. Slip the large bead onto the twisted wire, and push it down on top of the small beads.

4. Twist together all of the wire above the large bead and bend it into a hook for attaching.

ILLUSTRATIONS BY HARRY DAVIS

Candle Stabilizer Disks

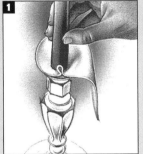

Here's a quick alternative to wrapping the bottom of a candle with aluminum foil or tape to make it fit snugly inside a candlestick cup. Instead, use a disk cut from the foam type of a used anti-static or fabric softener sheet. The padding will keep the candle upright and wobble-free. One 2½" x 8" sheet will yield three disks. In addition to the used dryer sheets, you'll need a pair of scissors. The candle shown here is ¾" in diameter, while the candle cup is ⅞" in diameter.

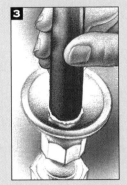

1. Place the dryer sheet on top of the candlestick, then insert the candle into the cup, gently pushing the dryer sheet down into the cup.

2. Remove the candle and the dryer sheet. You should be able to see two faint concentric impressions in the dryer sheet. Using scissors, cut around the larger circle to make one disk.

3. Center the foam disk over the candle cup, then push the candle down into the cup until the disk disappears from view.

Make-Your-Own Sanding Block

If you find you need a sanding block, but don't have one on hand, you can improvise using a cigar box or a smooth scrap block of wood. The cigar box shown here measures 5½" x 3½" x 1". You'll also need masking tape, scissors, a ruler, and a pencil.

1. Measure, mark, and cut a strip of sandpaper the same width as the cigar box or wood block, and twice as long. Lay the strip rough side down, and center the box or block on top.

2. Fold the sandpaper around one end of the box or block, making a firm crease at each edge. Tape both end flaps to the top surface.

Making a Knotted Trim

Skeins of perle cotton, either purchased new or left over from other projects, can easily be fashioned into a novelty knotted trim for edging pillows, valences, or other soft furnishings. The trim shown is made up of fifteen strands of a single color thread, but you can combine various colors to suit your decor. In addition to the perle cotton, you'll also need scissors, a ruler, a needle, and matching thread.

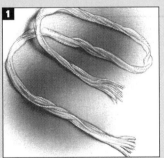

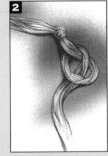

2. Starting 4" from one end, tie an overhand knot in the rope. Make an identical knot 2" from the first one. Continue until the entire rope is knotted at 2" intervals.

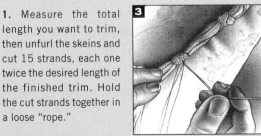

1. Measure the total length you want to trim, then unfurl the skeins and cut 15 strands, each one twice the desired length of the finished trim. Hold the cut strands together in a loose "rope."

3. To attach the trim, work from behind the edge you're trimming, and tack each knot in place with a needle and thread.

Create a Triple Trim

By combining three different upholstery trims—such as bullion fringe, loop trim, and braid—you can create decorative edging that would be difficult or expensive to buy. Each trim is topstitched in succession. Calculate the yardage for each as you would for a single trim. You'll need pins, thread to match the trim, scissors, and a ruler or measuring tape.

1. Pin the bullion fringe to the bottom edge of the fabric, and topstitch with matching thread.

2. Lay the loop fringe on top, butt or overlap the edges, then topstitch it in place.

3. Pin the braid on top to conceal the previous overlap, and topstitch along the top and bottom edges.

ATTENTION READERS: RECEIVE A FREE SUBSCRIPTION IF WE PUBLISH YOUR TIP. Do you have a unique technique that you would like to share with other readers? We will give you a one-year complimentary subscription to *Handcraft Illustrated* for each Quick Tip that we publish. Send a description of your special technique to Quick Tips, *Handcraft Illustrated*, P.O. Box 509, 17 Station Street, Brookline Village, MA 02147-0509. Please include your name, address, and daytime phone number. Unfortunately, we can only acknowledge receipt of tips actually used in the magazine. In case the same tip is received from two readers, the one postmarked first will be selected.

Gingerbread Birdhouses

Using these fast, easy gingerbread and royal icing recipes, you can make a trio of birdhouses in an afternoon's time.

These gingerbread houses are an ideal project for children aged six and up.

Creating these gingerbread birdhouses involves five simple steps: making up a batch of gingerbread and rolling it out on a cookie sheet, tracing around the templates on page 7 with a plastic knife, baking the gingerbread pieces, "gluing" the birdhouses together using royal icing, and adding decorative icing squiggles, swirls, and dots (*see* "Decorating with Royal Icing," page 8) to the roof, walls, or base.

Before you get started, here are a few tips regarding gingerbread. The recipe below yields enough dough for three birdhouses. To fit all the pieces on two cookie sheets, butt and cut all the like pieces together. For each house, you'll need three of the roof/base pieces, two of the side pieces, and two of the front/back pieces, or a total of twenty-one pieces for three birdhouses. Before rolling the dough, remove it from the refrigerator and let it warm up to just below room temperature. (Dough taken directly from the refrigerator can be difficult to roll.) Rolling out and cutting the dough directly on the cookie sheet eliminates the need to move the pieces of dough around, and helps you avoid breaking or distorting them. Put a clean bath towel under the cookie sheet to keep it stable while you roll out the dough. When shaping and rolling out the dough, choose the area that is smoothest and most free of cracks for the birdhouse roof, since these pieces are most visible.

Use a serrated plastic knife to cut out the pieces. The blunt, thick blade leaves a separation between the cut pieces and prevents the dough from stretching. The blade of a regular kitchen knife will be too thin, and the pieces will run together when you bake them. (If this occurs, run the blade between the pieces to separate them after they've been cooked and while the dough is still hot.)

When assembling the house, turn each piece so the side that faced the cookie sheet during bak-

MAKING THE BIRDHOUSES

1. Lay the cardboard templates on the gingerbread dough and cut around each shape using a serrated plastic knife. For each house, cut three roof/base pieces, two side pieces, and two front/back pieces.

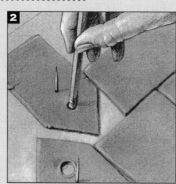

2. Break a toothpick in half and cut off the sharp ends with a pair of scissors, then stick the broken end into the front piece for a perch as shown. Use a new pencil eraser to bore a hole above the perch.

3. Squeeze a vertical line of icing on each inside edge of the back piece, then stand the back piece upright and press the side pieces into the icing as if it were glue.

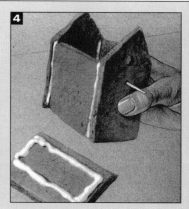

4. Hold the partially assembled house over the base to see where the walls will sit, then pipe the icing directly onto the base to correspond to the bottoms of the walls. Position the house on top of the icing and press gently to adhere.

ILLUSTRATIONS BY NENAD JAKESEVIC/PHOTOGRAPH BY STEVEN MAYS

Pattern Pieces

Trace these templates onto tracing paper, then lay the tracing on the cardboard. Using a ruler and ballpoint pen, go over the traced lines, pressing firmly to make an impression on the cardboard. Remove the tracing and darken the impressions with a pencil, then cut out the templates along the marked lines.

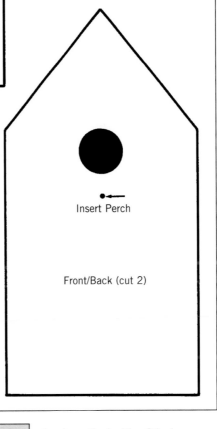

Roof/Base (cut 3)

Side (cut 2)

Front/Back (cut 2)

Insert Perch

pump, so the last icing to come out will be harder to control and may appear drippy. When this begins to happen, switch to another chilled bag of icing.

Be sure to decorate the base, front, and sides of the house before you put on the roof. (For tips on decorating, *see* "Decorating with Royal Icing," page 8.) If you need to make repairs or corrections on any of the icing swirls or squiggles, carefully remove any big globs with a damp cotton swab. Dip a second cotton swab in water and rub it over the remaining icing to partially dissolve it, then dab the rest away with a dry cotton swab.

If your children take part in this project, take care that they don't approach the hot oven, or touch the just-baked gingerbread.

GINGERBREAD BIRDHOUSES

Gingerbread
8 tablespoons (one stick) unsalted butter or margarine, softened
½ cup loosely packed dark brown sugar
¼ cup unsulfured molasses
¼ cup dark corn syrup
3½ cups sifted all-purpose flour
1 teaspoon baking soda
2 teaspoons ground ginger
1 teaspoon ground cinnamon
¼ teaspoon ground nutmeg
¼ teaspoon ground cloves
¼ teaspoon cardamom
¼ teaspoon salt
¼ cup water
2 toothpicks

Royal Icing
3 egg whites
1½ pound confectioners' sugar

You'll also need: lightweight cardboard or poster board; pencil with new eraser; tracing paper; paper plates; ball-point pen; ruler; scissors; two rimless 13" x 15" cookie sheets; plastic serrated knife; bath towel slightly larger than cookie sheet; 2 large zip-lock freezer bags; 4 or 5 sandwich-sized zip-lock freezer bags; twist ties; sifter; electric mixer; wooden rolling pin; and kitchen knife.

Other items, if necessary: cotton swabs for cleaning up mistakes when applying icing.

ing is on the inside of the house, as the other side is generally smoother. (Ultimately, you can conceal uneven texture or defects with the royal icing decorations.)

The royal icing should be mixed up and then stored in four or five sandwich-size zip-lock freezer bags, closed with twist ties. The bags have to withstand considerable pressure when you squeeze them to pipe the icing, so be sure to use freezer-weight bags rather than ordinary plastic bags, and be sure to tie the tops with twist ties instead of relying on the zip-locks, otherwise the bags may burst or split open. Chilled icing is easier to pump and direct, so store your bags in the refrigerator until you're ready to use them. Your hands will warm up the bags a little as you

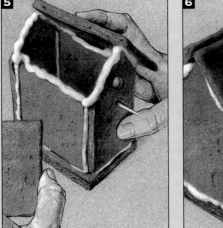

5. To attach the roof, squeeze a continuous line of icing on the tops of the walls and position the roof sections one at a time.

6. Squeeze the icing onto the roof sides and peak to suggest shingling or accumulated snow and icicles.

Preparing the Gingerbread and Royal Icing

1. *For the gingerbread:* Using electric mixer, cream butter or margarine and dark brown sugar together in large mixing bowl. Add molasses and corn syrup and continue mixing on medium speed until well combined.

2. Sift dry ingredients together. Add to sugar mixture, a little at a time, alternating between dry ingredients and water and mixing until well combined.

3. Lightly flour hands and gather dough into ball. Divide ball in half, place each half into one of the large zip-lock bags. Shape dough inside into rough cubes using palm of hand. Zip bag closed and refrigerate for at least 1 hour. While dough is chilling, prepare royal icing.

4. *For the royal icing:* Clean beaters, then set mixer on high speed and beat egg whites until fluffy. Add confectioners' sugar, ½ cup at a time, until icing is stiff. Test icing by running knife blade through it. When the walls of the cut area hold, the icing is ready. Icing should have a slight sheen to it. Transfer icing to four or five sandwich-size zip-lock freezer bags, then close each bag with a twist tie and refrigerate.

Making the Birdhouses

1. Trace templates onto tracing paper. Lay tracing on cardboard. Using ruler and ball-point pen, go over traced lines, pressing firmly to make impression on cardboard. Remove tracing and darken impressions with pencil. Cut along lines to make templates.

2. Preheat oven to 325 degrees. Coat cookie sheets with butter and lightly dust with flour. Take dough from refrigerator and remove from bag; place on cookie sheet. (Let dough warm up for about 10 minutes before rolling.) Put bath towel on work surface, then put cookie sheet on top of towel. Lightly flour rolling pin, then roll out dough to ¼" thick, or until dough covers cookie sheet.

3. Lay templates on top of dough and cut around each using serrated plastic knife. For each house, cut two front/back pieces, two side pieces, and three roof/-base pieces. Repeat process on

Decorating with Royal Icing

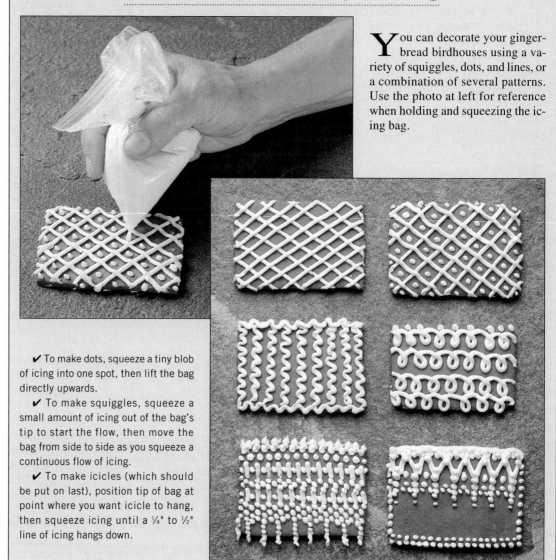

Y ou can decorate your gingerbread birdhouses using a variety of squiggles, dots, and lines, or a combination of several patterns. Use the photo at left for reference when holding and squeezing the icing bag.

✔ To make dots, squeeze a tiny blob of icing into one spot, then lift the bag directly upwards.

✔ To make squiggles, squeeze a small amount of icing out of the bag's tip to start the flow, then move the bag from side to side as you squeeze a continuous flow of icing.

✔ To make icicles (which should be put on last), position tip of bag at point where you want icicle to hang, then squeeze icing until a ¼" to ½" line of icing hangs down.

second cookie sheet.

4. Break toothpicks in half and cut off sharp ends with scissors. Using pattern as reference, stick broken end into each front piece to serve as a perch. Use new pencil eraser to make hole above perch, moving in a circular pattern until desired size is reached.

5. Bake all gingerbread pieces for 10 to 15 minutes. Test for doneness by inserting knife blade into base piece; if blade comes out clean, gingerbread is done. If necessary, trim any rough edges or pieces which have run together. Let gingerbread cool at least 20 minutes.

6. Remove one bag of icing from refrigerator. Using scissors, make a ⅛" diagonal snip across

one corner of bag. Twist bag gently so icing flows down to cut area. Squeeze small amount of icing onto paper plate to test how quickly it flows and what shape the beaded line takes.

7. Squeeze a vertical line of icing on each side of back piece from roofline to floor. Stand back piece upright, and using these lines of icing as glue, attach two side pieces to back.

8. Squeeze a vertical line of icing on each side of front piece. Stand front piece upright and attach to three-sided assembly from step 7 using icing as glue, then allow to set about 5 minutes.

9. Carefully lift partially assembled house and set on base. Note its position, then lift away

and pipe icing onto base so that it corresponds to house bottom. Position house on top of icing and press very gently to adhere. Pipe icing around base of birdhouse as desired to suggest snowbanks. Decorate sides, front, and back pieces as desired. (*See* photographs and "Decorating with Royal Icing," above.)

10. To attach roof, squeeze a continuous line of icing around top edges of walls and position roof pieces one at a time. Gently press into icing, then let set about 10 minutes. (Don't worry about making perfect joints, as the royal icing will conceal any gaps.) Squeeze icing onto roof sides and peak to suggest shingling or accumulated snow and icicles. ◆

How to Antique Fabric

Transform inexpensive fabric into antique cloth using tea-staining techniques.

BY PAT CASTKA AND SUSAN WILSON

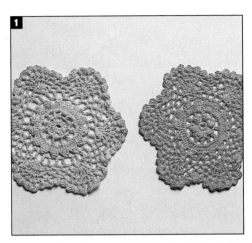

1. Lace doily submerged in Lipton tea for 5 minutes (left) and 30 minutes (right).

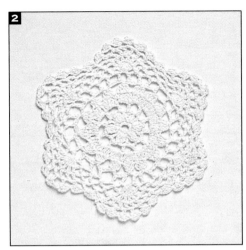

2. Lace doily before dyeing.

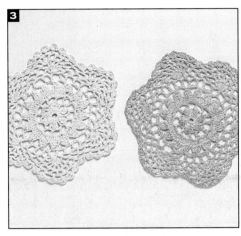

3. Lace doily submerged in mint tea for 5 minutes (left) and 30 minutes (right).

Staining fabric using tea, a natural dye, is one of the simplest means of obtaining an aged or antiqued look. Two easy techniques, which we tested with a variety of fabrics and tea types, can produce dramatic results in less than five minutes.

Tea-stained fabrics can be used in several ways. An aged lace runner or doily lends a vintage look to a dresser or table, while tea-stained ribbon on a bedspread gives a certain warmth. Tea-stained worsted wool makes a nice choice of fabric for a teddy bear, while stained satin is ideal for sewing sachets or assembling tiny roses. Dyed muslin or cotton works well for quilt squares or soft furnishings such as pillows.

For this article, we narrowed the field of fabrics to those that look most natural with an antiqued finish. We tested a white cotton lace doily, squares of unbleached muslin, a section of polyester ribbon, a polyester lace runner, a piece of cream-colored worsted wool, and squares of off-white polyester satin. Tea dyeing works best on light-colored, natural fibers such as cotton, linen, or wool. The higher the synthetic fiber content, the more resistant the fabic is to dye. Fabrics such as polyester and nylon are sometimes difficult to dye, although we had some beautiful results with the polyester ribbon and the polyester lace runner shown in photographs 14 and 15, page 11.

There is an endless variety of tea on the market. We chose two that are commonly available—Lipton and Tetley Orange Pekoe—and tested them on our fabrics for five, ten, twenty, and thirty minutes each. The photographs show the two extremes on most of the fabrics. Naturally, a wide range of shades is possible, depending on the particular tea, the fabric selected, and the soaking time.

Certain fabrics, such as muslin and polyester satin, were tested with two staining techniques, each of which produced different results. In the first technique, the fabric was dyed, then rinsed with cold water, then laid flat and allowed to dry. In the second, the fabric was dyed, then *not* rinsed but simply crumpled into a ball while still wet and allowed to dry that way. The first technique produced an even overall color, while the second produced veins of tea stain, almost like tie-dyeing (*see* photographs 4 and 5, page 10).

We also soaked the lace doily (one of the best choices for dyeing) in four other teas to give an idea of the range of shades possible. In an effort to stick to a true antiqued look, we tested brown teas and, with the exception of Red Zinger, steered clear of those with other distinct colors. Naturally, a wide variety of colors, shades, and effects are possible by using green, yellow, red, or purple teas.

Getting Started

Many of the guidelines which apply to commercial dyes (such as Rit or Tintex) also apply to tea: The darker you want the fabric, the more tea bags you should use and the longer the object should soak. (Remember, the fabric will look several shades darker when wet.) Soaking tea and fabrics in hot water dye baths generally works better than soaking them in cold, although cold baths can be used if you want a light shade, or if the fabric requires a long dyeing time. (The one exception to this rule is wool. As hot water will cause wool to shrink a great deal, we recommend cool water for dyeing wool. Expect longer dyeing times as a result.) To retain a darker stain, don't rinse the fabric after dyeing. For lighter shades, rinse the fabric in cold running water.

To set the dye, add a small amount of vinegar to your tea bath. The vinegar acts as a mordant to fix the color.

Newly purchased fabric is generally coated with size, a finish which can prevent dyes from taking, so wash your fabrics before dyeing them, and be aware that most fabrics shrink when washed. Take special care when washing wool, as shrinkage can be extreme.

Once you've placed your fabric in the tea bath, move it around with a paint stirring stick or an old wooden spoon. (The tea will stain the wood, so use something you won't need again for cooking.) We also recommend purchasing a clean pair of rubber gloves and wearing those while dyeing. The gloves will protect your hands from the hot water and tea stain when you're squeezing out the extra dye.

If you're dyeing a fabric other than those we tested, and you want to be certain of your results, run a test by soaking a small corner or scrap of the fabric using different teas and dye-

4. Muslin, soaked in Tetley tea, and left crumpled while drying. Clockwise from left: 30 minutes, 5 minutes, and undyed.

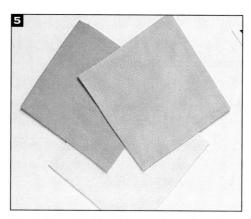

5. Muslin, soaked in Lipton tea for various times and dried flat. Clockwise from left: 30 minutes, 5 minutes, and undyed.

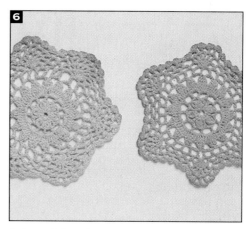

6. Lace doily submerged in Red Zinger tea for 5 minutes (left) and 30 minutes (right).

ing times. If you use one of the fabrics and teas we've used here, we've already done your testing for you.

Before moving to the tea-staining directions on page 11, it's important to understand how different fabrics react to the process.

Cotton Lace Doily

Cotton doilies absorb dye quickly and require only a short dyeing time of five minutes or less for light hues and a slightly longer dyeing time for darker colors.

In the test results shown on these various pages, we submerged a lace doily in each of the teas for five minutes, and then for thirty minutes. We did this with Red Zinger, Lipton, mint tea, black tea, Tetley, and Constant Comment. You can see how the results varied. Soaking the doily in Lipton for thirty minutes produced the darkest tone (*see* photograph 1, page 9). Black tea was somewhat disappointing, as we had expected more dramatic results (*see* photograph 9, page 11).

Red Zinger, like other colored teas, takes tea staining in an entirely new direction. Whereas most teas are brown and produce

varying shades of brown stain, Red Zinger produces a red stain. We liked the results on the lace doily (*see* photograph 6, above). However, when we tested crumpled satin in Red Zinger we ended up with what looked like a blood-stained rag.

For a subtle tint, submerge the doily in tea, then immediately remove it, squeeze the excess dye from the fabric, and rinse. For darker shades, use longer dyeing times and eliminate rinsing. Doilies tend to dry unevenly, resulting in some variation in hue, even when you have rinsed them and dried them flat. For the most part, drying flat (versus crumpling the doily) worked best.

Muslin

Muslin is an excellent choice for tea-staining, because the results are easy to control. Muslin is lightweight by nature and its cotton fibers are very absorbent, so it takes the tea dye well. Of all the fabrics tested, muslin was most affected by subtle changes in dyeing times.

We achieved an even overall color by rinsing out the excess tea and drying the muslin flat. It's possible to achieve darker tones by

drying the cloth flat without the benefit of rinsing. Muslin is also a good candidate for the crumpled approach to tea-staining (*see* photographs 4 and 5, above). We were able to achieve consistent, subtle veins of color with a range of soaking times.

Worsted Wool

We tested the wool with Tetley tea to achieve a golden brown color for use in sewing a wool teddy bear (*see* photograph 10, below). Thick and absorbent, worsted wool absorbs dye quickly. For best results, dampen the fabric slightly beforehand, as this makes the dye take more evenly. Dry wool took the dye unevenly. To assure even coverage, submerge the dampened wool completely, then squeeze the fabric with gloved hands to saturate all the fibers.

When dyeing wool, we had best results using a cool bath with double the amount of tea. In general, wool needs less dyeing time than other fabrics.

Polyester

Tea dye is excellent for toning down bright white polyester satin. It mellows and ages the

10. Teddy bear head sewn from wool soaked for 30 minutes in Tetley tea.

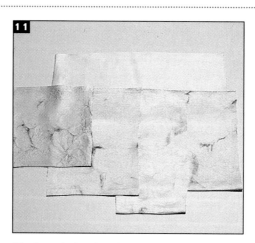

11. Crumpled satin before dyeing (top), and after soaking (left to right): Lipton, 5 minutes; Tetley, 30 minutes; Tetley, 5 minutes; Lipton, 30 minutes.

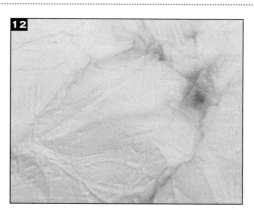

12. Polyester satin may repel tea to a certain extent, causing the tea to collect in some areas. The resulting darker veins and patches like those shown here can be intensified using the crumpled method of drying.

PHOTOGRAPHS BY DAVE HENDERSON

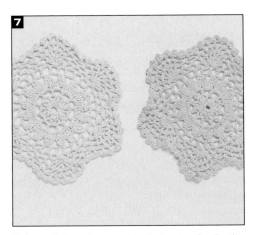

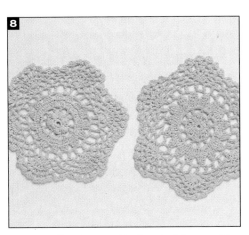

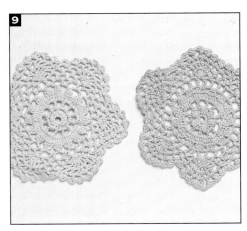

7. Lace doily submerged in Tetley tea for 5 minutes (left) and 30 minutes (right).

8. Lace doily submerged in Constant Comment tea for 5 minutes (left) and 30 minutes (right).

9. Lace doily submerged in black tea for 5 minutes (left) and 30 minutes (right).

fabric effectively without taking away its satiny sheen.

Unlike cotton or wool, however, the man-made fibers in polyester satin prevent it from absorbing dye well or quickly. To achieve the mottled effects shown in photograph 12 on page 10, we crumpled the satin, left it submerged for thirty minutes (a time that would have resulted in deep shades of brown on cotton or muslin), then crumpled it in a ball and set it aside to dry. (For a comparison of five-minute and thirty-minute submersions, *see* photograph 11, page 10.)

Other forms of polyester were also difficult, as most polyester fibers are resistant to dye. Even after thirty minutes of soaking, they never achieve the dark tones of tea-stained cotton or muslin. The fabric repels the tea, and when rinsed, most of the dye washes out. However, it's possible to create a subtle tint which is quite pleasing, as shown on the polyester lace runner in photograph 15, below, or the polyester ribbon shown in photograph 14, below.

You can also use the "repelling" nature of polyester to your advantage. As the fibers in the fabric repel the tea, the tea collects in other areas of the cloth, creating darker or patchy areas of stain. To enhance this effect, we recommend using the crumpled technique of dyeing. (*See* photograph 12, page 10.)

ANTIQUING FABRIC WITH TEA

The following materials and directions will dye about one yard of light muslin cotton. For larger quantities of fabric, simply multiply each supply below by the number of yards of fabric (i.e., double the ingredients for two yards, triple them for three yards, and so on) and use a container large enough for the fabric to move freely in the bath. (If the container is too small, you'll have wrinkles in your fabric which the hot water can set permanently.)

1 yard prewashed fabric for dyeing
5 tea bags
1 tablespoon white vinegar
2 cups water

You'll also need: small to medium-size metal pan; two teaspoons; paint stirring stick or old wooden spoon; and a pair of rubber gloves.

Other items, if necessary: sink for rinsing fabric; iron for pressing crumpled fabric.

1. Heat 2 cups water to rolling boil; add tea bags and turn off heat. (Use cool water when dyeing wool.)

2. Let tea bags soak about 10 minutes; remove tea bags using two teaspoons, and squeeze excess tea from bags between spoons. Add vinegar.

3. While dye bath is still very hot, submerge fabric, stirring occasionally with paint stirring stick or wooden spoon to ensure fabric is fully saturated. Let fabric sit in bath for desired amount of time.

4. Pull on rubber gloves. Lift out fabric with stirring stick or wooden spoon, and squeeze out excess dye. For even overall color, rinse fabric in sink with cold running water and dry flat. For mottled look, do not rinse, crumple wet fabric in ball and set aside to dry. When dry, iron flat. ◆

Pat Caska, a professional seamstress, lives in West Sayville, New York. **Susan Wilson** is a directions editor for *Handcraft Illustrated*.

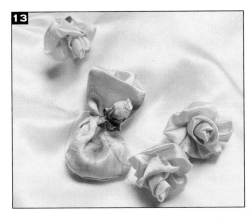

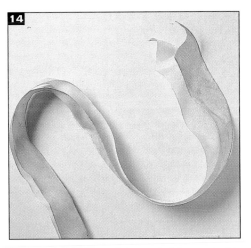

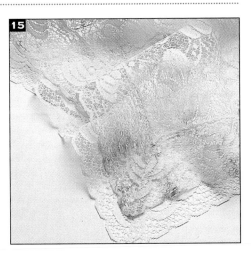

13. Satin roses and sachet assembled from fabric that was soaked for 30 minutes and left crumpled to dry. Left to right: Mint tea; Lipton; Constant Comment; Tetley.

14. Undyed polyester ribbon and ribbon soaked in Lipton tea for 30 minutes.

15. Polyester lace runner before dyeing and after dyeing in Tetley tea for 30 minutes.

Heirloom Mantel Skirt

Two quick calculations yield a custom-fit holiday mantel skirt.

BY MARY FRAZIER

This holiday season, instead of decorating your mantel with greens or candles, make an elegant, custom-fit mantel skirt for a fraction of the cost of what professional decorators charge.

Before you shop for materials, you'll need to measure the depth and width of your mantel and do a few quick calculations. In this case, depth refers to the distance from the front edge of the mantel to the wall, and width refers to the distance from side to side across the front of the mantel. This mantel skirt can be adapted to fit just about any width rectangular mantel, but it *will not* fit rectangular mantels with a depth greater than 12", or mantels that are curved, scalloped, or ornately shaped. (To further coordinate your holiday decorations, sew the matching Tree Skirt on page 30. While the two projects are presented separately, many of the techniques are the same, and I used the same fabrics and trim for both.)

This heirloom Victorian mantel skirt can be customized to fit rectangular mantels no deeper than 12".

Because this skirt is designed to be customized, this project differs from ordinary sewing projects in three key places. First, both the side and front patterns have a dotted line marked "adjust here." This is where you'll make any adjustments in the width of the pattern in order to ensure a perfect fit for your mantel. Second, although the top pattern piece is found on the cutting diagram on page 13, you'll need to create your own top piece based on the measurements of your mantel. Third, unlike most patterns, the mantel skirt pattern pieces here *do not* include seam allowances, since customizing is much easier without them. Once you've adjusted the pattern pieces to fit your mantel and you've laid them out on your fabric, you'll need to add seam allowances by cutting ½" beyond the edges of the pattern pieces (except those edges placed on folds).

Once you've measured your mantel, three possible scenarios will arise:

(1) If your mantel's depth measures greater than 12", this pattern will not fit. (2) If your mantel width measures 53" wide or less, and the depth measures 12" or less, you can use the patterns and cutting diagram found on page 13. You will be able to fit the pattern pieces on the crosswise grain of 54"- or 60"-wide fabric. (3) If your mantel width measures 54" wide or more, and its depth measures 12" or less, use the pattern pieces on page 13, *but use the cutting diagram on page 15.*

For mantels falling into this third scenario, you'll need to "railroad" the fabric to avoid having a seam in the front of the skirt. Railroading means cutting the pieces on the lengthwise grain of the fabric rather than on its crosswise grain. (The crosswise grain runs at a right angle to the fabric's selvage, a narrow, tightly-woven border found along two sides of the fabric. Lengthwise grain runs parallel to the fabric's selvage.) Many upholstery fabrics are specially designed with the pattern running lengthwise and are meant to be railroaded. Other fabrics can also be railroaded, as long as they don't have an obvious one-way pattern or a design that will look funny when turned sideways. To determine the amount of fabric you'll need when railroading, add 2" to your mantel width. (For example, for a 70" mantel, you'll need 72"—2 yards—of fabric.)

Upholstery fabrics come in two standard widths: 54" and 60". However, some fabrics that are labeled 54" actually measure a few inches more, depending on the manufacturer. If your mantel is 54" wide, and you want to avoid railroading, measure the fabric width yourself rather than relying on the label. You may be able to fit the pattern across the fabric width. One important note: You must cut each pattern piece from both the facing and lining fabrics, and if you railroad the facing fabric, you must also railroad the lining. If you don't, the opposing grains will pull at each other, and the skirt will not hang properly.

For all three scenarios mentioned above, you must use your own depth and width measurements to create a pattern piece for your mantel top. To do this, lay brown wrapping paper or butcher paper on a flat surface and draw a rectangle that measures half your mantel's width by its full depth.

With a copying machine, enlarge the front and side pattern pieces found on page 13 until each square measures 1", taping together pieces as necessary. Trim off any extra paper. To adjust the width of the front and side patterns, *see steps 4 and 5 on page 14.*

Note that the front and side pattern pieces are also marked "lengthen here." The skirt is designed so that it can be lengthened by up to 3". Once you've cut out your pattern pieces and adjusted the width, I recommend taping the front and side pattern pieces to one half of the mantel and assessing the mantel skirt's length. You may need to lengthen the pattern, depending on the height and shape of your fireplace opening. (Keep in mind that the tassel will be attached to the center, adding another 6" to 8" drop; you can adjust the skirt or the tassel as necessary so the tassel doesn't dangle near the fire.) To add length, tape scrap paper extensions onto the pattern. Be sure to cut or add the same amount to both the front and side pieces, and tape the altered pattern to the mantel to double-check the new length.

Once you've adjusted your pattern pieces, use them to cut out one front, two sides, and one top piece from both the facing and lining fabrics, for a total of eight pieces in all.

Three of the trims used in this project must be purchased by the yard. Two trims—the gold ½"-thick twisted rope welting and the ⅜"-thick green-cranberry twisted cord—are attached to the scalloped edge of the mantel skirt. The gold welting is sewn in place, while the green-cranberry cord is glued on. To determine how much of each of these two trims to buy, add together the mantel's width and twice the mantel's depth, then multiply that number by 1.15 to get the total yardage. (For example, for a mantel measuring 60" wide and 12" deep, buy 97"—60"+24"=84", and 84"x1.15=96.6"—or about 2¾ yards of trim.) All mantels, regardless of size, require ⅝ yard of the third trim, the ½"-thick gold metallic braid.

For the finishing trims, I purchased nine 27" cable cord chair ties with tassels at each end. (Any fabric store with an upholstery section should carry these.) Some of these ties will be used with the tassels attached, while others will be used without the tassels. You can save the extra tassels for another project, or attach them elsewhere on the mantel skirt.

When selecting fabrics, I recommend heavier-weight fabrics with a lot of body, such as damasks, heavy-weight brocades, or upholstery-weight silks. For the project pictured, I used a hefty green damask called Serenity/Ivy for the facing fabric, and cranberry upholstery fabric called Gibson/Crimson for the lining. I recommend using a heavyweight fabric for the lining (instead of a traditional, lighter-weight lining) to add more body to the skirt.

A few other notes regarding trims. Be sure to tape any exposed ends of the trim and cording with masking tape to prevent unraveling. For the finishing steps, you'll glue a variety of trims in place. When attaching the green-cranberry twisted cord along the lower edge of the skirt, I recommend using washable fabric glue. Use tacky glue to attach the cords and insignia in the center. Fabric glue remains flexible when dry, so the draped edge will be pliable instead of stiff. Tacky glue tends to be stiff when it dries, but items pressed into it adhere immediately. This will help when pressing the pretzel knots into place—they won't pop up, and you can arrange them and glue them in place without having to use pins.

HEIRLOOM MANTEL SKIRT

Fabric
For mantel up to 53" wide:
1⅛ yard 54" dark green fabric (for facing)
1⅛ yard 54" cranberry fabric (for lining)

For mantel 54" or wider:
1 piece each of dark green and cranberry fabric, railroaded so fabric yardage equals mantel width plus 2" (*see* introductory discussion, page 12)

Trim
For all mantels: add together mantel width and twice the depth, then multiply that number by 1.15 for total trim yardage:
½"-thick gold twisted rope welting
⅜"-thick green-cranberry twisted cord

5 gold 27" cable cord chair ties
4 wine 27" cable cord chair ties
⅝ yard ½"-thick gold metallic braid
1 gold metallic filigree-style appliqué, about 2¾" across
Green, cranberry, and gold cotton-covered polyester thread
White fabric glue
White tacky glue

You'll also need: Access to a copying machine; sewing machine with zipper foot attachment; hand sewing needles; straight pins; scissors; iron; scrap paper; pencil; fabric marking pencil; ruler or yardstick; transparent tape; masking tape; 6" saucer or plate; and brown wrapping paper or butcher paper.

Customizing the Mantel Skirt Pattern
1. Measure mantel depth and width to determine necessary yardage of fabric and trims.
2. Start by making the top pattern piece. Lay brown wrapping paper or butcher paper on flat surface, then use pencil and ruler or yardstick

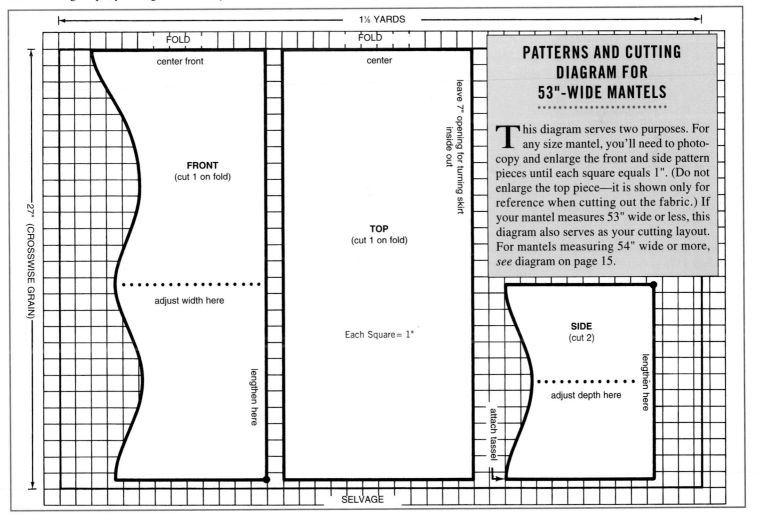

1⅛ YARDS

FOLD · center front · FOLD · center

leave 7" opening for turning skirt inside out

27" (CROSSWISE GRAIN)

FRONT
(cut 1 on fold)

adjust width here

lengthen here

TOP
(cut 1 on fold)

Each Square = 1"

PATTERNS AND CUTTING DIAGRAM FOR 53"-WIDE MANTELS

This diagram serves two purposes. For any size mantel, you'll need to photocopy and enlarge the front and side pattern pieces until each square equals 1". (Do not enlarge the top piece—it is shown only for reference when cutting out the fabric.) If your mantel measures 53" wide or less, this diagram also serves as your cutting layout. For mantels measuring 54" wide or more, *see* diagram on page 15.

SIDE
(cut 2)

lengthen here

adjust depth here

attach tassel

SELVAGE

to draw a rectangle that measures half of your mantel's width by its full depth. (The long side of the rectangle should equal half the width, and the shorter side should equal the mantel's depth.) Cut out along edges using scissors.

3. With copying machine, enlarge front and side pattern pieces on page 13 so each box measures 1", taping sheets together as necessary. (*Do not enlarge top pattern piece.*) With scissors, cut out patterns along marked outlines.

4. To adjust the mantel's width, line up long, straight edges of top and front pattern pieces on flat surface. Cut front piece into two sections along line marked "adjust width here."

To enlarge width of front pattern piece, pull two sections of front pattern piece apart, keeping cut edges parallel, until width of front piece matches width of top piece. Fill gap created by pulling two sections apart by arranging sheet(s) of scrap paper with top edges aligned, and tape in place. Using pencil, draw freehand the mantel's lower edge across scrap paper, then cut

paper along marked line to complete pattern.

To reduce width of front pattern piece, overlap two sections of front piece until width of front piece equals width of top piece. Tape in place. If lower edge of new pattern is uneven, slip a sheet of scrap paper underneath, tape in place, then draw a new edge. Cut on marked line to complete pattern.

5. To adjust depth of side pattern pieces, use principles in step 4. Lay top and side pieces side by side, with corresponding straight edges matching. Cut side piece into two sections along line marked "adjust depth here."

To shorten depth of side pattern piece, overlap two sections of side piece, tape in place, and redraw edge. Cut out along marked lines. (*Note: Widening the depth of the side pattern piece is not an option, as this pattern will not work on mantels deeper than 12".*)

6. Tape front and side pattern pieces to one half of mantel to assess length. *To lengthen skirt,* tape scrap paper extensions to front and

side pattern pieces. (*Note: Take care to add or cut the same amount from both pattern pieces to ensure a perfect fit.*) Tape new pattern pieces to mantel and double-check length.

Cutting the Pattern Pieces

1. Choose a cutting layout that corresponds to your mantel's width (53" wide or less, use the cutting diagram on page 13; 54" or wider, use the cutting diagram on page 15).

If following diagram for mantels 53" wide or less, fold facing (green) fabric in half lengthwise, wrong sides facing. Lay pattern pieces on fabric, lining up front and top pattern pieces with fold. Allow at least 1" between pattern pieces. Pin in place.

If following diagram for mantels 54" wide or more, fold facing fabric in half crosswise, then lay top and front pattern pieces on fold. Allow at least 1" between pattern pieces. Pin in place.

2. Cut out all pattern pieces ½" beyond pattern lines to add seam allowances. Using fab-

Making the Mantel Skirt

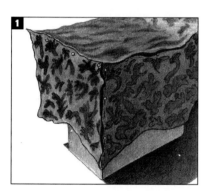

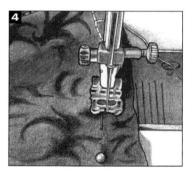

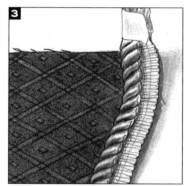

1. To double-check the fit of the cut pattern pieces, pin them together and position them on the mantel.

2. This diagram shows the short, straight edge of the side piece attached to the short, straight edge of the front piece.

3. Before stitching the gold welting to the lining fabric, allow 1" of excess trim to extend beyond the fabric at each end. Once the mantel skirt is turned right side out, these ends are inserted into a 1" unsewn opening, resulting in a neatly finished edge.

4. Once the facing and lining pieces have been pinned together (with the gold welting sandwiched in between), begin stitching 1½" in from the end of the fabric. This creates an opening through which to insert the cord ends once the mantel skirt is turned right side out.

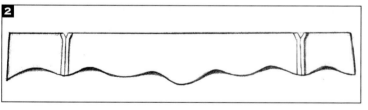

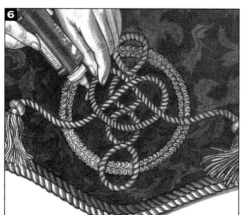

6. Form a continuous piece of wine-colored cord by gluing together the ends of a wine-colored chair cord right behind the tassels, and then cutting the tassels off. Twist this piece into four 2" loops, creating what looks like two stacked figure eights. Apply a small dot of tacky glue to each place where the cord overlaps, then glue the double figure eight on top of the gold braid circle. Arrange one gold chair tie in a loose pretzel shape inside the gold braid circle, allowing the tasseled ends to fall outside the circle at each side, then glue the tie in place.

5. Insert the taped end of the green-cranberry twisted cord into the 1" unsewn opening, then glue the cord in place with fabric glue along the scalloped edge.

7. Position the two smaller wine-colored pretzels between the gold pretzel and the edge of the gold braid circle, with the tassels falling outside the lower edge of the gold braid circle. Glue the tie in place.

ILLUSTRATIONS BY WENDY WRAY

ric pencil, transfer small dots at corners to wrong side of fabric. If desired, pin cut facing fabric pieces together and place on mantel to double-check fit. (*See* illustration 1, page 14.)

3. Repeat steps 1 and 2 with lining (cranberry) fabric. You should have a total of 8 pieces: 1 top, 1 front, and 2 sides in each color.

Assembling the Mantel Skirt

For steps 1, 2, 3, and 6, use a regular presser foot on your sewing machine. For steps 4 and 5, use a zipper foot attachment.

1. Thread machine with cranberry thread. Using illustration 2 on page 14 as reference, pin short, straight edge of lining side pieces to short, straight edge of lining front piece, right sides together, and stitch making ½" seams. Start at curved edge and stitch toward straight edge, stopping at dot (½" from top straight edge), with needle in down position. Backtack (sew backwards for a few stitches) to secure each seam. With iron, press seams open.

2. Pin sewn piece from step 1 to lining top piece, right sides together, and matching one long and two short edges. With front piece on top, stitch together. Make a separate seam for each edge, and break off thread before starting a new line of stitching. Backtack at dots that begin or end a line of stitching. Press seams open.

3. Thread machine with green thread. Repeat steps 1 and 2 with facing (green) fabric pieces.

4. Install zipper foot attachment on sewing machine. Thread machine with gold thread; thread bobbin with cranberry thread. Wrap both ends of gold rope welting with masking tape to prevent raveling. Pin welting to lower edge of front and side lining pieces, right side of welting facing right side of fabric and flat edge of welting matching curves of skirt. Allow welting to extend 1" beyond fabric at each end (illustration 3, page 14). Sew welting to fabric, getting needle as close to edge of welting as possible. Begin stitching 1½" in

from end of fabric.

5. Thread sewing machine with cranberry thread; thread bobbin with green thread. Pin facing and lining pieces together, right sides facing and curves and seams matching. As in step 4, begin stitching 1½" in from end of fabric (illustration 4, page 14). With lining fabric on top, stitch over previous stitching along curved edge and through all layers, getting needle as close to edge of welting as possible. Continue along entire edge.

6. Reinstall regular presser foot on sewing machine. Stitch remaining seams all around facing and lining pieces, leaving 7" open where marked along top edge. Turn piece right side out through opening and press. Insert ends of welting into unsewn openings at edge of skirt. Slipstitch 7" opening closed using green thread.

Applying the Final Trims

1. Tape one end of green-cranberry twisted cord with masking tape to prevent raveling. Insert end of cord into unsewn opening at one edge of skirt (illustration 5, page 14). Working 4" to 6" at a time, apply fabric glue to facing fabric just above sewn-on welting. Press cord into glue, securing with pins if necessary until dry. At other end of skirt, wrap cord with tape 1" beyond edge of fabric, then cut through middle of tape for clean edge. Insert end of cord into unsewn opening, then slipstitch both openings closed using green thread.

2. Center 6" saucer or plate face down on mantel front. Using saucer or plate as template, apply line of tacky glue around saucer or plate edges. Lift saucer or plate straight up off fabric and set aside, then press gold braid into glue to form circle. For a clean finish, overlap ends of braid and cut through both layers at once before gluing in place.

3. Twist tasseled ends of one wine-colored chair tie around each other for 1" to 2", then glue twisted pieces together with tacky glue. When dry, cut off tassels. You should now have one continuous piece of wine-colored cord. Lay this cord on flat surface and twist into four 2" loops, creating what looks like two stacked figure eights (illustration 6, page 14). Apply small dot of tacky glue to each overlap. When dry, lay this double figure eight atop gold braid circle, with 1" of top and bottom loops overlapping gold braid circle. Glue in place with tacky glue, gluing small sections at a time from top to bottom, but leave loop closest to skirt edge unglued.

4. Arrange one gold chair tie in a loose pretzel shape inside gold braid circle and atop the double figure eight. Allow tasseled ends to fall outside circle at each side, then glue in place (illustration 6, page 14).

5. Tie two small pretzel shapes near center of

one wine tie, and position these between gold pretzel formed in step 4 and gold braid circle. Position tassels outside lower edge of gold braid circle, and glue entire length of tie in place (illustration 7, page 14).

6. (For steps 6 and 7, *see* photograph on page 12 as reference.) Apply glue to end of one gold tie just above tassel. Let dry, then snip off tassel (the glue will prevent the tie from unraveling). Glue cut end of tie behind gold tassel positioned in step 4, then pull tie loosely across front of skirt towards side, creating a drape. Pin tie to fabric about 4" above tassel, allowing tassel to hang loosely. (Exact position of tassel will vary, depending on size of mantel.) Repeat on opposite side. Adjust both ties as necessary to match, then glue to fabric at pins using tacky glue. (Do not glue draped section of tie.)

7. Twist and glue ends of two wine ties together and cut off tassels as in step 3 to form longer version of chair tie. Center tie at top edge of front piece, concealing front-top seam, and glue in place at several points. Allow tassels to hang free. Cut gold tie in half. Glue tassel close to wine tassel on top edge of front piece, then drape gold cord around corner of mantel skirt and glue to side piece. Cut one tassel off remaining gold tie; trim gold tie to 12" and re-attach tassel to end of cord. Loop gold tie through unglued figure eight loop so tassels hang in front of fireplace opening. Glue appliqué to center of circle arrangement. ◆

Mary Frazier is a professional seamstress based in New York.

Assorted trims and chair ties are used to finish off the mantel skirt.

CUTTING DIAGRAM FOR MANTELS MEASURING 54" OR WIDER

36" (UNFOLDS TO 2 YARDS)

If your mantel measures 54" wide or more, this diagram serves as your cutting layout. Note that the pattern pieces are cut on the lengthwise grain rather than crosswise grain of the fabric, a practice known as railroading.

RAW EDGES (CROSSWISE GRAIN)

54" FOLD (CROSSWISE GRAIN)

SIDE (adjusted smaller) (cut 2)

fold — Leave 7" opening for turning skirt inside out — TOP (cut 1 on fold)

fold — FRONT (expanded layer) (cut 1 on fold)

SELVAGE (LENGTHWISE GRAIN)

Victorian Place Cards

Cut out and personalize your own nineteenth-century Christmas and floral place cards using our special insert.

❧ BY JUDITH WINSLOW ❧

This issue's insert features a collection of place cards assembled from antique Victorian images. You can cut out and use the place cards as they are, make multiple copies of them using a color copier, or follow the Victorian tradition of decorating place cards with tassels, silk fringe, or gilding.

These place cards represent two different Victorian traditions: an interest in the symbolism and language of flowers, and the practice of collecting small, often sentimental images of flowers, birds, or children for use in decoupage projects or scrapbooks.

Although in this day and age floral images are not typically associated with the holiday season, flowers and plant materials of all kinds held great interest for Victorians. Like needlework, flower identification and collection was an accepted pastime of genteel Victorian ladies, and the sending and receiving of bouquets was the custom. Out of this floramania emerged the "language of flowers," which assigned particular meanings to each kind of flower. These meanings were codified and published in popular books that enabled the giver of flowers (or the person who set the table, in this case) to send discreet messages. (Consult the chart below for the meanings of the flowers used in these place cards.)

Flowers were also symbols of luxury and renewal in the midst of winter's gloom, and were extensively used in Victorian Christmas imagery and decoration.

Victorian women were also fond of collecting scrap, a variety of colorful, embossed images depicting such items as birds, flowers, animals, children, well-dressed ladies, politicians, or historical figures. Such images were used to decoupage boxes or screens, or collected in albums or scrapbooks along with bits of poetry, dried flowers, or autographs. Much of this fascination with color images can be attributed to the introduction of chromolithography in the first half of the nineteenth century. Rich pieces of art, some containing as many as twelve colors or gilding, were printed from reverse images skillfully rendered on separate plates. Toward the end of the nineteenth century, scrap was available in sheets of specialized images designed especially for Victorian collectors.

Victorians were also fond of ornate objects, and you can decorate your place cards in that tradition by gluing on tassels, a cluster of three or four satin roses, tiny stamped metal ornaments, decorative cord or trim, or miniature bows tied from lace or gold mesh ribbon. Many of the ideas for decorating the folded boxes found in the September/October 1994 issue of *Handcraft Illustrated* (see "Fold Your Own Decorative Boxes," page 16 of that issue), such as outlining figures or borders with a fine-point Pilot gold marker, will also work on these place cards.

To use the place cards, cut around the square edges using household scissors, then write in each guest's name with a fine-line permanent marking pen. (While your own printing or script is the most personal inscription for a place card, you may wish to try calligraphic lettering. If you're not skilled in this area, purchase a felt-tip calligraphy pen at a stationer

This place card has been decorated with a fine-point gold marker.

or office supply store and practice on scrap paper.) Then, using manicure scissors and starting somewhere near the upper edge of the image, trim the image away from the back portion of the place card following the trim lines (*see* diagram on the insert). The place card can then be folded in half and placed on the table.

VICTORIAN PLACE CARDS

Place cards (*see* Special Insert, following page)

You'll also need: manicure scissors; household scissors; and fine-line marking pen.

Other items, if necessary: Access to color copier if making multiple copies; felt-tip calligraphy pen if using calligraphic lettering; decorative objects or markers, as noted above for decorating; and white tacky glue or hot-glue gun and glue sticks for attaching objects.

1. If making multiple copies, copy place cards onto heavyweight, glossy paper using color copier. Cut out place cards around square edges using household scissors. Write name using calligraphy or marking pen. If decorating cards with glue-on objects or markers, complete decorations before proceeding to step 2.

2. Insert tip of manicure scissors along solid cutting line, then neatly trim along contour of image. Do not cut along dashed fold line. Fold place card in half along dashed line and stand up on table. ◆

Judith Winslow designs a variety of crafts, gifts, and paper products.

THE LANGUAGE OF FLOWERS

Flower or Plant	Meaning
Apple blossoms	Preference, perpetual concord, temptation
Coral bells	Challenge, scholarship, hard work, or dainty pleasures
Ferns	Fascination or sincerity
Holly	Foresight, good will, or domestic happiness
Holly berries	Christmas joy or protection
Pansy	Loving thoughts
White daffodils	Regard, respect, chivalry, or grace
Yellow rose	Friendship, highest mark of distinction, jealousy, unfaithful, or forgive and forget

Make Your Own Victorian Place Cards

You can cut out these place cards and use them as they are, make copies of them using a color copier, or decorate them with gilding, tassels, fringe, or beading. If you're making copies, copy them onto heavyweight, glossy paper.

To make the place cards, start by cutting out each one along the square border using

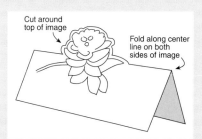

Cut around top of image

Fold along center line on both sides of image

scissors, then write each guest's name on the card. Decorate the cards if desired, then insert the tip of your manicure scissors somewhere on the solid cutting line and trim along the contour of the image. Do not cut along the dashed fold lines. Fold the card in half along the dashed lines and stand the card up on the table.

Silk Screen Photo Mat

Using a beginner's silk screen technique and our decorative border, you can print your own photo mats for use as greeting cards.

BY GABRIELLE NANCY STERBENZ

Whether you've tried silk screening before, or you're new to the process, this article will teach you a simpler method of silk screen printing. After careful experimentation, I've found several places where you can substitute commonly found items for more specialized silk screen equipment, and I've come up with a number of practically foolproof techniques.

For starters, you can assemble your silk screen from any existing wooden frame; you'll just need to purchase a piece of sheer polyester curtain fabric to use for the "silk." As a substitute for expensive silk-screening squeegees, I used an expired credit card, which is flexible, gets into the corners of the frame, and is just the right size. (If you don't have an expired credit card, I recommend a three-inch-wide plastic paint scraper.)

While many silk screening projects use two or more ink colors, this project is designed for just one, which keeps it simple. Furthermore, after testing several different colors of water-based printer's ink, I recommend printing with gold ink, as the metallic grains thicken the ink to a very dependable consistency, and the resulting image looks crisp.

Every silk screen project requires a means of transferring the image to be printed to the screen. More advanced techniques include tracing the outline of the design onto the screen and painting the background area with block-out fluid, but this requires good freehand painting skills. In this project, I've chosen an easier way: photocopy the selected artwork onto acetate, then coat the printing screen with an emulsion and photographically transfer the artwork to the screen. Although this emulsion takes approximately forty-five minutes to expose, I recommend using it with this project because it yields the most consistent results. (As you gain more experience, you may want to try products that are faster and more light-sensitive but require a darkroom to use.)

Silk screen printing is especially suited to producing small quantities of a single design. The project shown here is a floating picture mat for use with a 3" x 5" photograph. You can print as many mats as you need, and then affix a photo in the open area of each one. The finished pieces can be framed or used as greeting cards, thank-you notes, or invitations.

Your first step is selecting an image for

Printed with gold ink, the border is well suited for making your own greeting cards, thank-you notes, or invitations.

printing. You can use the border provided on page 18, or find one of your own. If using your own image, look for line drawings or black and white pictures that have distinct black and white areas. The best pieces will have solid shapes and lines that are neither too thin nor too complicated. Closely spaced lines tend to print together and turn into a mass of color, losing any delicacy or detail. Take your image (or the border we've provided) to a photocopy shop and have it copied onto clear acetate.

I assembled my silk screen using an old wooden picture frame, but you can also use artists' stretcher strips. They are sold in most art supply stores. The screen for silk screening is not actually silk, but a piece of sheer polyester curtain fabric which can be found in any fabric store. Look for very sheer fabric, often referred to as "denier," with at least 120 threads per inch. Fabrics with lower thread counts will allow too much ink to pass through the screen. Since the fabric is stretched taut over the frame, it should also be strong and durable.

Once the frame and fabric are assembled, you'll cover the screen with photographic emulsion in order to expose the image. Wet emulsion can take as little as fifteen minutes or as long as twenty-four hours to dry, depending on the temperature and humidity. On a dry day, you can speed up the drying time a small amount by carefully fanning the screen up and down. (Don't use a hair dryer, as emulsion

should not be exposed to heat.) Remember to keep the emulsion-covered screen out of direct or bright light. If you're not in a hurry, put the screen in a closet and let it dry overnight in complete darkness.

Just as the emulsion on ordinary camera film makes it possible to "take" a picture, emulsion applied to your screen allows it to "take" an image on acetate. To make the exposure, the acetate is laid on top of the prepared screen, and both are placed twelve inches below an adjustable desk lamp fitted with a 150-watt bulb. While the film in a camera is exposed with a quick opening and closing of the shutter that lasts only a fraction of a second, the screen requires a full forty-five minutes of exposure. It's important that the rest of the room be dark during this step and that the bulb be no closer than twelve inches to the screen. Extra light from other sources or light too close to the screen can cause white scorch marks on the final image, which affects the quality of the prints.

When the forty-five–minute exposure is up, the screen is rinsed under running water. The emulsion exposed to the light will stay in place, but the emulsion that was protected by the acetate image can be worked loose with an old, soft-bristled toothbrush and washed off. Don't rub too briskly, or you may strip off the surrounding emulsion. Examine the emerging image closely, and you should be able to make out the fibers in the screen fabric. It is through this mesh area that the ink will pass to print the image. Let the screen dry overnight in a dish rack before using it for printing. Although the fabric portion will feel dry to the touch in one or two hours, the frame may still contain moisture that could leach onto your paper.

Printing through the screen requires special printer's inks, which are sold in art supply stores. Their consistency allows them to pass through fine fabric without drenching it. Regular inks bleed once they touch the paper, creating smudges and blurs, and acrylic paints with the consistency of printer's ink may clog the screen. When inking the screen, it's better to use less ink and more pressure on the credit card to force the ink through the screen. If you don't put enough ink on the screen the first time, you can always add more.

I chose water-based printer's ink because it is easy to clean up and it works well on paper (but not on fabric or other material). While it is available in tubs, jars, or tubes, the jar and tub variety are runnier, which can result in blurred lines. I found the tube variety to have the best consistency. I chose metallic gold for my cards, but you can substitute just about any color except black, which smudges easily. The best paper to print on is a heavy bristol stock with a plate finish.

SILK SCREEN PHOTO MAT

2 each 10" and 12" artist's stretcher strips, *or* one 10" x 12" wooden frame
½ yard sheer polyester denier fabric, 120-thread count
   Speedball photo emulsion No. 4573
   Speedball sensitizer No. 4574
   Gold metallic water-based printer's ink (in tube)
   9" x 12" bristol paper with plate finish
   White tacky glue

You'll also need: access to copying machine; expired credit card or 3"-wide plastic paint scraper; transparent tape; plastic cup; plastic spoon; adjustable desk lamp with 150-watt bulb; staple gun and staples; old soft-bristled toothbrush; scissors; plain white paper for testing; kitchen timer with loud alarm; clothesline and clothespins; newspaper; and latex gloves.

Other items, if necessary: screwdriver for removing staples; and straightedge and X-Acto knife for cutting out center of mat.

Making the Screen

1. Cut a 4½" x 3" piece of white paper and tape over center of border (below) to cover text. Photocopy border onto acetate. Trim off text above and below border.

2. If using stretcher-strip frame, assemble to form 10" x 12" frame. Lay denier fabric on flat surface, then lay stretcher–strip or wooden frame on top of fabric. Trim fabric 2" beyond frame edges.

3. Fold excess 2" of fabric up and around frame edge on one side. Stand frame upright on opposite edge and staple through fabric into frame at center of topmost edge. Turn frame upside down, pull fabric taut across center of frame, and staple to center of edge that is now topmost. Staple fabric to center of two remaining edges in same way, pulling taut before stapling. Working from center out, continue stapling opposite edges every ¾" until fabric is secured and surface is drum-tight and smooth. If a bump develops, remove staple(s) with screwdriver, adjust tension, and restaple.

4. Trim excess fabric even with frame edge, then seal edge of fabric with bead of glue to prevent loose threads from getting on screen.

Applying the Emulsion

1. Work in dim place, such as garage or basement. Spread thick layer of newspaper over work surface. Lay screen on top of newspaper, fabric side up. Put on latex gloves. In a plastic cup, stir 4 teaspoons photo emulsion (blue) and 1 teaspoon photo sensitizer (yellow) together until green.

2. Drizzle one spoonful of green mixture across the "window" area of screen. Tilt credit

USING THIS BORDER

Cut a 4½" by 3" piece of white paper and tape it over this text. Photocopy this border onto acetate at your local photocopy store and then trim off the text above and below the border.

card or paint scraper at an angle and distribute mixture in a thin, even coat over screen surface. Add additional green mixture if necessary, and smooth with credit card or scraper.

3. Lift screen and set on end. Taking care not to touch wet area of screen or to rest wet area on newspaper, repeat step 2 on reverse side of screen. If sufficient green mixture has leached through screen, smooth mixture already present across surface.

4. Set screen back down on newspaper, fabric facing up. Repeat step 2 to add a very thin second coat on fabric side only.

5. Let screen dry (15 minutes to overnight, depending on conditions). Do not expose to light during drying. Proceed when surface is completely dry to touch. Clean up with water.

Exposing the Image on the Screen

1. Select a dim area in basement or garage near electrical outlet, and plug in (but don't turn on) desk lamp. Position lamp so bulb is 12" above work surface. Lay screen, fabric side up, on work surface directly under bulb.

2. Hold acetate so image facing you is the view you want to print. Flip and center image on screen with correct side face down.

3. Turn on lamp and adjust position as necessary so light shines on screen. Set timer for 45 minutes, but plan to return every 5 or 10 minutes to make sure lamp has not slipped out of position. Do not move or touch screen or acetate during exposure.

4. When timer goes off, turn off lamp, then slip acetate off screen. (You can now move to a lighted area.) Hold screen under running water, and using an old soft-bristled toothbrush, rub gently up, down, and sideways to remove emulsion in image areas. Continue rinsing and rubbing screen on both sides until image appears as clean, bare fabric, but take care not to overscrub. To see image more clearly, hold screen up to light. Set wet screen upright in a dish rack and let dry several hours or overnight until both fabric and frame are bone dry.

Printing the Image

1. Set up clothesline for drying. Spread thick layer of newspaper over work surface. Lay sheet of scrap paper on top of work surface. Center screen, fabric side down, on paper.

2. Squeeze a narrow line of ink across one edge of screen. Press down on screen with one hand to prevent shifting. With other hand, squeegee credit card up, down, and across screen to distribute ink evenly and force it through open mesh areas.

3. Lift screen (the paper should stick to it) and turn over. Slowly lift up one corner of paper and peel off screen in slow, continuous motion. Do not allow paper to fall back onto screen, as wet ink may end up outside the border on the screen. (If this happens, you must clean all the ink off the screen and let the screen

dry thoroughly before proceeding.) If image is satisfactory, begin printing with good paper. Repeat steps 1 through 3 for desired number of prints. Hang finished prints on clothesline and let dry 24 hours.

4. Clean up by rinsing screen and credit card under steady stream of hot water. Do not scrub screen with brush, as additional emulsion may come off. Hold screen to light and double-check that all mesh areas are free of ink. Let

screen dry and store upright.

5. When prints are dry, mount photos directly on them, centering photos within borders, or cut a traditional mat opening slightly smaller than your photos using X-Acto knife and straightedge. ◆

Gabrielle Nancy Sterbenz is a student at New York University who enjoys silk screening, painting, and quilting.

Key Steps of Silk Screening

1. Fold the excess fabric up and around the frame edge on one side. Stand the frame upright on the opposite edge and staple through the fabric into the frame at the center of the top edge. Turn the frame upside down, pull the fabric taut across the center of the frame, and staple to the center of the new top edge. Repeat for the other two edges. Working from the center out, continue stapling opposite edges every ¾" until the surface is drum-tight and smooth.

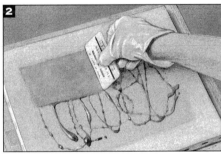

2. Drizzle the green emulsion mixture across the screen. Tilt the credit card at an angle and distribute the mixture in a thin, even coat. Expose the screen and the acetate image.

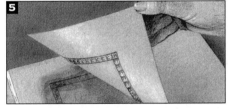

3. After exposing the screen, hold it under running water and use a toothbrush to remove the emulsion from the image areas. Continue rinsing on both sides until the image appears as clean, bare fabric, but take care not to over-scrub. Let the screen dry.

4. Squeeze a narrow line of ink across the edge of the screen surface. Squeegee the credit card up, down, and across the screen to distribute the ink evenly and force it through the open mesh areas.

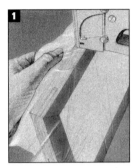

5. Lift the screen (the paper should stick to it) and turn it over. Then slowly lift up one corner of the paper and peel it off the screen in a slow, continuous motion.

EVALUATING COMMON MISTAKES

1. If the lines of your printed image are broken, try adding more ink or distributing the ink more evenly. If that doesn't help, check the screen image. It may be flawed, either because the emulsion wasn't applied evenly or because the original artwork had lines that were too thin or too closely grouped.

2. If the lines of the image are thick and fuzzy, or are running together, you have probably used too much ink or the wrong type of ink, or you may have rubbed the ink too many times across the screen.

3. If the ink printed in places outside of your image, you'll need to find the corresponding areas on the screen and fill them in with screen filler from an art supply store. Before you apply the filler, make sure the screen is dry and free of ink. Dip a small artist's paintbrush into the screen filler and brush it onto the side of the screen to which you apply the ink. Work carefully, since the filler adheres firmly to any screen surface it touches. Let it dry completely.

Victorian Christmas Cornucopia

Use our vintage design to decorate your Christmas tree with cornucopia ornaments.

Decorate the cornucopia as shown, or outline the pansies with a gold or silver Pilot marker and line the cone with fabric.

This pansy cornucopia, which you can make in less than thirty minutes, represents two Victorian traditions. Its cone-shaped design and ornate decoration are reminiscent of a vintage Victorian ornament. In addition, it reflects the Victorian fondness for flowers no matter what the season.

Decoration of Christmas trees first became popular in the late 1840s when the *Illustrated London News* published an engraving and an elaborate description of Queen Victoria's and Prince Albert's Christmas tree. Among the treasures hanging from its branches were little cornucopias used as "receptacles for sweetmeats" and tiny gifts.

This cornucopia can be hung on a tree or in a window just as it is, or you can fill it with small gifts or wrapped candies. We've trimmed it with paper lace, draped it with tiny pearl swags, and attached a cherub. For the filling, we wrapped several foil-covered candies in white tulle, then gathered the tulle into a soft pouch, tied it with white wire-edged ribbon, and added a silk pansy for decoration.

For variation, consider decorating the cornucopia by gluing on pink and purple seed beads; miniature roses, voilets, or pansies; tiny gold and silver tassels; cream-colored fringed trim; assorted lace decorations from the bridal section of a fabric store; or appliques. You could also decorate the scalloped edge with a fine-point Pilot gold or silver marker, or fill in the pansies using a squeeze bottle of fabric paint. For creative fillings, consider foil-wrapped coins, Hershey Kisses, or hard candy.

To avoid cutting up this magazine, take the pansy image on the facing page to a copy shop with a color copier and copy the image onto medium-weight, glossy paper. (Don't use text-weight paper, as the cornucopia won't be strong enough to hold the decorative items.) To decorate a tabletop tree or topiary, you could reduce the image by 50 percent and make miniature cornucopias. The materials below will yield one cornucopia.

VICTORIAN CHRISTMAS CORNUCOPIA

Pansy pattern (*see* facing page)
½ yard 1"-wide, embossed, silver paper lace
½ yard 1"-wide, mauve wire-edged ribbon
½ yard ³⁄₁₆", silver metallic trim
½ yard 3mm pearls on a string
1 gold or brass cherub stamping
8–10" metallic gold thread or ribbon

You'll also need: scissors; rubber cement; hot-glue gun and glue sticks; sewing or darning needle; and access to a color copier.

Other items, if necessary: transparent tape for securing glued edge of cornucopia; ¼ yard white tulle for candy pouch; ¼ yard 1"-wide white wire-edged ribbon for tying pouch closed; silk pansies for decorating candy pouch; and candy of choice.

1. Using color copier, make copies of pansy cornucopia on medium-weight, glossy paper. Using scissors, cut out image(s) along edges.

2. Place cornucopia on flat surface, wrong side facing upwards. Using illustration at right as guide, crease paper lace to form zigzag or crimped pleats. Using rubber cement, glue crimped edge of lace along scalloped edge of cornucopia. Trim off any extra lace.

3. Turn cornucopia over (pansy side up) and hot-glue mauve wire-edged ribbon along scalloped edge. Hot-glue metallic trim in place directly below wire-edged ribbon.

4. Place cornucopia face down with point toward you. Brush a ¼"-wide strip of rubber cement along right edge. Pick cornucopia up, turn it over in your hand, and with point still toward you, apply a second ¼"-wide strip of rubber cement along the new right edge.

Allow cement to dry for 1 minute. Carefully roll pansy image into cone, overlapping glued edges. Press glued edges together with your fingertips. Set aside to dry for several minutes. If necessary, reinforce this seam by applying tape on inside of cone.

5. Using photograph on page 20 as reference, swag about half the string of pearls and hot-glue in place at 1½" intervals. Repeat with remaining pearls for second swagged row. Hot-glue cherub in place.

6. To create a hanging loop, using sewing or darning needle, pierce a tiny hole in one side of the cornucopia beneath the silver metallic trim. Knot one end of the gold metallic thread or ribbon, then thread the other end from inside of cornucopia through hole and pull knot up against hole. Reinforce hole and knot with hot glue. Pierce hole in opposite side of cornucopia, and insert free end of metallic thread or ribbon through it from outside of cornucopia. Knot that end and hot glue it in place.

7. If desired, form candy pouch by centering foil-wrapped candies on tulle, then gathering tulle into pouch and tying with white wire-edged ribbon. Using photo as guide, hot-glue silk pansy in place and insert in cornucopia. ◆

ILLUSTRATION AT TOP BY JUDITH LOVE

Celestial Ornaments

Creating professional-looking ornaments is a snap with fine-grade glitter.

These celestial ornaments, which may look complicated, are actually quite simple to make using three primary ingredients: fine-grade glitter, cardboard, and wire. You can make one ornament, or a half dozen. Start by shaping the wire around an ordinary soup can to form orbits, then trace the star and moon templates provided on this page onto cardboard (e.g., poster board or the back of a notepad). Glue the pieces together at various points, cover them with fine-grade glitter, and you've got a matching set of celestial ornaments for use at Christmas, Hanukkah, or New Year's.

If you've used glitter in the past, you may be familiar with the chunky, sprinkle-on glitter of old. However, in the last few years, glitter has come of age. Fine-grade glitter works well for this project, as it's cut much smaller than traditional glitter, yielding a granulated surface with a more subtle sparkle. It can be bought in craft stores in three forms: in a spray can, loose (for sprinkling), and mixed with a binding medium in a squeeze bottle.

We tested the squeeze bottle variety against spray-on and sprinkle-on, and the squeeze bottle glitter won hands down. It's easy to apply, and when finished, looks as if the glitter is intrinsic to the metal, not simply stuck to the surface. Spray-on glitter did not stick to the metal. Sprinkle-on glitter went on quicker than expected (remember that you have to brush tacky glue on the surfaces first), but the look is not nearly as smooth as the squeeze bottle variety, and the glitter-covered piece is awkward to handle even when dry, because pieces of glitter keep falling off. The other advantage to squeeze bottle glitter is that you don't need to apply adhesive beforehand.

When shopping for glitter, look for brands that are designed for use on a variety of craft materials, versus those made specifically for painting or drawing on fabric. The latter type, which comes in a squeeze bottle with a fine tip, usually contains more water, which can result in drips. If you cannot find the generic type of glitter, you can use those designed for drawing on fabric, but be sure to apply a very thin coat, let dry, and recoat. If you still get drips, gently squeeze them out with your fingers after the first coat is partially dry.

Although squeeze bottle glitter is milky white when first applied, it shrinks and becomes clear after several hours, leaving behind a hard, glittery surface. Unlike sprinkle-on glitters, which sit on the surface, squeeze bottle glitters appear to fuse and become part of the surface. They are especially suited for concealing different materials, such as the metal wire and cardboard used in this project.

We chose gold and silver glitter for these ornaments, but you can use any number of combinations, such as red and green or silver and blue.

These ornaments are made using fine-grade squeeze bottle glitter, which yields a more finished look than sprinkle-on glitter. Spray-on glitter didn't stick to the metal.

CELESTIAL ORNAMENTS

69" 16-gauge galvanized steel wire
1 sheet cardboard
  Gold squeeze bottle glitter
  Silver squeeze bottle glitter
2 6mm (¼") round, flat-backed acrylic jewels
  Gold metallic thread
  Heavy-duty sewing thread
  White tacky glue
  Florist wire
  Tracing paper

You'll also need: 3"-diameter soup, vegetable, or tomato sauce can; 2½"-diameter can; wire cutters or pliers; scissors; permanent felt-tip marker; pencil; ball-point pen; X-Acto knife; small brush; ruler; and tape measure.

Making the Moon Ornament

1. Cut a 39" length of wire with wire cutters or pliers. Using permanent marker, make two marks to divide wire into three 13" lengths. Hold one end of wire against 3"-diameter can and wind tightly around can several times to make a coil.

2. Cut coil at two marked points. Overlap ends of each piece by ½" to form circle about 4" in diameter. Bind overlapping ends tightly with 5" length of heavy-duty thread, winding thread around joint several times. Tie ends in square knot and snip off excess. Apply small drop of white tacky glue to knot and smear along entire joint with fingertip. Let set 15 minutes. Repeat process to make three rings.

PATTERNS BY ROBERTA FRAUWIRTH, PHOTOGRAPH BY STEVEN MAYS

3. Using illustration 3 as reference, lay one wire ring on cardboard and trace inside edge with pencil. Remove ring and set aside. Mark a point 1" in from traced circle. Place second ring on top of traced circle, slightly off-center and touching 1" point. Trace outer edge of second ring to make a crescent within the circle.

4. Trace moon face template on page 22. Lay tracing on crescent, matching dashed lines with crescent as closely as possible. Pressing firmly with a ball-point pen, trace nose, mouth, and eye to make impression in cardboard. Remove tracing and darken impression with pencil.

5. With scissors, cut out moon. Apply thin bead of glue to outside edge of crescent and set into one wire ring. Let dry ½ hour.

6. To form orbits, arrange two remaining wire rings around ring with moon. Bind all wire intersections except those along edge of moon with heavy-duty thread, wrapping horizontally and then vertically to secure. Knot ends, trim excess thread, and apply a small dot of glue to each joint as in step 2.

7. Trace faceted star pattern A (page 22) and transfer twice to cardboard, repeating process outlined in step 4. Being careful not to cut through cardboard, score dashed lines lightly using X-Acto knife and ruler, then cut out both stars. Fold along scored lines to add facets (see illustration 6). Apply generous dots of glue to concave side of each star and position over two wire intersections. Let dry ½ hour.

8. Apply heavy coat of silver glitter to both sides of moon, excluding wire or orbit's edge.

9. Cut 5" to 8" length of florist wire and make a temporary hook and hang ornament. Squeeze gold glitter along all 3 wire rings, onto small stars, and inside eye area of moon. Use a small brush to remove drips and cover any missed spots. Let dry overnight.

10. Remove florist wire hook. Attach 1½" loop of gold thread to top of ring in which crescent is mounted. Glue one jewel in gold portion of eye; repeat on opposite side.

Making the Star Ornament

1. Repeat step 1, on page 22, but cut a 30" length of wire. Using permanent marker, make two marks to divide wire into three 10" lengths. Tightly wind wire around 2½"-diameter can to make a coil.

2. Repeat step 2 on page 22, cutting coil at two marked points and forming 3 circles, each about 3" in diameter. Bind overlapping ends with thread, and glue in place.

3. Repeat step 4 above, but trace, transfer, and cut out large star template on page 22. Apply a dot of glue to each point of star and affix to one wire circle. Let dry ½ hour.

4. Repeat appropriate parts of steps 6 through 10 above, substituting faceted star pattern B in step 7. Coat wire circles and faceted stars with gold glitter and large star with silver glitter. ◆

Making the Moon Ornament

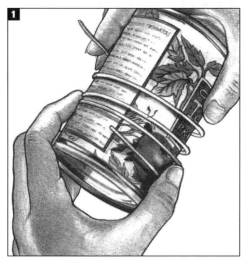

1. Holding one end of the wire against the 3" can, wind the other end around the can several times to form a coil.

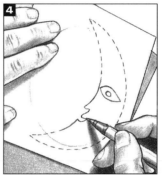

2. Overlap the wire ends by about ½", then bind the overlapping ends together using heavy-duty thread.

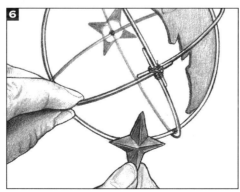

3. Place one wire ring on the cardboard and trace the inside edge with a pencil. Mark a point 1" in from the traced circle, then place the second ring on top of the traced circle, slightly off-center, touching the 1" mark. Trace the outer edge of the second ring to create a crescent.

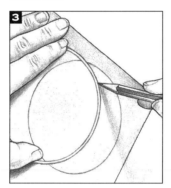

4. Lay the tracing of the moon template on the crescent, matching the dashed lines as closely as you can. Using a ball-point pen, trace the silhouette of the moon's nose, mouth, and eye to make an impression in the cardboard. Remove the tracing and darken the impression with a pencil.

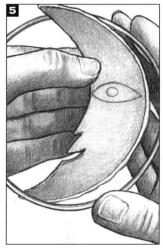

5. Cut out the crescent with scissors, then apply a thin bead of glue to the crescent's outside edge and set it into one wire ring.

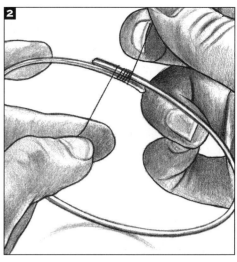

6. To form the orbits, arrange the two remaining wire rings around the ring with the glued-in moon, and bind all the intersections with heavy-duty thread. Trace and cut out the stars, fold along dotted lines to add facets, then glue in place over wire intersections on either side of the moon.

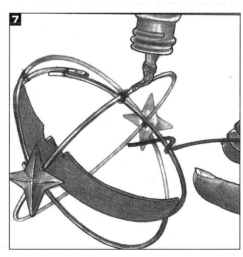

7. Put gold glitter along all three wire circles, the small stars, and inside the eye area.

Trash Bag Garland

An ordinary trash bag serves as a flexible and durable base for this evergreen garland.

BY URTE TUERPE WITH SUZANNE GUZZO

To make longer versions of the garland, knot additional trash bags together. Aim for a length two times that of your space.

The base of this swagged garland, which can be used to decorate a banister, a mantel, or a doorway, consists of an ordinary black trash bag. We chose black trash bags for several reasons: they're strong, they're inexpensive, and they're flexible, meaning the garland can be draped and twisted easily. Though the materials and directions here yield one five-foot garland, doubling, tripling, or even quadrupling that length is as simple as knotting additional bags together. When making swagged garlands, we've found that making the garland twice as long as the area to be covered yielded the best results.

The color scheme we chose is red, white, and green, and our theme revolves around birds. Most craft and garden stores stock a variety of small feathered birds, birdhouses, and birds' nests around the Christmas season. But consider substituting bouquets of preserved flowers or foliage for the bird-related items, or develop a theme of your own based on color, specific objects, or your decorating scheme.

Certain greens are better suited for use in garlands such as this one, because they keep their leaves or needles longer and provide good texture, shading, and variety. Our list of recommended greens includes laurel, berried holly, white pine, and boxwood. Incense cedar can be substituted for the holly, but it may be harder to find. We spray painted our birch branches white for a nice contrast. It's best to assemble your garland as soon as you obtain your greens, as fresh greens are much easier to work with. As they dry, they become sharp and brittle. Holly is sharp even when fresh, so wearing gloves is a good idea.

To assemble the garland pictured, we assembled four bouquets of each green; each bouquet contained four to six stems bound with florist wire or waxed string. (For instructions for making your own waxed string, *see* "How To Make Waxed String," *Handcraft Illustrated*, September/October 1994, page 9.) If your stems are short, you may need additional bouquets. One other note: Don't use white garbage bags, as the white background could be visible through the greens.

TRASH BAG GARLAND

1 heavy black plastic trash bag, 3' long (30-gallon size)
3 6"-long red cardinals
2 birds' nests, 4" to 6" in diameter
1–2 miniature birdhouses, 4" high
   Green waxed string or florist wire
   Stems or branches, 16 to 24 each of berry holly, laurel, white pine, and birch
4–6 red ribbon bows
   White spray paint

You'll also need: garden gloves; newspaper; and scissors.

1. Cut trash bag open on both sides and unfold to form 6' plastic sheet.
2. Cover workspace with newspaper, lay down birch branches, and spray paint each branch white. Let dry following manufacturer's guidelines, then turn branches over and spray paint opposite side.
3. Put on garden gloves to protect hands. Make 4 bunches of each foliage by bundling 4 to 6 stems together for a total of sixteen bouquets. Stagger lengths of stems and bind base of each bunch with waxed string or florist wire.
4. Lay 6' length of trash bag flat on newspaper and bunch width together to create a loose rope. Lay first bouquet on top of plastic with heads of foliage covering end of plastic. Bind to plastic using waxed string or florist wire. Lay next bunch parallel to first bunch with heads slightly overlapping stems of first bouquet, and secure in place. Continue attaching bouquets in same manner along trash bag rope. When all bouquets are attached, wrap any visible parts of plastic with waxed string or florist wire.
5. Attach cardinals, birds' nests, bows, and birdhouses using waxed string or florist wire. (The garland will be swagged, so exact symmetry is not necessary.)
6. Position garland wherever it will be used, and tie in place using waxed string. Adjust decorations or foliage as necessary. ◆

Urte Tuerpe is the owner of Village Flowers in Huntington, New York. **Suzanne Guzzo** is a freelance writer based in New York.

Position first bouquet on top of the plastic so the "heads" of the foliage cover the end of the plastic bag; secure in place using florist wire or waxed string. Lay the next bunch parallel to the first, with the heads slightly overlapping the stems of the first bouquet. Secure with florist wire or waxed string, then repeat with remaining bouquets.

ILLUSTRATION BY NENAD JAKESEVIC/PHOTOGRAPH BY STEVEN MAYS

Tufted Footstool

Transform an ordinary pine stool into an elegant ottoman using a simple tufting technique.

BY MARY FRAZIER

Unlike traditional tufting techniques, which involve compressing a spring base under several layers of padding, this footstool's foam and batting "stuffing" is easily tufted using a five-inch needle and dental or embroidery floss. Using the pattern provided on page 26, mark and drill tufting holes in the top of the stool, then sew through the holes, attaching covered buttons on top of the padding and anchoring them underneath. Finish the stool by stapling on a pleated skirt and hot-gluing fringe in place. The result is an elegant reproduction of an upholstered ottoman at a fraction of the cost.

For this project I used a ten-inch-high footstool with a top that measured eleven by fourteen inches. Footstools with a brace attaching the legs to the top of the stool will not work for this project, as you would not be able to drill the necessary holes (*see* photograph, below).

I recommend purchasing batting on rolls, as it is thicker than the kind that comes in packages. For the tufting process, you'll need the help of a friend.

TUFTED FOOTSTOOL

1   unfinished pine footstool,
        11" x 14" x 10" tall
1¾ yards 56" or 60" upholstery fabric
1½ yards coordinating fringe or braid trim,
        at least ½" wide
4   yards heavy-weight dental floss, 6-strand
        embroidery floss, *or* other strong,
        thin cord
10 matching covered buttons (*see* "How to
        Cover Buttons," page 26)
10 plastic, 2-hole, ⅝" buttons
        1¾"-wide Stitch Witchery
1   piece high-density foam, 12" x 24" x 2"
⅝   yard 60"-wide, 1"-thick batting
        Matching thread

You'll also need: 5" dollmaking or upholstery needle; electric drill with ¼" bit; safety glasses; quilter's 1¾" ball-head pins; staple gun and staples; hot-glue gun and glue sticks; sharp, serrated knife; iron; pencil; blunt permanent marker; fine-point permanent marker; ruler or yardstick; scissors; 11" x 14" tracing paper (or size to match top of stool); and sewing machine.

Preparing the Stool

1. Working with ruler and pencil directly on top of stool, divide both 11" edges of stool into four equal segments, each measuring 2¾". Draw three parallel lines connecting points to form lines 1, 2, and 3. (*See* diagram 1, page 26.)

2. Divide lines 1 and 3 into four equal segments, each measuring 3½". Mark these points A, B, and C. Draw a diagonal line to connect point B on line 1 with point A on line 3. Draw a second diagonal line to connect point C on line 1 with point B on line 3 (diagram 2, page 26).

3. Mark points where diagonal lines cross line 2 as B and C. Measure up from point B 3½" and mark point A; measure down 3½" from point C and mark point D (diagram 3, page 26). You should have a total of ten points, each of which represents a spot for drilling. Examine the stool top to make certain no point is directly above a leg or brace. If there is an obstruction, adjust spacing between points as necessary to avoid it, while keeping overall pattern intact.

4. Lay tracing paper on stool top and make tufting pattern by tracing marked points with pencil. Remove pattern and set aside for use in steps 3 and 4 of tufting process.

5. Put on safety glasses. Using electric drill and ¼" bit, drill through stool top at each marked point.

6. Lay stool topside down on foam. Using blunt permanent marker, trace outline of stool top onto foam. Remove stool from foam. Stand foam up on end and cut around outline using serrated knife. Set foam aside.

7. Lay stool topside down on 1"-thick batting. Using blunt marker, draw a line 4" beyond edges of stool. Cut along this line with scissors. Set batting aside.

8. Stand stool upright; set foam on top. Center batting on top of foam. Carefully turn stool upside down, holding batting and foam in place. Lift one edge of batting around to underside of stool and staple in place at midpoint of batting edge. Lift opposite edge of batting around to underside of stool, pulling batting

Though this footstool's tufting may look complicated, it's actually very quick and simple. You can even use dental floss to form the tufts.

firmly but not stretching it, and staple into place at midpoint of batting edge. Repeat on two remaining sides.

9. Staple batting at ½" intervals on all sides. Turn stool over occasionally to be sure padding is smooth and even. Ease batting around corners for as few wrinkles as possible. With scissors, trim off excess batting under corners.

Cutting the Fabric

1. Cut three panels of fabric (these are the skirt panels), each measuring 12" x 56", and set aside. Cut from selvage (finished edge of fabric) to selvage.

2. Lay remaining fabric wrong side up on work surface. Lay stool with padding topside down on fabric. Using fine-tip marker, draw a line on fabric 5" beyond all edges of stool. Cut out along this line and set aside.

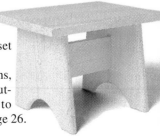

3. To cover buttons, follow directions outlined in "How to Cover Buttons," page 26.

Upholstering and Tufting the Footstool

1. Place rectangle of cut fabric on work surface, wrong side up. Lay stool top-side down, with padding against fabric. Using method outlined in steps 8 and 9 of "Preparing the Stool," pull each edge of fabric around to stool's underside and staple in place at midpoint. When each edge is attached, continue stapling at ⅛" intervals from midpoint out, stopping 3" from corners.

2. To secure fabric around corners, work from left to right as follows (reverse if left-handed): Place fingers of left hand on fabric edge near staple. Hold excess fabric between thumb and fingers of right hand. Smooth fabric in right hand up over the batting, making a small ⅛" pleat as you near the edge. Hold down pleat with left hand. Repeat, making second small pleat to right of first pleat and fanning it slightly to ease in fullness. When you have completed four or five pleats (totaling ½" altogether), staple in place. Repeat this process until you have rounded the corner. Trim off excess fabric with scissors.

3. Stand stool upright. Center tufting pattern on padded top; secure at corners and edges by inserting quilter's pins straight down into padding until ball heads rest on surface.

4. Cut ten 14" lengths of dental or embroidery floss, or other cord. Thread one length into 5" dollmaking or upholstery needle. Insert needle into one drilled hole in stool underside, and push up through padding so it emerges at corresponding point on pattern. (You may have to remove and reinsert the needle several times to get it to come out at the right point.) Pull needle out through top, leaving a 3" to 4" tail on underside. Slip needle through covered button shank, reinsert needle approximately 1/16" from exit hole, and push back through padding and out original hole. Adjust tails so button rests snugly on top. Repeat process with remaining nine holes. Remove quilter's pins; tear pattern off stool.

5. Turn stool on side. Have a partner push in on a button, compressing padding about ¾". Insert tails of threads on stool underside through holes of plastic ⅝" button. Slide button up tight against stool underside. Tie thread tails securely against button. Repeat process with remaining nine buttons, turning stool over occasionally to check for even tufting.

Pleating and Attaching the Skirt

1. Sew the three 12" x 56" skirt panels together with ½" seam to make one panel approximately 164" long. (Exact length will vary, depending on selvage waste.) Press seams open, then press to one side.

2. Lay panel on work surface right side up with 12" side facing toward you. Place ruler along one long raw edge so it crosses a seam line. Make two small marks 2" apart with one mark on each side of seam line. Continue marking every 2" along entire edge. If a seam line

Tufting Diagrams

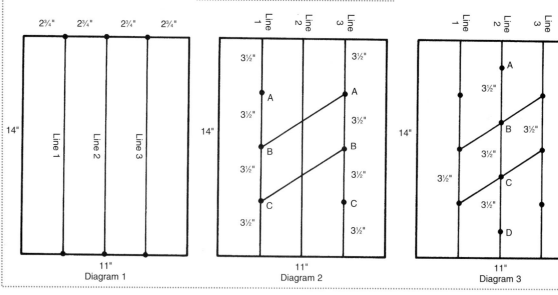

Diagram 1

Diagram 2

Diagram 3

How to Cover Buttons

You will need the following supplies: a button covering kit (Dritz, Prym, or equivalent) with ten 9/16" half-ball buttons; several scraps of fabric from covering the stool; a miniature screwdriver; scissors; a small bowl or cup of water; a fine-tip marker; and a wooden spool.

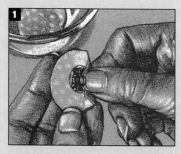

1. Use the marker and the pattern on the back of the package of self-covering buttons to trace ten 1⅜" diameter circles on the fabric. Cut out circles and wet them in water for easier handling. Place each circle, right side out, over a half-ball button.

2. Turn the button over and smooth the excess fabric around the edges onto the prongs lining the rim. To help the prongs grip the fabric, push the allowance under the rim with a miniature screwdriver. Turn the button right side up, and smooth out any wrinkles.

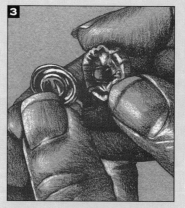

3. Slip the backplate into position so the shank emerges out the back slot.

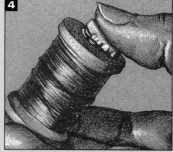

4. Set the button on top of the wooden spool so the backplate rests on the rim and the shank drops into the hole. Press down firmly on the button until you hear the backplate snap into place.

ILLUSTRATIONS BY TONY DELUZ/DIAGRAMS BY ROBERTA FRAUWIRTH

and mark coincide, restitch the seam 1½" from ends of these two joined fabric panels instead of ½", trim off excess allowance and press open as before. Continue marking remainder of panel edge.

3. Position fabric right side up with marked edge at right and short edge at top. Insert pins into fabric at third mark from top. Continue inserting pins every third mark down length of panel, checking seam placement as you go. A seam that falls between a pin and the second mark below it will be concealed when pleats are formed, but a seam that falls between the second mark and the pin below will show when pleats are formed. To prevent this seam from showing, remove pins, reinsert first pin either two or four marks from top, and try same sequence again. If no arrangement works, you will have to resew the problem seam, as in step 2, to avoid having it show.

4. Fold unmarked long edge 1" to wrong side, and press. Fold again by 1" to form double hem. Fuse in place with Stitch Witchery, following package directions. (*Note:* Stitch Witchery may not work with heavy upholstering fabrics. If necessary, stitch hem in place using sewing machine.)

5. Lay panel right side up on ironing board with hem at left and long raw edge at right. Fold top of panel back at first pin, wrong sides together and edges matching. Remove pin, and press across panel from raw edge to hemmed edge to set crease. Repeat at every pin to create a series of creases 6" apart.

6. To form pleats, bring pressed-in crease toward you until it touches second mark below it. Align raw and hemmed edges, then press to set pleat. With pin, secure raw edge of pleat just formed. Continue in this manner to form 2" pleats along entire length of panel, ending by folding back.

7. Stand stool upright on work surface. Starting at midpoint of one 14" side, pin unfinished edge of pleated skirt around padded top so hem of skirt reaches work surface. Overlap ends neatly at back. Staple edge of skirt through pleats and padding to wooden edge of top of stool. Remove straight pins as you staple along entire edge.

8. Wrap fringe or braid trim around stool to conceal staples and unfinished edge of skirt. Pin at corners. Overlap neatly at back, tucking unfinished edges under. Measure up from work surface on all sides to check for even length, and adjust as necessary. Lay stool on side. Working one side at a time, lift trim away from stool and apply hot-glue under it in a straight, even line, getting as close to corners as possible. Quickly press trim to glue to adhere in place. Repeat on remaining three sides. Tuck unfinished edges under before gluing in place.◆

Mary Frazier is a professional seamstress living in New York.

PREPARING THE STOOL

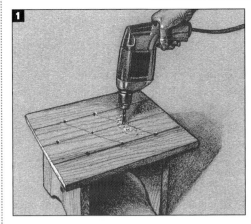

1. Using an electric drill and a ¼" bit, drill holes at each marked point, making certain to drill completely through the top of the stool.

2. Pull one edge of the batting to the underside of the stool and staple it in place at the midpoint. When all sides have been attached this way, continue stapling the batting at ½" intervals, starting from the midpoint on each side. With scissors, trim off the extra batting under the corners.

TUFTING THE FOOTSTOOL

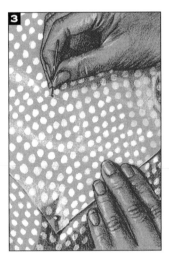

3. Insert the needle from the underside of the stool, pushing it up through the padding so it emerges at the corresponding point on the pattern.

4. Slip needle through the covered button shank, reinsert it at a point approximately 1/16" from where it came up through the pattern, and push it back down through the padding and out through the hole.

5. Insert the tails of the thread through the holes of a plastic ⅝" button. Slide the button up until it rests against the underside of the stool. Have a friend compress the padding while you pull the thread tight and tie it.

PLEATING AND ATTACHING THE SKIRT

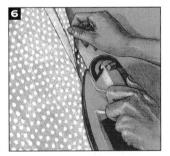

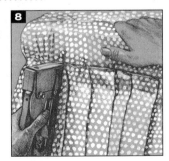

6. Fold the unmarked long edge 1" to the wrong side, and press it down. Turn up a second 1" to form a double hem. Fuse the hem in place with Stitch Witchery.

7. To form the pleats, bring the pressed-in crease toward you until it touches the second mark below it. Align the raw and hemmed edges, then press the panel to set the pleat. With a pin, secure the raw edge of the pleat just formed.

8. Staple the edge of the skirt through the fabric and padding to the wooden edge of the stool top, securing each pleat. Remove the straight pins as you go.

Field Guide to Watercolor Brushes

BY NANCY JOHNSON

I am often reminded, upon seeing well-conceived and well-executed watercolor paintings, that results are due not only to the painters' talents, but also to their skill with materials. Since there is no eraser at the end of a watercolor brush, and white paint is not used to cover mistakes, I recommend that beginning watercolorists focus most of their time and money on their most important piece of equipment—the paintbrush.

Watercolors are made of finely-ground pigments suspended in a water-soluble binder. Not unlike a musical score, the artist lays down colored notes in a certain pattern, that when assembled, can represent a landscape or a portrait. The color combinations are limitless, as are the type of brush strokes. In order to understand how a style or subject matter evolves, it's important to chose the correct brushes. A beginner's watercolor palette should be supplied with three brushes: a one-inch-wide flat brush for washes and large areas; a large, round #12 brush; and a script liner, which is used to paint delicate lines. Before rushing out to buy these brushes, read on to learn how brushes are categorized, priced, and used.

Choosing Your Brush: Size, Cost, and Type

Watercolor brushes are used only with water-based pigment, never with oil or acrylic paint, which would damage the brush. Unlike an oil paint brush, where the artist uses the long handle for leverage and holds it away from his canvas, the watercolor brush has a short handle and is held like a pencil, allowing the artist to work closer to the painting.

While it would be nice if all paintbrush manufacturers used the same codes to indicate brush sizes, they don't. Some use the width of

Paintbrushes, from left to right: (Type, size, manufacturer, and name)

A. Round #8. Rekab #013K Pure Kolinsky.
B. Round #12. Princeton Art & Brush Co. #4050 R.
C. Flat #12. Isabey #6236 Petit Gris.

D. Bright #8. Artec #124 Pure red sable.
E. Bright #10. Artec #124 Pure red sable.
F. Filbert #8. Artec #128 Pure red sable.
G. Filbert #10. Artec #128 Pure red sable.

H. Script Liner #2. Windsor & Newton Cotman #222.
I. Fan #6. Grumbacher #8807.
J. 1" Wash brush. Rekab #123 Golden Taklon.

PHOTOGRAPH BY STEVEN MAYS

the brush (for instance, the one-inch-wide wash brush mentioned above), while others use the more familiar # sign to indicate sizes. In this latter scheme, brush sizes range from #000 (smallest) to #14 (largest). When you look at the field guide to the right, you'll see the various brush sizes. In general, #1 or #2 brushes will be very small, perhaps one-eighth-inch in width, whereas larger brushes (e.g., #12 or #14) may be as large as one-inch across.

There are three major parts to a brush: the handle; the ferrule, or metal casing which holds the hair; and the hair itself (also referred to as the bristles). Cost is largely determined by the type of hair. In general, the higher the quality of the hair, the higher the cost. When buying brushes, it's always better to have one high-quality brush than a number of inferior ones, so purchase the finest brushes you can afford.

Kolinsky sable, also called Russian sable, is the finest hair used in watercolor brushes. It comes from a small, weasel-like animal. The hairs are long and are bigger at the base (thus forming a "belly" in the mid-section of the brush) and taper to a point at the tip. Sable hair is prized for several of its attributes, including its toughness, flexibility, and ability to spring back to its original shape. Brushes made from Russian sable are versatile enough to cover large areas when doing a wash or color blocking, or come to a sharp point to render a line as narrow as an eyelash. Kolinsky sable watercolor brushes range from about $5 for a #3 to an amazing $750 for a #12.

If your budget doesn't allow for Russian sable, consider brushes made from squirrel, which are more reasonably priced. They have consistent performance when rendering washes, large areas of color, or fine lines. The hair is soft and fluffy and doesn't shed on the surface of your painting. They lack the "spring" of a sable brush, however. Average prices for squirrel brushes range from $4 for a #2 to approximately $60 for a #12 or #14.

If sable or squirrel are out of your price range, consider a blend of sable and synthetic fiber, also known by the name sabeline. These brushes give adequate performance; average prices vary from $3 for a #1 or #2 to $25 for a #12 or #14.

The least expensive watercolor brushes are made of all synthetic fiber. I find them too soft, and the bristles are often stained by the pigments. The least desirable brush is a camel hair brush, which, interestingly enough, is not made from camel hair, but rather from a mix of hairs. They have very little spring and shed when painting.

Types of Watercolor Brushes

Once you've selected your price range, determine your main use. The major types of watercolor brushes and their distinguishing characteristics are outlined in the chart, above.

Common Types of Watercolor Brushes

TYPE AND SIZE	DESCRIPTION	USE	BRUSH SAMPLE
Round (#8)	Round ferrule; very fine-pointed end.	Details, fine lines, features.	
Round (#12)	Round ferrule; pointed end.	Lines, wash, area drawing with color.	
Flat (#12)	Flat ferrule; square end; medium to long length.	Bold, sweeping strokes.	
Bright (#8)	Flat ferrule; square end; short length.	Short, sweeping strokes.	
Bright (#10)	Flat ferrule; square end; short length.	Short, sweeping strokes.	
Filbert (#8)	Thick, flat ferrule; oval end.	Firm, controlled painting with color-loaded brush.	
Filbert (#10)	Thick, flat ferrule; oval end.	Firm, controlled painting with color-loaded brush.	
Script Liner (#2)	Round ferrule; long point; medium to long length.	Thin to thick stroke; delicate lines.	
Fan (#6)	Flat ferrule; fan shape; spread hairs.	Special effect; dry brush; use fan tips only.	
Wash (1")	Thick, flat ferrule; square end.	Applying wash to large areas.	

Caring For Your Brushes

All watercolor brushes can be cleaned with mild soap and warm water. Choose a soap that contains no pumice, as this abrasive will wear out the bristles. After all the pigment has been rinsed from the hair, gently stroke the brush on a soft cloth, shake to remove excess water, and lay flat in a protected place such as a drawer or box to dry. Never store a brush upright with the handle stuck into a jar or can, as water can seep into the ferrule, causing mold to grow or the handle to warp.

Purchasing Paint and Paper

A few notes about watercolor paints and paper: Watercolor paints come either in tubes or in pans, which are shallow metal or plastic containers of paint. Both work equally well. I recommend that beginning watercolorists purchase student-grade watercolors, manufactured by such firms as Windsor & Newton, by the tube (average price, $3.80) or by the set (average price, $28). Check other manufacturers (such as Grumbacher) for price and quality comparison. As with brushes, buy the best paint you can afford.

When purchasing paper, ask for a medium-weight (#140) paper by the block (average price, $42) or by the sheet (average price, $4). If your budget is tight, shop around for better prices.

Once you have assembled your materials, spend some time practicing painting with your brushes on scrap paper or newsprint (inexpensive paper without news type). Remember—there are no rules to follow. Give free reign to your nature, and have fun! ◆

Nancy Johnson is an artist specializing in painting, pottery, and silversmithing.

Low-Sew Tree Skirt

A simple quarter pattern yields a scalloped Victorian tree skirt.

This article will teach you how to make a richly-colored, scalloped tree skirt that you'll use again and again. To further coordinate your holiday decorating scheme, make the matching Heirloom Mantel Skirt on page 12, using the same fabrics and trims and similar techniques.

The skirt shown here is assembled from two similar pieces of fabric, which are sewn together, turned right side out, and finished with trim. The quarter-pattern found below is designed for use on fabric that has been folded in half, then in half again to form quarters. This eliminates the need to cut four separate pieces and stitch them together.

Bind the ends of the gold twisted rope welting with tape to prevent them from unraveling. This is easier if you tape the trim, and then cut it right through the tape. For further reference, *see* the illustrations on page 14.

LOW-SEW TREE SKIRT

1½ yards 54"-wide dark green fabric
1½ yards 54"-wide cranberry fabric
5¼ yards gold ⅜"- to ½"-thick twisted rope welting
5½ yards decorative green-cranberry ⅜"-thick twisted cord
Green, cranberry, and gold cotton-covered polyester thread
3 gold frog closures
White fabric glue

You'll also need: access to a copying machine; sewing machine with zipper foot attachment; straight pins; scissors; iron; ruler; transparent tape; and masking tape.

Cutting the Tree Skirt

1. Using a copying machine, enlarge pattern below until each square measures 1", taping sheets together as necessary with transparent tape. Cut out pattern along marked outlines.
2. Fold lining (cranberry) fabric in half lengthwise, then crosswise into quarters. Place pattern on folded fabric with fold lines of pattern matching folded edges of fabric and small cutout quarter circle at folded corner. Pin in place, then cut out along pattern outlines.
3. Repeat step 2 to cut second skirt from facing (green) fabric.
4. Unfold both skirts and lay flat with either skirt on top and edges matching. Cut a long, straight slit through both pieces from outer edge to inner circle.

Assembling the Tree Skirt

1. Thread sewing machine with gold thread; thread bobbin with cranberry thread. Position welting with extra 1" extending beyond opening cut in step 4, above. Pin welting to outer edge of lining skirt piece, right side of lining facing wrong side of welting, flat edge of welting tape matched to curved edge of skirt. Using a zipper foot, sew welting to fabric, starting 1½" in from end of skirt and getting needle as close to edge of welting rope as possible. Stop 1½" from other end. Wrap welting with masking tape 1" beyond end of fabric to prevent raveling, then cut through middle of tape with scissors.
2. Thread sewing machine with cranberry thread; thread bobbin with green thread. Pin green and cranberry skirts together, right sides together and curves and edges matching, with welting sandwiched in between. Position cranberry lining on top. Using zipper foot, stitch over previous stitching, sewing through all layers and staying as close to welting rope as possible. (As in step 1, leave 1½" of fabric unstitched at each end.)
3. Switch to regular presser foot. Stitch remaining seam all around, but leave a 7" opening along one straight edge. When finished stitching, turn skirt right side out through opening and press. Slipstitch 7" opening closed.
4. Insert both ends of gold rope welting into unsewn openings at edges of skirt. To prevent raveling, tape end of green-cranberry twisted cord with masking tape and poke into one opening. Working 4" to 6" at a time, apply fabric glue to green side of skirt above gold welting. Press green-cranberry cord into glue, securing it with pins if necessary until dry. When you reach end of skirt, wrap cord with tape 1" beyond fabric edge, then cut through middle of tape. Insert end into second unsewn opening. Slipstitch both openings closed.
5. Glue frog closures in place over back opening. ◆

This low-sew tree skirt uses the same fabric, trims, and sewing techniques as the Mantel Skirt on page 12.

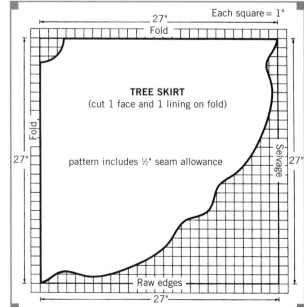

TREE SKIRT
(cut 1 face and 1 lining on fold)

pattern includes ½" seam allowance

Each square = 1"
Fold
Fold
27"
27"
27"
27"
Selvage
Raw edges

PATTERN BY ROBERTA FRAUWIRTH/PHOTOGRAPH BY STEVEN MAYS

SOURCES
AND RESOURCES

Most of the materials needed for the projects in this issue are available at your local craft supply, hardware or paint store, florist, fabric shop, or bead and jewelry supply. Following are specific mail-order sources for particular items, arranged by project. Suggested retail prices listed below are current at press time. Contact suppliers directly to confirm up-to-date prices and availability.

Notes From Readers; pages 2–3
Paint Choices for Stenciling: Large selection of acrylic paints available from $2.50, from Co-op Artists' Materials, Jerry's Artarama, New York Central Art Supply, and Ott's Discount Art Supply. Japan paints from $6.25 per ½ pint from Johnson Paint Company. Turpenoid for $5.55 per quart from Ott's Discount Art Supply. *Fast Fix for Roll-up Shades:* Selection of ribbon from 70¢, laces from 75¢, decorative trims from $1, drapery and upholstery trims from $3.75, hot-glue gun for $12.95, glue sticks for $3, and variety of beads from 95¢ per package, all from Newark Dressmaker Supply. Large selection of precut stencils from $3 from Stencil World. *The Definition of Nontoxic:* General information on the safety of products from the Center for Safety Coalition in the Arts. Information on products that have been certified by an authority on toxicology from the Art and Craft Materials Institute. *Using Edible Flowers in Ice Cubes:* Variety of edible flower seeds from $1.60 per package from Shepherd's Garden Seeds. *Tips on Caring for an Amaryllis:* Variety of amaryllis from $15 from White Flower Farm. *Protecting a Newly Refinished Table:* Selection of furniture wax and cleaners from $4.95 from The Woodworkers' Store. *Types of Watercolor Paper:* Large selection of watercolor papers from $1 from Daniel Smith. *Rejuvenating Older Furniture:* Odorless mineral spirits $4.50 per pint from Daniel Smith. Antiquax polish (containing carnauba and beeswax) for $5.95 per 2.8 ounces from The Woodworkers' Store. *Tips on Sanding Intricate Items:* Handsanding blocks for $5.95, sanding cords for $9.95, and bronze wool for $4.95 per 3 pads from The Woodworkers' Store. *How to Make a Greeting Card Puzzle:* Peacock 100% Sulfite Construction Papers in a variety of colors from $1.15 per 50 sheets, Surgrip Utility (X-Acto) Knife for $4.99, Tag boards from $3.54, Grumbacher flat brushes from $2.96, and Sharpie permanent marker for $1.09, all from Co-op Artists' Materials. Plaid's Tacky Glue for 89¢ and selection of stencils from 98¢ from Craft King. Wooden dowels from

20¢ from Pearl Paint. *Origins of Raffia:* Selection of raffia from $2.65 per 50 grams from Mills Floral Supply. Natural Raffia for $3.45 per 8-ounce package from Craft King.

Quick Tips; pages 4–5
Making a Starched Fabric Bow: Muslin for $2.15 per yard and selection of ribbons and bows from 70¢ from Newark Dressmaker Supply. Plaid's Tacky Glue for 89¢ and rubber gloves for $1.23 per 5 pairs from Craft King. Storage containers from 55¢ from Earth Guild. *Building a Beaded Tassel:* 24-gauge beading wire for $4.99 per 5 feet, 8mm bead strands from $4.80, 4½" side cutter pliers for $7.99, and a variety of 20mm beads from $2 per package, all from Enterprise Art. *Candle Stabilizer Disks:* Selection of candles from $4 and candle cups from $6 from Pottery Barn. Laser Scissors for $7.41 from Craft King. *Making a Knotted Trim:* Perle cotton in a variety of colors for $5 for 157-yard tube from Newark Dressmaker Supply. *Make-Your-Own Sanding Block:* 1¼" solid wood blocks for 2.50 per 12-piece pack, 12" wooden ruler for 39¢, and Laser Scissors for $7.41 from Craft King. Masking tape for $1.35 at Ott's Discount Art Supply. *Create a Triple Trim:* Selection of upholstery trims from $3.75, pins for $1.75 per box of 350, variety of thread from $1.65, measuring tape for $1.25, and scissors from $10.75, all from Newark Dressmaker Supply.

Gingerbread Birdhouses; pages 6–8
14" x 16" Cushionare Pro Cookie Sheets for $15, KitchenAid 5-Speed Mixer for $59, Kaiser Flour Sifter for $14, all from Williams-Sonoma. Bakery Rolling Pin for $9 and kitchen utility knife for $7.60 from A Cook's Wares. New Cut-Rite Scissors for $3.50, Pentel Superball Pen for $1.29, illustration boards from $1.80, Canson 82 Tracing Paper for $3.99 per 50 sheet pad, and Stainless Steel Corkback Rulers from $3.35, all from Co-op Artist' Materials. Reclosable Zip Plastic Bags from $1.55 per 100 from Craft King.

How to Antique Fabric; pages 9–11
Selection of teas from $2.50 from San Francisco Herb Company. Lace doilies from 90¢, polyester ribbon from $1.65 per yard, satin ribbon roses for $2.40 per 10, satin ribbon bows for $1 per 10, and muslin for $2.15 per 5 yards, all from Newark Dressmaker Supply. Worsted wool for $29.95 per yard and polyester fabric from $2.98 per yard from G Street Fabrics. Selection of dye handling equipment from Earth Guild,

including storage containers from 55¢, scoopula spatula for $4.50, and syringes to measure and apply dye from $2. Irons from $12 from Service Merchandise. Rubber gloves for $1.23 per 5 pairs from Craft King.

Heirloom Mantel Skirt; pages 12–15
Shangri-La 54"-wide, cotton fabric in dark green (willow) and cranberry (wine) for $11.98 per yard from The Fabric Center. Gold filigree-style appliqué for $8.89 for 144 pieces, Bond's fabric glue for $1.59, Plaid's tacky glue for 89¢, all from Craft King. Green, cranberry, and gold polyester thread for $1.65 per 300 yards, ¼" gold middy braid for $1.10 per 5 yards, straight pins for $1.75 per box of 350, scissors from $10.75, fabric-marking pencil for 95¢, C-thru plastic ruler for $3.75, all from Newark Dressmaker Supply. Selection of craft cords from $2.69 per 27 yards from Enterprise Art. Variety of colored cord from $2.50 per 4 yards from Home-Sew. Zipper attachment for $4.75 from G Street Fabrics. Transparent tape for $3.95 and masking tape for $1.45 per 1 from Jerry's Artarama. 18" brown wrapping paper for $25.95 per roll from Reliable. Selection of sewing machines from $140 and irons from $12 from Service Merchandise.

Victorian Place Cards; page 16
Fabric paint for $5 for 24-color set, selection of fringes from $3.75, decorative pearls and beads from 75¢ per package, Low Temp Glue Gun for $12.95 and glue sticks for $3 for 8, scissors for $10.75, and tacky glue for $2.10, all from Newark Dressmaker Supply. Sharpie extra fine permanent marker for 82¢ and calligraphy pens for $3.53 for set of 3 from Ott's Discount Art Supply. Selection of art paper from $1.50 and gold leafing kit for $14.99 from Jerry's Artarama.

Silk Screen Photo Mat; pages 17–19
Speedball sensitizer for $5 per 8 ounces, Speedball photo emulsion for $13.20 per quart, paint scraper for $6.10, Speedball screen filler for $6.37 per 8 ounces, and polyester "denier" fabric from $6.60 per yard, all from Pearl Paint. 10" stretcher strip for 36¢, 12" stretcher strip for 41¢, Metallic Richgold Ink for $19.98 for 1-pound can, Olfa utility knife for $6.78, and Matline measuring tool for $6.65, all from Daniel Smith. Selection of brushes from $1, Bristol paper for $8.25 per 20 sheet pad, transparent tape for $1.65, New Cut-Rite Scissors for $3.50, Halogen Drafting Lamp for $169.50, and plastic

tub from $4.95, all from Co-op Artists' Materials. Swingline 101 Staple Gun for $14.99 and staples for $2.29, Sobo glue for $1.89 per 4 ounces, and Strathmore 400 Sketch Pads for $2.89 per 100 sheets, all from Jerry's Artarama. Clothespins for $2.58 for 40 pieces and rubber gloves for $1.23 for 5 pairs from Craft King.

Victorian Christmas Cornucopia; pages 20–21
Selection of paper lace from $1.49 per 6 yards and Laser scissors for $7.99 from Sunshine Discount Crafts. White tulle for $6.25 per 25 yards, selection of wire-edged ribbon from $1.65 per yard, 3mm pearls for $1.95 per 60" string, metallic thread for $3.75 per 200 yards, metallic ribbon from $1.60 per 5 yards, mini glue gun for $6.25 and mini glue sticks for $1.50 per 20, all from Newark Dressmaker Supply. Rubber cement for $1.96 per 4 ounces and Bond clear tape for $1.41 from Ott's Discount Art Supply. Brass Filigrees in various sizes and shapes from 95¢ from Craft King.

Celestial Ornaments; pages 22–23
Selection of acrylic jewels from $1.29, white tacky glue for $1.99, and galvanized wire from $2.79 per 40 yard spool, all from Enterprise Art. Gold and silver glitter with precision applicator for $2.49 each from Sunshine Discount Crafts. Heavy-duty sewing thread for $1.60 per 55 yards, gold metallic thread for $3.75 per 200 yards, florist wire for $1.15 per 10-yard spool, tape measure for $1.25, 11½" x 9½" tracing paper for $1.55 per 6 sheets, and C-thru plastic ruler for $3.75, all from Newark Dressmaker Supply. Wire cutters for $6 from Earth Guild. Variety of paintbrushes from 75¢, Sharpie permanent felt-tip marker for $1.09, Pentel Superball Pen for $1.29, Utility knife for $3.75, all from Co-op Artists' Materials.

Trash Bag Garland; page 24
4½" wood birdhouse for $1.99, 5" red cardinal for $1.99, 4" flying cardinal for 99¢, and 2½" flat red cardinal for 65¢, holly-berry pick for 69¢, pine picks for 69¢ per 9 tips, green stem wire for 69¢ per 16 pieces, DMC embroidery floss for 39¢, and 2" red bows for 79¢ per 2 pieces, all from Sunshine Discount Crafts. 4" pine straw nests for $4.70 per 4 and birch branches for $9.65 per 25 pieces from Mills Floral Supply. Laser Scissors for $7.41, and white spray paint for $2.75 per 6 ounces, all from Craft King. Garden gloves for $19.95 from White Flower Farm. 30-gallon trash bags for $22.19 per case from Reliable.

SOURCES
AND RESOURCES

Tufted Footstool; pages 25–27
Large selection of 54" upholstery fabric ranging from $2.49 to $100 for ¾ yards from The Fabric Center. 1"-thick batting for $3.65 for 45" x 60" precut from The American Needlewoman. Green, cranberry, and gold polyester thread for $1.65 per 300 yards, 1"-wide fringes from $3.75 for 4 yards, Glo-tone crochet cotton for $2.55 for ball of 300 yards, ⅝" 2-hole buttons for 85¢ per dozen, ½" wooden spool for $3.95 for 100 (also ¾" and 1⅛" available), 5½" doll needles for 50¢ for 2, variety of scissors from $10.75, low-temp glue gun for $12.95, and low-temp glue sticks for $3.00 for 8, all from Newark Dressmaker Supply. ⁷⁄₁₆" or ¹¹⁄₁₆" half ball buttons to cover for $1.30 for package of 5, ¾" stitch witchery for $1.65 for 20 yards , and Dritz covered button kit for $1.70, all from G Street Fabrics. 1¾" quilting pins for $4.50 for 200 from Quilts & Other Comforts. 18" non-slip ruler for $5.99, retractable utility knife for $3.29, staple gun for $14.99 and ⁵⁄₁₆" staples for $2.19 per box of 1000, and 11" x 14" parchment tracing pad for $9.40 per 100 sheets, all from Jerry's Artarama. Variable-speed reversible drill for $32.99 and safety glasses for $3.99 from Northern. Large selection of irons from $12.00, selection of sewing machines from $140, and 6-piece screwdriver set for $9.97, all from Service Merchandise. Permanent fine-point marker for $1.09 from Co-op Artists' Materials. 12" x 24" x 1" foam for $2.50 from Pearl Paint.

Field Guide to Watercolor Brushes; pages 28–29
Kolinsky Sable Rounds from $8, Red Sable Rounds from $4, variety of other watercolor rounds from $3, selection of watercolor flats from $5.25, and script brushes from $7.45, all from New York Central Art Supply. Large selection of watercolor brushes, including flats, rounds, script liners, wash brushes, filberts, fan brushes, and brights, from $3 from Co-op Artists' Materials. Selection of Rekab, Winsor & Newton, Princeton, Isabey, and other watercolor brushes from $2.50 from Jerry's Artarama. Also, variety of watercolor brushes and sets from $1.70 from Ott's Discount Art Supply and Daniel Smith.

Low-Sew Tree Skirt; page 30
Shangri-La 54"-wide, cotton fabric in dark green (willow) and cranberry (wine) for $11.98 per yard from The Fabric Center. Green, red, and gold polyester thread for $1.65 per 300 yards, straight pins for $1.75 per box of 350, scissors from $10.75, fabric-marking pencil for 95¢, C-thru plastic ruler for $3.75, all

from Newark Dressmaker Supply. Bond's fabric glue for $1.59, green and red metallic craft cord for $2.08 each per 27 yards from Craft King. 20" x 36" cardboard for 72¢ from Pearl Paint. Variety of colored cord from $2.50 per 4 yards from Home-Sew. Transparent tape for $3.95 and masking tape for $1.45 from Jerry's Artarama. Selection of sewing machines from $140 and irons from $12 from Service Merchandise.

Quick Projects; page 33
Tablecloths from $15 and 20"-square napkins for $10 per set of 4 from Williams-Sonoma. Variety of scissors from $10.75 from Newark Dressmaker Supply. 18" non-slip ruler for $5.99 from Jerry's Artarama. *Ferns, Snapdragons, and Daises:* 2½" Gold wire-edged ribbons for $3.95 per 4 yards, 18" silk feather fern for 85¢, eucalyptus for $2 per 1-ounce bundle, and a variety of ribbons from 70¢ from Newark Dressmaker Supply. Daisy stems for $4.50 per set of 4, snapdragon for $3.40 per stem, and holly and ivy garlands for $11.90, all from May Silk. *Fresh Roses and Silk Berries:* Florist wire for $1.15 per 10-yard spool and Floratape for $1.15 from Newark Dressmaker Supply. Fresh roses for $35 per half dozen from Village Flowers. *Golden Pinecones, Pods, and Leaves:* Large selection of silk leaves and flowers from $1.90 from May Silk. Pinecones for $2.49 per pound, florist wire for $1.09, metallic ribbon for $6.75 per 50-yard spool, and gold spray paint for $3.75 per 6 ounces, all from Craft King. Mini artichokes for $5.45 per 8-piece package and selection of pods from $3 from Mills Floral Supply. *Ivy, Holly, Berries, Stars, and Gold Balls:* Ivy for $9.65 per bunch, mini holly for $5.65 per 4 ounces, and red berries for $6.75 per 12 ounces, all from Mills Floral Supply. Star sequins for 49¢ per 400-piece bag and aluminum filigree balls for $1.19 per 12 pieces or Styrofoam ball shapes (to paint) for 85¢ per 12 pieces from Enterprise Art. *Eucalyptus and Dried Foliage:* Wire-edged ribbon from $1.60 from Newark Dressmaker Supply. Eucalyptus from $7.75 per pound and selection of foliage leaves from $3.50 from Mills Floral Supply. Craft cord from $2.08 per 27 yards from Craft King.

Fruit and Ivy Wreath; back cover
12" Oasis floral ring wreaths for $18.79 per case of 12 (other sizes available) and sheet moss for $22.25 per 5-pound case from Mills Floral Supply. Selection of ivy house plants from $7.90, 10" green grapes for $4.90, and assortment of plastic fruit for $4.90, all from May Silk. Natural Dried Fruit Apples for $5.95

per 10-piece bag, florist wire for $1.15 per 10-yard spool, and floral pins for $1.65 per 400, all from Newark Dressmaker Supply. 10" round bubble bowl for $6.95 and candles from $2.50 from Crate and Barrel.

....

The following companies are mentioned in the listings above. Contact each individually for a price list or catalog.

A Cook's Wares, 211 Thirty-seventh Street, Beaver Falls, PA 15010-2103; 412-846-9490
The American Needlewoman, P.O. Box 6472, Fort Worth, TX 76115; 800-433-2231
Art and Craft Materials Institute, 100 Boylston Street, Suite 1050, Boston, MA 02116; 617-426-6400
Center for Safety Coalition in the Arts, 5 Beekman Street, New York, New York 10038; 212-227-6220
Co-op Artists' Materials, P.O. Box 53097, Atlanta, GA 30355; 800-877-3242
Craft King Discount Craft Supply, P.O. Box 53097, Lakeland, FL 33804; 800-769-9494
Crate and Barrel, P.O. Box 9059, Wheeling, IL 60090; 800-323-5461
Daniel Smith, P.O. Box 84268, Seattle, WA 98124-5568; 800-426-6740
Earth Guild, 33 Haywood Street, Asheville, NC 28801; 800-327-8448
Enterprise Art, P.O. Box 2918, Largo, FL 34648; 800-366-2218
The Fabric Center, P.O. Box 8212, Fitchburg, MA 01420-8212; 508-343-4402
G Street Fabrics, 12240 Wilkins Avenue, Rockville, MD 20852; 800-333-9191
Home-Sew, P.O. Box 4099, Bethlehem, PA 18018-0099; 215-867-3833
Johnson Paint Company, 355 Newbury Street, Boston, MA 02115; 617-266-5210
Jerry's Artarama, P.O. Box 1105, New Hyde Park, NJ 11040; 800-U-Artist
May Silk, 13262 Moore Street, Cerritos, CA 90703; 800-282-7455
Mills Floral Supply, 4550 Peachtree Lakes Drive, Duluth, GA 30136; 800-762-7939
Newark Dressmaker Supply, 6473 Ruch Road, P.O. Box 20730, Lehigh Valley, PA 18002-0730; 800-736-6783
New York Central Art Supply, 130 East Twelfth Street, New York, NY 10003; 800-950-6111
Northern, P.O. Box 1499, Burnsville, MN 55337-0499; 800-533-5545
Ott's Discount Art Supply, 102 Hungate Drive, Greenville, NC 27858; 800-356-3289

Pearl Paint, 308 Canal Street, New York, NY 10013; 800-221-6845
Pottery Barn, 100 N. Point Street, San Francisco, CA 94133; 800-922-9934
Quilts & Other Comforts, P.O. Box 394, Wheat Ridge, CO 80034-0394; 303-420-4272 ext. 100
Reliable, 101 W. Van Buren, Chicago, IL 60607; 800-735-4000
Service Merchandise, P.O. Box 25130, Nashville, TN 37202-5130; 800-251-1212
San Francisco Herb Company, 250 14th Street, San Francisco, CA 94103; 800-227-4530
Shepherd's Garden Seeds, 30 Irene Street, Torrington, CT 06790; 203-482-3638
Stencil World, P.O. Box 1112, Newport, RI 82840; 800-274-7997
Sunshine Discount Crafts, P.O. Box 56, Litchfield, CT 06759-0050; 203-496-9600
Village Flowers, 297 Main Street, Huntington, NY 11743; 516-427-0996
White Flower Farm, P.O. Box 50, Litchfield, CT 06759; 203-496-9600
Williams-Sonoma, P.O. Box 7456, San Francisco, CA 94120-7456; 800-541-2233
The Woodworkers' Store, 21801 Industrial Boulevard, Rogers, MN 55374-9514; 800-279-4441 ◆

The Dried Rose Bouquet featured on the back cover of the July/August 1994 issue of *Handcraft Illustrated* is available as a kit including all the necessary materials. The cost is $19.95 plus $1.50 shipping and handling. To order the kit, send a check or money order for $21.45, or send your credit card number (we accept American Express, VISA, and Mastercard), the expiration date, and an authorized signature to: Rose Kit, *Handcraft Illustrated,* P.O. Box 509, Brookline Village, MA 02147-0509.

Quick Projects

Golden Pinecones, Pods, and Leaves

Instead of creating an elaborate centerpiece for your holiday table, consider making plate crowns—a half wreath of decorative foliage that arches around and crowns the top of a plate. The effect is delicate and colorful and takes a minimum of effort.

Some of the plate crowns shown below have been laid directly on the tablecloth, while others are placed between the dinner plate and a charger. You can create arc-shaped crowns to place at the top of the plate, or to encircle the entire plate. Plate crowns made from fresh flowers will last only a few hours, but those assembled from dried or silk foliage can be used over and over.

Ferns, Snapdragons, and Daisies

Ferns, Snapdragons, and Daisies—Crimp one edge of a length of 2"-wide gold wire-edged ribbon, then place the crimped edge just under the plate rim. Arrange sprigs of any green foliage, such as fern, eucalyptus, ivy, or holly above the plate, then position snapdragons and daisies in an arc over the greens. For an added touch, encircle the folded napkin with a band of ribbon and accent with a small piece of green foliage.

Fresh Roses and Silk Berries—Form an arc-shaped base by covering heavy wire with green florist tape. Cut the stems of four fresh pink roses to 3", then bind the roses, green foliage, and berries onto the base using florist tape.

Ivy, Holly, Berries, Stars, and Gold Balls

Golden Pinecones, Pods, and Leaves—Cover the workspace with newspaper; arrange an artificial artichoke and assorted miniature pinecones, nuts, pods, leaves, and silk flowers on an old cookie rack. Spray paint each item gold. When dry, wire the pods or seeds by pushing a length of stem wire directly through the lower third of the piece. To wire the pinecones, wrap the wire around the stem or lower portion of the cone. Then bend both ends of the wire under the object and twist them together to form a false stem. Make an arc-shaped base from two short branches of the silk flower stems, and bind each piece to the base using stem wire to form an arch. Accent the arrangement as desired with narrow metallic ribbon.

Fresh Roses and Silk Berries

Ivy, Holly, Berries, Stars, and Gold Balls—Arrange sprigs of ivy and holly on the rim of the charger, then position red berries, metallic stars, and gold balls on top of the foliage. Accent the napkin with a sprig of ivy.

Eucalyptus and Dried Foliage—Bend an arc from two types of eucalyptus, then wind silk-twisted cord around the arc, followed by wire-edged ribbon. Curl the ends of the ribbon. Make cone-shaped "lace lilies" by rolling skeletonized leaves, then wiring them at the base to secure them. Insert each "lace lily" into the arc between stems of the foliage and wire it in place. ◆

Eucalyptus and Dried Foliage

Fruit and Ivy Wreath

S oak an Oasis floral ring wreath until wet throughout, then cover the ring with sheet moss, attaching it with thin floral wire. Cut a large ivy houseplant into 3" to 5" sections and cover the wreath with ivy by poking the stems through the moss into the Oasis. Attach five red apples, four green pears, and three to five green apples using floral picks. Attach three to four bunches of green grapes (about 1½ pounds) by wiring each bunch with floral wire, then inserting the wire into the wreath. Place a fishbowl and candle in the center of the wreath. (Because of its weight, this wreath should not be hung.)